'*Social Movements and Civil War* is an ambitious and exceptionally original book. It analyses four cases of civil war through the prism of contentious politics and pushes our understanding of political violence forward significantly through 'the authors' imaginative use of the analytical concepts and tools of social movement research.'

—*Niall Ó Dochartaigh, National University of Ireland*

'Many studies have tried to explain why nonviolent movements for democratization in authoritarian states succeed, yet much less attention has been paid to the mechanisms through which such democratic uprisings fail. This timely and important book looks into a particularly alarming type of failure: escalation into civil war. Studying the causal mechanisms in nonviolent social movements' path to large-scale political violence, the authors provide new empirical insights and a theoretical understanding of failed movement-driven democratization processes. This new book employs a compelling dynamic approach that seeks to move beyond the unfruitful dichotomy between structural and agency-based explanations which has, for too long, permeated research on nonviolent uprisings.'

—*Isak Svensson, Uppsala University, Sweden*

'As mass uprisings in key Arab states have escalated into vicious and obdurate civil wars, this volume could not be timelier. *Social Movements and Civil War* is the first major work that comprehensively bridges Social Movement Theory with the study of civil war. It draws on theoretical rigor and deep empirical insights, providing sophisticated analyses of the wars in Syria, Libya, Yemen and the former Yugoslavia. This book is sure to become a major reference work for those grappling with the tragedy of democratic aspirations degenerating into large-scale violence.'

—*Reinoud Leenders, King's College London, UK*

SOCIAL MOVEMENTS AND CIVIL WAR

This book investigates the origins of civil wars which emerge from failed attempts at democratization.

The main aim of this volume is to develop a theoretical explanation of the conditions under which and the mechanisms through which social movements' struggles for democracy end up in civil war. While the empirical evidence suggests that this is not a rare phenomenon, the literatures on social movements, democratization and civil wars have grown apart from each other. At the theoretical level, *Social Movements and Civil War* bridges insights in the three fields, looking in particular at explanations of the radicalization of social movements, the failure of democratization processes and the onset of civil war. In doing this, it builds upon the relational approach developed in contentious politics with the aim of singling out robust causal mechanisms. At the empirical level, the research provides in-depth descriptions of four cases of trajectory from social movements for democratization into civil wars: in Syria, Libya, Yemen and the former Yugoslavia. Conditions such as the double weakness of civil society and the state, the presence of entrepreneurs of violence as well as normative and material resources for violence, ethnic and tribal divisions, domestic and international military interventions are considered as influencing the chains of actors' choices rather than as structural determinants.

This book will be of great interest to students of civil wars, political violence, social movements, democratization, and IR in general.

Donatella della Porta is Professor of Political Science and Dean of the Institute for Humanities and the Social Sciences at the Scuola Normale Superiore, Florence, Italy.

Teije Hidde Donker is a postdoctoral researcher in the Department of Comparative Politics at the University of Bergen, Norway.

Bogumila Hall has a PhD in Sociology from the European University Institute, Florence, Italy.

Emin Poljarevic is a PDRA Research Fellow at Qatar University.

Daniel P. Ritter is Assistant Professor of Sociology at Stockholm University, Sweden.

Routledge Studies on Civil War and Intrastate Conflict

Series editors: Edward Newman, *School of Politics and International Studies, University of Leeds*; and Patrick Regan, *Kroc Institute for International Peace Studies, University of Notre Dame*.

This series publishes theoretically rigorous and empirically original scholarship on all aspects of armed intrastate conflict, including its causes, nature, impacts, patterns of violence, and resolution. It welcomes work on specific armed conflicts and the micro-dynamics of violence, on broad patterns and cross-national analyses of civil wars, and on historical perspectives as well as contemporary challenges. It also seeks to explore the policy implications of conflict analysis, especially as it relates to international security, intervention and peacebuilding.

Understanding Civil Wars
Continuity and change in intrastate conflict
Edward Newman

Territorial Separatism in Global Politics
Causes, outcomes and resolution
Edited by Damien Kingsbury and Costas Laoutides

Armed Group Structure and Violence in Civil Wars
The organizational dynamics of civilian killing
Roos Haer

Social Movements and Civil War
When Protests for Democratization Fail
*Donatella della Porta, Teije Hidde Donker, Bogumila Hall,
Emin Poljarevic and Daniel P. Ritter*

SOCIAL MOVEMENTS AND CIVIL WAR

When Protests for Democratization Fail

*Donatella della Porta, Teije Hidde Donker,
Bogumila Hall, Emin Poljarevic and
Daniel P. Ritter*

Routledge
Taylor & Francis Group

LONDON AND NEW YORK

First published 2018
by Routledge
2 Park Square, Milton Park, Abingdon, Oxon OX14 4RN

and by Routledge
711 Third Avenue, New York, NY 10017

Routledge is an imprint of the Taylor & Francis Group, an informa business

© 2018 Donatella della Porta, Teije Hidde Donker, Bogumila Hall, Emin Poljarevic and Daniel P. Ritter

British Library Cataloguing-in-Publication Data
A catalogue record for this book is available from the British Library

Library of Congress Cataloging-in-Publication Data
A catalog record for this title has been requested

ISBN: 978-1-138-22417-9 (hbk)
ISBN: 978-1-138-22418-6 (pbk)
ISBN: 978-1-315-40310-6 (ebk)

Typeset in Bembo
by Apex CoVantage, LLC

CONTENTS

ABOUT THE AUTHORS

Donatella della Porta is Professor of Political Science and Dean of the Institute for Humanities and the Social Sciences at the Scuola Normale Superiore in Florence, Italy, where she directs the Center on Social Movement Studies (Cosmos). She directs a major ERC project, Mobilizing for Democracy, on civil society participation in democratization processes in Europe, the Middle East, Asia, and Latin America. Among her very recent publications are: *Late Neoliberalism and its Discontents* (Palgrave, 2017); *Movement Parties in Times of Austerity* (Polity 2017); *Where Did the Revolution Go?* (Cambridge University Press, 2016); *Social Movements in Times of Austerity* (Polity, 2015); *Methodological Practices in Social Movement Research* (Oxford University Press, 2014); *Spreading Protest* (with Alice Mattoni, ECPR Press, 2014); *Participatory Democracy in Southern Europe* (with Joan Font and Yves Sintomer, Rowman & Littlefield, 2014); *Mobilizing for Democracy* (Oxford University Press, 2014); *Can Democracy be Saved?* (Polity Press, 2013); *Clandestine Political Violence* (edited with David Snow, Bert Klandermans, and Doug McAdam, Cambridge University Press, 2013); *Blackwell Encyclopedia on Social and Political Movements* (Blackwell, 2013); *Mobilizing on the Extreme Right* (with Manuela Caiani and Claudius Wagemann, Oxford University Press, 2012); *Meeting Democracy* (edited with Dieter Rucht, Cambridge University Press, 2012); *The Hidden Order of Corruption* (with Alberto Vannucci, Ashgate 2012). In 2011, she was the recipient of the Mattei Dogan Prize for distinguished achievements in the field of political sociology and PhD honoris causa from the universities of Lausanne, Bucharest, and Goteborg.

Teije Hidde Donker is a postdoctoral researcher in the Department of Comparative Politics at the University of Bergen, Norway. He holds a PhD from the European University Institute in Florence, Italy. He is the author of a number of articles on the interaction between state actors and Islamist activists in Syria and Tunisia, building on extensive ethnographic research in these two countries. His research has appeared in *Mediterranean Politics*, in *Middle East Critique*, and in an edited volume from Stanford University Press.

Bogumila Hall received her PhD from the European University Institute, Florence, Italy. Focusing on the geographical Middle East, her work explores issues of subaltern politics and agency, knowledge production and representation, social movements, and transnational activism. She has conducted extensive ethnographic fieldwork in Yemen, Palestine/Israel, and Syria.

Emin Poljarevic is currently a PDRA research fellow at Qatar University, Doha, Qatar. He is a sociologist of religion with current research interest in contemporary Salafi activism. He has published articles, book chapters, and scholarly analyses on a range of issues related to Islamism, Salafism, and religious mobilization among youth in the Middle East and North Africa, including northern Europe.

Daniel P. Ritter is Assistant Professor of Sociology at Stockholm University, Sweden. His primary research interests are revolutions and social movements, and, in particular, the international contexts in which domestic contentious politics play out. His first book, *The Iron Cage of Liberalism: International Politics and Unarmed Revolutions in the Middle East and North Africa* (Oxford University Press, 2015), sought to explain why some nonviolent revolutionary movements are able to oust dictators while similar movements elsewhere either falter or degenerate into violent conflict. Daniel earned his PhD in sociology from the University of Texas at Austin in May 2010.

ACKNOWLEDGEMENTS

The idea for this book came from two (inter-linked) observations, one empirical and one theoretical. As for the former, after the hope of the Arab Spring, there was the shock of the increasingly brutal civil wars that, in some countries, had followed failed social movements' mobilization for democracy. As for the latter, the understanding of these specific forms of escalation into political violence seemed thwarted by a lack of dialogue between research on civil wars and research on social movements, which had proceeded quite apart from each other.

The Advanced Scholars' grant from the European Research Council for my project on Mobilizing for Democracy provided the theoretical background as well as the resources for the empirical work. In the intellectually rich environment of the Center on Social Movement Studies (Cosmos), located first at the European University Institute and now at the Scuola Normale Superiore in Florence, was most important for the development of our work, providing innumerable stimuli during the various stages of our work. Donatella della Porta is also grateful for a stimulating visit at the Hertie School of Governance in Berlin.

As always, Sarah Tarrow contributed with care and commitment in making this volume more readable.

1

INTRODUCTION

Social movements in civil wars

Donatella della Porta

Introduction

The main aim of this volume is to develop a theoretical explanation of the conditions and mechanisms through which the struggles for democracy of social movement end in civil war. While the empirical evidence suggests that this is not a rare phenomenon, scholars in the social science fields of social movements and civil war, as well as democratization and nonviolent revolutions – all of whom can contribute to address to this question – have grown quite apart from each other. In particular, while social movements and civil wars have empirical overlaps, the respective fields of study rarely consider each other. As Elisabeth Wood (2015, 457) noted:

> [S]cholars who work primarily on social movements and on civil wars largely work in isolation from one another, with too few analyzing the relationship between the two forms of political opposition as instances of the broader field of contentious politics . . . Yet scholars of social movements and civil wars share an emphasis on the dynamics of escalation of violence and social mobilization.

This lack of dialogue is also evident if we look at the fields of democratization and of nonviolent resistance (della Porta 2014; 2016).

The first theoretical task we want to address in this volume is the bridging of insights in the four above-mentioned fields of study, looking in particular at explanations for the onset of civil wars, the failure of democratization processes as well as of nonviolent resistance, and the radicalization of social movements. In doing so, we will build upon the relational approach developed in contentious politics, with the aim of singling out robust causal mechanisms (della Porta 2013). Our discussion of the main theoretical contributions to the above-mentioned topics will distinguish between structuralist and agentic orientations, pleading for a relational approach that aims to overcome the limits of both, within a process-oriented, dynamic perspective. This means reflecting on the ways in which conditions are activated and individual motivations transformed through intense interactions among different players within emerging arenas (Jasper and Duyvendak 2015). As intense times, the moments we analyse are structurally underdetermined, with a fluidification of relations that unsettles the rules and norms that are established in normal times (della Porta 2016).

Combining explanations that address the radicalization of social movements, the onset of civil wars, and the failure of democratization as well as of nonviolent repertoires, the chapter will introduce some main mechanisms in the trajectory from social movements to civil wars. Considering trajectories of escalation as moments of time intensification, we will point to the need to analyse these as contingent and open-ended processes. Conditions such as the double weakness of civil society and the state, the presence of entrepreneurs of violence as well as normative and material resources for violence, ethnic and tribal divisions, and domestic and international military interventions must therefore be considered as factors that influence the chains of actors' choices, rather than as structural determinants.

From the empirical point of view, the volume aims at providing in-depth descriptions of four cases of the trajectory from social movements for democratization into civil wars. The study of civil wars has been characterized by a search for global explanations, with an initial focus on structural conditions, then combined with strategic approaches, often based on rational choice theory. However, researchers have identified the limits to 'large-N' studies, including reliability and validity of indicators, endogeneity and direction of causality, as well as omitted variables and observational equivalents (Kalyvas 2008). On the side of the dependent variable, different measures used to operationalize the concept of civil war (number of deaths, especially among civilians) affect the results of various explanatory models, while gross domestic product (GDP) is used as a proxy for a broad range of independent variables (Sambanis 2004). The consideration of these limits, which explain the inconsistent results, has triggered more research aimed at singling out relational causal mechanisms rather than structural causes. This will be the approach in our study, which will undertake an in-depth analysis of trajectories from movements for democratization to civil war in Syria, Libya, and Yemen, which are then compared with the former Yugoslavia. We will present fieldwork as well as desk-top research on these cases, pointing to the relational mechanisms at the basis of a transformation from nonviolent to violent forms of protest and then to civil war.

In this chapter, we will first review some existing explanations in the social science literatures on the onset of civil war, the failure of democratization processes, unsuccessful nonviolent revolutions, and the radicalization of social movements. Considering the limits of static and structuralist explanations, we will suggest a relational, dynamic and constructed model. In a methodological section, the research design will be justified. In particular, we will explain how the search for robust mechanisms oriented the choice of relevant cases, showing the trajectory from social movements to civil war within a most-different research design. The chapter ends with a presentation of the content of the volume.

At the onset of civil wars

A civil war has been defined as an 'armed combat within the boundaries of a recognized sovereign entity between parties subject to a common authority at the outset of the hostilities' (Kalyvas 2006, 17). Civil wars develop around political aims. If war is 'a political act of organized violence to obtain some advantage or goal in term of power, territory or security' (Olson Lounsbery and Pearson 2009, 4), *civil* war is a 'sustained combat between relatively organized forces with the goals of changing government or boundaries' (ibid.). The duration in time distinguishes civil wars from riots as, while a riot is characterized by a short duration, a civil war is 'protracted internal violence aimed at securing control of the political and legal apparatus' (Evans and Newman 1998, 54). The main difference concerning forms of clandestine political violence is the need to assess territorial control and therefore, to a certain extent, not only to challenge an existing order but also to reconstitute an emerging one – in fact, 'civil wars are political contexts where violence is used both to challenge and to build order' (Kalyvas 2008, 406). In civil wars, challengers usually exert territorial control of some areas, with the presence of multiple armed actors fighting each other: 'Civil war occurs if a group of people forms a private military organization that attacks government forces and ordinary civilians on a large scale and with a high degree of persistence' (Collier *et al.* 2003, 54). The intensity of the violence is also a defining characteristic, as civil wars create large numbers of victims – for example, according to Sambanis (2004, 829), we can talk of a civil war when there are at least 500/1,000 deaths.

A great deal of research on civil wars has attempted to single out the macro-level conditions under which these are more likely to develop, looking at sets of economic, social, political, and cultural variables at the domestic but also at the transnational level. Large-N studies have identified conditions that increase the risks of civil war at the *economic level*, particularly economic strains, including deep poverty, massive unemployment, economic stagnation, and low GDP (Fearon and Laitin 2003). The expectation is that poverty increases the risk of civil war, while rapid economic development reduces it. In particular, 'political violence occurs in states in which assets are immobile and unequally distributed' (Boix 2008, 216). In relatively equal societies, peaceful, democratic means of solving conflict are advantageous to all parties.

At the *social* level, researchers have discussed the effects of various potential sources of divisions. Economic inequality is relevant especially if associated with ethnic, religious, or cultural belonging. Population diversity, with related ethnic nepotism, makes ethnic identities relevant. In particular, the presence of two main ethnic groups produces a higher likelihood of civil war (Henderson and Singer 2000). However, ethnic divisions also have an indirect effect (Blimes 2006). Ethnicity counts when linked with acute social uncertainty, a history of conflict, fear

(Lake and Rothchild 1998, 7), as well as politicized religious identities. The probability of civil war increases with long-lasting (especially communal) deprivation and failure to attend to grievances (Kogan Iasnyi and Zissernan-Brodsky 1998, 212).

From the *cultural* point of view, according to Huntington's (1993) debated theory, the intrinsic incommensurability of the values of civilizations leads to wars. Others have referred instead to the ideological power of organized ideas. More specifically, a history of internal conflicts is said to fuel exclusive identities, with the potential for narratives of group suffering and revenge.

At the *political* level, civil wars are favoured by an ill-disciplined and corrupt military (Herbst 2000). When minority rights are repressed, demands for self-determination are more likely where large minority groups are territorially concentrated, where ethnic networks exist. Accommodation and decentralization can help in diffusing the conflict (Sambanis 2003). Partial democracies present the highest risks, especially in low-income countries (Eliot, *et al.* 2003). If some ethnic and religious conflicts are more dangerous than others, this depends on the historical paths that lead institutions to negotiate on some issues, but not on others (Wilkinson 2008). Moreover, scholars have addressed the government's capability to use repression. In this regard repeatedly, the formation of the state has been linked to violence, which can remain high in cases of incomplete state building (Mann 2012; Tilly 1993).

All these dimensions are affected by *external* interventions, which can cause the onset of civil war (Sambanis 2003) – with the highest risk of weak democracy, especially in low-income countries – as well as contributing to prolonging the conflicts (Elbadawi and Sambanis 2002). Conflicts tend in fact to cluster geographically (Sambanis 2001), spreading through migrant diasporas, criminal organizations, or terrorist networks (Collier and Hoeffler 2004). As states can more easily repress their populations at home, rebels often choose to position themselves outside of the state's reach. This happens especially if the neighbouring states are weak, when they are rivals, or in the presence of massive waves of refugees (Salehyan 2009). Rebellions are indeed more likely and longer in duration when there are rival or weak states on the borders, and ethnic groups are more likely to rebel when they are located near the border. An important role is played by refugee warriors (ibid.): civil wars interact with wars, as new conflicts imply more and more loosely organized actors (Kaldor 1999).

Moving then towards the micro-dynamics of conflicts, analyses of insurgent violence and civilian responses in civil wars have addressed the reasons behind the compliance among the population at large (Kalyvas 2006), and of the different levels of brutality (e.g. Weinstein 2007). In this field, as in others, rational choice models have provided the theoretical basis for the search for causes at the macro-level. According to Collier and Hoeffler's influential model (2004), participation in civil war is a rational decision based on economic cost and expected utility. While traditional theories had stressed grievances (e.g. Gurr 1970), recent studies have made a significant turn towards an emphasis on greed as a motivation. Explanations based on greed look at the possibility for groups to capture lucrative resources.

Civil war is seen as a move to capture lucrative resources – a massive predation of productive economic activity (Eliot *et al.* 2003). Civil wars are expected to unfold when the expected net gains employing violence exceed the expected net gains in maintaining the status quo, especially in cases of increasing inequalities and immobile assets (as in agrarian societies) (Boix 2008, 199).[1]

As we will see, some of the preconditions identified by scholars of civil war emerge as relevant in our cases as well – including economic inequality, social fragmentation, political instability, and international interventions. However, these factors need to be activated during long-lasting and open-ended mobilization processes.

Failed democratization

The social science literature on democratization and democratic consolidation has also been characterized, first, by structuralist approaches and then by more strategic ones: the outcomes of the democratization processes have been explained, based on some of the characteristics of the previous regimes, as well as by the dynamics of the transition. In general, the literature on democratization has singled out several favourable or unfavourable conditions, in some cases extending the reflection to the conditions for non-consolidation. Some of these explanations are relevant to understanding the shift from peaceful movements for democracy into civil war.

In research on democracy as well, mirroring the expectations developed in civil war studies, *economic* conditions have traditionally been considered an important predictor of democratization, with economic development and modernization creating a favourable terrain for democracy. In contrast, poverty, inequalities, and a backward economy have been considered as conditions jeopardizing democratic consolidation. In a broad synthesis of the determinants of democratization, Jan Teorell (2010) recently suggested that socioeconomic modernization helps to prevent downturns, as does economic freedom. While modernization facilitates the regime survival, economic crises trigger democratization processes, as they (especially under recessionary policies) tend to divide the elites, often causing private sector defection while producing mass protests on social issues.

From the *political* point of view, the characteristics of the previous authoritarian regimes are also significant: for instance, military dictatorships and multiparty autocracies have long been considered more likely to democratize than single-party regimes. Periods of liberalization are expected to facilitate consolidation, as they support the development of a civil society. Reversed liberalization is instead linked to the presence of a strong executive (either a president or a monarch) or to military intervention. Consolidation is considered easier when there is a simple transition, that is, only political democratization. It is more complicated when it involves, at the same time, transformations of the economic model (in particular, from state socialism to a free market) and/or the (re)emergence of an issue related to state sovereignty (Linz and Stepan 1996).

Other conditions that either favour or jeopardize consolidation are seen at the *international* level. Diffusion from neighbours' imitation as well as membership of regional organizations tend to promote democracy. However, foreign interventions only sometimes work in the expected direction, and they can even be the reason for failed democratization. Violence and wars have also been linked to globalization, as they fuel inequalities (Malesevic 2010).

Even though attempts to explain democratization through models based on large-N research are still ongoing, what is called the transitologist tradition has expressed disappointment with the endless search for preconditions, proposing instead to look at actors' behaviour during transitions. Using game theory, negotiations towards democracy are explained by the attitudes of the defenders and the challengers of the regime, as they are linked to the public preferences as well as to the positions of relevant actors, both domestic and international ones (Casper and Taylor 1996). Important elements for consolidation are the positions of the military, the judiciary, public service, the church, and civil society. As for the attitudes of the political elites, their ability to encapsulate conflicts and work within democratic institutions has been mentioned. In sum, the analytic framework 'focuses squarely on the strategic choices of elites, and popular action is considered relevant primarily for its indirect effects on intra-elite bargaining in situations in which a transition is already underway' (Ulfelder 2005, 313).

According to the widespread moderation thesis, consolidation is easier when civil society demobilizes, leaving space for the emergence of representative institutions. Masses are in fact presented as vulnerable to elite co-optation or manipulation, often focusing on very instrumentally defined purposes (see Przeworski 1991, 57; for a critique, see Baker 1999). Mass mobilization is thus conceived of as a short phase, while the analysis addresses

> the process by which soft-line incumbents and moderate opposition party leaders reach some implicit or explicit agreement on a transition from an authoritarian regime. To a substantial extent this is a model of democratization in which collective actors, mass mobilization and protest are largely exogenous.
>
> *(Collier 1999, 6)*

The *transición pactada* in Spain was considered (explicitly or implicitly) the model for successful democratization, with civil society's declining role perceived not only as inevitable – given the re-channelling of participation through the political parties and the electoral system – but also as desirable, in order to avoid frightening authoritarian soft-liners into abandoning the negotiation process with pro-democracy moderates. Moderation was therefore seen as a positive evolution, as the attitudes and goals of the various actors are changed through the process (Huntington 1991, 589).

Criticizing this vision, however, other scholars have considered social movements to be the main promoters of democratization. During the *transition*, old movements and new social movements have been seen as participants in large coalitions asking for democratic rights and social justice (Jelin 1987; Tarrow 1995). The mobilization of a pro-democracy coalition of trade unions, churches, and social movements has often been pivotal in supporting the movement towards democracy when faced with contending counter-movements that oppose liberalization. Protests can then be used by modernizing elites to push for free elections (Casper and Taylor 1996, 9–10; Glenn 2003, 104). Protests and the social cohesion of the opposition facilitate democratic consolidation (Bratton and van de Walle 1997). Radical insurgencies might even be necessary for democratization. This is the case in oligarchic societies in which 'economic elites rely on extra-economic coercion of labour by the state for the realization of incomes superior to those possible under more liberal, market-based arrangements' (Wood 2000, 6–7).

In sum, as we will see, our cases of failed democratization evolving into civil wars will confirm the importance of the absence of some (economic as well as political) conditions for democratization, as singled out in this stream of literature. In particular, they will confirm the difficulty in constructing long-term stability in the situation of the double weakness of the state and of civil society. However, they will also indicate that violence ensues from specific causal mechanisms, including strategic choices by civil society actors.

The demise of nonviolence

Agency is considered of pivotal importance in many theories on nonviolent resistance against authoritarian regimes. In this regard, Kurt Schock has defined unarmed insurrections as 'organized challenges to government authorities that depend primarily on methods of nonviolent action' (2005, xvi). Considering power as relational, studies on nonviolence resistance stress the importance of non-cooperation. Creative nonviolent interventions upset the normal order and forge new autonomous relations (ibid., 40). Nonviolent action is not just passive: non-institutionalized, it involves risks, not a simple compromise, and it is not necessarily oriented towards a moderate aim.

Moreover, some scholars link the success of nonviolence for democratization to its capacity to bring about elite division and regime defection. Nonviolent strategies, involving methods of protest and persuasion, non-cooperation, and nonviolent intervention, act according to the logic of a political jujitsu: in the presence of state repression, nonviolence is expected to reduce support for the regime, as it produces doubts about state legitimacy, divisions within the elites, and support by other (also international) actors. Methods of organizational dispersion (with loose coordination in networks, coalitions and decentralization) are considered to reduce the risks of repression, while concentration in public spaces helps to build solidarity and show support (ibid., 51).

Nonviolence diffuses power, thus maximizing the segments of the population who can take part in collective protests (ibid., 22). In fact, it is observed that rulers are undermined if citizens devise strategies of non-cooperation by refusing to acknowledge the rulers' legitimacy: contesting the mentality of obedience; failing to obey laws and cooperate with the regime; withdrawing material resources by refusing to use their skills to support the regime's activities; or undermining the state's sanctioning power (in particular, by persuading soldiers and police to side with the citizens) (Nepstad 2011). There is then an emergent dynamic, as 'When concessions are made by the authorities, mobilization is usually encouraged. Recognizing that even larger concessions might be wrought with larger numbers of participants in collective action, more people are mobilized, and with each new concession mobilization increases' (Schock 2005, 31). Importantly, this literature considers opportunities as created in action, as 'Divisions among political or military elites, for example, might be the consequence of rather than the precondition for mass mobilization' (ibid., 262).

Nonviolence, however, is not always successful. While much of the literature on nonviolent social change focuses on strategic factors (Chenoweth and Stephan 2011), some scholars have sought to explain unarmed revolutionary success with due attention to structural factors.

Divisions in the opposition challenge the chances for victory. As Schock noted, 'In nondemocratic contexts, the forging of oppositional networks is vital to successfully challenging the state and developing civil society and democratic relations' (2005, 29). The capacity to unite the opposition is considered particularly pivotal. So, 'the effect of repression on dissent is not merely a function of its level or intensity, but also a function of the configuration of opportunities in which it occurs as well as the attributes of the challenge' (ibid., 117). For instance, in China, nonviolence failed during the Tiananmen Square protests due to the absence of coalitions of the opposition; instead, divisions increased with a lack of leverage for support from abroad, and the regime maintained control of the military. While resilience in fact requires decentralized structures, which, being more democratic, strengthen oppositional consciousness although allowing for coordination, attempts at domination by one part have the opposite effect. Besides a non-totalizing oppositional consciousness, respectful of diversity, success is facilitated by the use of different methods of protest, persuasion, and non-cooperation. Acting on multiple spaces and places of resistance increases the capacity to disrupt the system's social reproduction in multiple locations (ibid., 167). Nonviolence is more likely to fail when these conditions are not present in the opposition. In particular, class or ethnic divisions in the opposition and, in contrast, the absence of cleavages in the military can undermine the chances of success (Nepstad 2011).

Research on civil resistance against authoritarian regimes has also pointed to the importance of the distribution of power within the elites – in the military, in particular – in determining the elites' responses. As Nepstad (ibid.) noted, while nonviolent revolutions that win the support of the military tend to succeed, when the military is composed of different ethnic groups, endowed with different amounts of power, it is difficult for the army as a whole to side with the opposition. Rather, there will be defectors, causing violent developments. At the international level, authoritarian regimes closely aligned with democratic powers are more likely to surrender power in the face of large protests. As Ritter (2015) explained, an 'iron cage of liberalism' pushes authoritarian leaders aligned with the West to simultaneously live up to the normative standards that they have appropriated in order to secure patronage, while at the same time remaining repressive enough to frighten the population into submission.

Our research will help to single out the particular effects of the strategic choices (such as the position of the military or of the civil society) that scholars of nonviolent resistances have identified to explain the failure of some nonviolent resistance. However, we will also suggest some specifications of the analysis with reference to the escalation of nonviolent conflict into violent forms.

The radicalization of social movements

Research on the radicalization of social movements has suggested structural as well as agentic explanations. First and foremost, previous research has indicated that radicalization often spreads during waves of protest, developing inside social movements. Most radical organizations have their roots in splits within social movement organizations, and most of the militants of underground organizations have previous experiences in them (della Porta 1995). In fact, social movements are networks of individuals and organizations, with common identities and conflictual aims, that use unconventional means (della Porta and Diani 2006, Chapter 1). Although they only very rarely advocate violence, they often use disruptive forms of protest that sometimes can escalate. Violence might, therefore, ensue from interactions on the streets with the police forces that are called upon to restore public order. Additionally, in specific historical contexts, some forms of protest have been considered violent per se, including the considerable use of physical force, stigmatized as illegitimate in the dominant culture (della Porta 1995, Chapter 1).

Social movement scholars have focused attention on the processes of radicalization in social movements, linking them to the interactions between these movements and the state (ibid.), the 'inversion' of collective actors (Wieviorka 1993), and the construction of exclusive identities (Goodwin 2004). Scholars of radicalization processes in the Middle East have increasingly referred to social movement studies (Gunning 2008; Karagiannis 2011; Wiktorowicz 2004). However, the space for developments in the field is still large (Goodwin 2004, 260).

Within the dominant paradigm of social movement studies, political violence can be explained as an outcome of the interactions between social movements and their opponents. In this field, in the 1970s and 1980s, great attention was paid to the impact of political opportunities and organizational resources, as well as framing, in explaining forms of action (della Porta and Diani 2006).

Within more structuralist approaches, radicalism or moderation is influenced by the available structure of *political opportunities*, which define the responses the movements meet in their environments, the reactions of the authorities, and the strength and postures of their potential allies and opponents. Violence is expected to develop, especially in periods of social transformation, which exacerbate political conflicts. In his influential model of collective action, Charles Tilly (1978, 52–5, 172–88) linked the use of violence to the emergence of new social groups, as violent actions tend to increase when new challengers fight their way into the polity and the old polity members refuse to leave. Stable formal characteristics of a political system, such as the degree of functional and territorial centralization, as well as experiences in the interactions with political and social opponents, are expected to have an impact on the development of political violence. The same can be said of more contingent political opportunities, such as those linked to the strength and strategies of allies and opponents. Countries with a strategy of exclusion (that is, repression of conflict) are expected to experience polarization of conflict with opponents, whereas a strategy of inclusion (co-optation of emergent demands) tends to moderate conflicts (della Porta 1995; 2013). In the same vein, social movement research has addressed the influence of a country's democratic history, noting that past authoritarianism often re-emerges in times of turmoil (della Porta *et al.* 2017). Young democracies tend to fear political protest and to have police forces that remain steeped in the authoritarian values of the preceding regime, with ensuing risks of radicalization (Flam 1994, 348; on Italy, see della Porta and Reiter 2004; Reiter 1998).

In a more strategic approach, the first answer about protest choices can be sought in the complexity and multiplicity of the objectives that protest is meant to achieve. An important characteristic of protest is the use of indirect channels to influence decision-makers since, as a political resource of the powerless, 'protest is successful to the extent that other parties are activated to political involvement' (Lipsky 1965, 1). Additionally, protest action has an important internal function: creating a sense of collective identity, which is a condition for action towards a common goal (Pizzorno 1993). As actions need to cover a plurality of sometimes contradictory objectives, the leaders of social movement organizations find themselves faced with a series of strategic dilemmas when choosing the form that protest should take (Jasper 2004; 2006). First, forms of action – such as violent ones – that are more likely to attract media attention are also more often stigmatized by potential allies. In addition, those actions that are more apt to produce internal solidarity might not find public approval. While leaders must often favour more radical actions in order to maintain rank-and-file support, these are precisely the kinds of actions that risk alienating potential allies.

Choices are influenced, then, by the resources available to particular groups. Social movement organizations need to *mobilize resources* in their environments and then invest them into various organizational tasks. The availability of some material and symbolic resources might push towards the use of political violence. The use of violence increases the probability of success of the challengers as the existence of 'radical flak' facilitates mobilization, insofar as the use of violence is a substitute for other resources (Gamson 1990; Piven and Cloward 1977). Organizational resources are not only material in nature: forms of action are culturally constrained. First, the repertoire of action that defines citizens' known choices when they want to resist or promote changes is finite, constrained in both time and space.

The 'technology' of protest evolves slowly, limited by the traditions handed down from one generation of activists to the next, and crystallized in institutions (Tilly 1986). Rooted in the shared subculture of the activists, repertoires contain the options considered practicable, while excluding others (ibid. 390). In addition to what is known, choices of forms of action are also constrained by what is considered to be right; that is, there are normative limits. Some forms of action are not even assessed in terms of their efficacy, as their moral implications are considered either dubious or plainly wrong.

Organizational resources and contextual opportunities are not just given: they exert their effects especially according to how they are *framed* by social movement actors. Scholars of social movements have used the concept of framing to address the way in which movement actors make sense of the external reality. Frames are schemata of interpretation that enable individuals 'to locate, perceive, identify and label' what happens within their life spaces and in the world at large (Snow *et al.* 1986, 464). Frame analysis focuses on the attribution of the meaning that lies behind the evolution of social movements by looking at the recognition of certain facts as social problems, the strategies to address them, and the motivations for action. Different collective actors might give different meanings to the same conditions, perhaps helping us to understand why similar contextual conditions meet with different reactions from different actors. So, the particular subcultures to which movements refer contribute to the creation of distinctive repertoires, while some framing that advocates or justifies violence can become resonant, as it is not only rooted in memories of previous struggles but also acquires credibility as the interpretation of a radicalized conflict.

Political opportunities, resource mobilization, and framing are central aspects of the theoretical tool-kit in social movement studies that are indeed analytically relevant in order to understand radicalization processes such as those that developed in our case studies. While paying them due attention, our empirical analysis will move towards a more dynamic approach, which has pointed to the importance of interactions within complex processes (della Porta 2014; McAdam, Tarrow, and Tilly 2001).

Developing a dynamic approach

As mentioned, social movement studies provide a tool-kit to build some relevant innovations in the research on political violence, but require some adaptations in order to understand how civil wars have developed out of failed democratization processes. First, they have tended to stress structure over agency, at the same time overemphasizing instrumental reasoning (see della Porta and Diani 2006, for a review). Explanations based on the political opportunities approach, in particular, have looked at the way in which contextual structures affect social movements by strongly limiting, if not totally determining, their extent, forms, and potential success. In addition to an emphasis on the dependency of social movement organizations upon external support, resource mobilization has also stressed rational reasoning, in its original version downplaying normative concerns or at least considering them exogenous to protest. Even framing approaches have been accused of adhering too closely to an instrumental logic. Additionally, social movement studies have focused on very specific social movements in a very specific geographical area and historical era, very rarely addressing authoritarian regimes or transitions to democracy – not to mention the extreme conditions of civil wars that develop in authoritarian regimes, or at least in imperfect, non-consolidated democracies.

In this project, we suggest that, in order to address the above-mentioned challenges, the use of social movement categories for research on political violence must be accompanied by some reflection on the relational, constructivist, and emergent aspects of violent developments (della Porta 2013).

Relational perspectives focus attention 'on interpersonal processes that promote, inhibit, or channel collective violence and connect it with nonviolent politics' (Tilly 2003, 20; see also McAdam *et al.* 2001, 22–4). In fact, as we will see, in civil wars, forms of action emerge, and are transformed, in the course of physical and symbolic *interactions* between social movements and their opponents, but also with their potential allies. Changes take place in encounters between social movements and the authorities, with reciprocal adjustments during more or less gradual processes, as 'actions of some kind associated with other actions and reactions, often expressed in some sort of reciprocal relationship' (Taylor and Horgan 2012, 130). Clashes with police or with political adversaries gradually, and sometimes imperceptibly, radicalize individuals and groups, justifying more and more violent forms of action. Within supportive environments, radical groups find logistical help as well as symbolic rewards (Malthaner 2010). Interpersonal processes 'promote, inhibit or channel collective violence and connect it with nonviolent politics' (Tilly 2003, 20).

Violence is constructed, in the sense that it is produced by and reproduces cognitive and affective processes. Cultural processes are particularly important for research on radicalization, as political violence affects collective identification by mobilizing symbolic resources. Cognition is then linked to emotions, which are particularly intense in social movements – defined indeed as passionate politics (Aminzade and McAdam 2001; Eyerman 2005; Goodwin, Jasper, and Polletta 2001). The role of narratives, dramaturgy, rhetoric, and rituals in intensifying commitment has been investigated for protest events in general (as an effect of an 'emotional liberation', see Flam 2005), as well as for specific critical transformative events (della Porta 2014). All of these elements are particularly relevant for an understanding of the emotionally intense experiences and specific cognitive processes in radical oppositional organizations and in highly conflictual times. In civil wars, justification frames emerge in action. Looking at El Salvador and South Africa, Elisabeth Wood observed that, during the war,

> political culture – the values, norms, practices, beliefs and collective identity of insurgencies – was not fixed but evolved in response to the experiences

of the conflict itself, namely previous rebellious actions, repression, and the ongoing interpretations of events by the participants themselves.

(2000, 19)

In the oligarchic regimes that Wood studied, the emergent character of the insurgency is stressed, as 'Rather than simply responding to new political opportunities extended by the state, the insurgent social movements create and expand the structure of political opportunity through their interim victories and ongoing struggles' (ibid., 12).

Violence therefore has an emergent character, which is not considered by causal models that neatly distinguish between dependent and independent variables. Choices of violence develop in fact in action, as they are tried and tested during times of intense action (della Porta 2016). As Beissinger noted:

> Not all historical eras are alike. There are times when change occurs so slowly that time seems almost frozen, though beneath the surface considerable turbulence and evolution may be silently at work. There are other times when change is so compressed, blaring, and fundamental that it is almost impossible to take its measure.
>
> *(2002, 47)*

First of all, opportunities are created in action. For instance, insurgent democratization in an oligarchic society can be explained not by static conditions, but by the activation of a group, which creates its own opportunities and resources. As Wood noted:

> In oligarchic societies, the exclusivist ideology of economic and regime elites (whether racially coded or not) toward subordinates (indeed, its explicit disdain for members of subordinate groups), together with the experience of repression, fuels deep resentments that can be mobilized by an insurgent group, providing a collective identity based on their claim to common citizenship that lessens the costs of collective action and contributes to the emergence of its leadership as an insurgent counter-elite.
>
> *(2000, 11)*

In fact, the political mobilization particularly affects the calculations of economic elites, through three main mechanisms: 'It may depress present profit rates (because of extended strikes or subsequent wage increases, for example), dampen expected profit rates (if mobilization is seen as likely to recur), or render expectations so uncertain that investors suspend investment' (ibid., 151).

Beyond the original cleavages, identities, and interests, new ones are created, weakened, or strengthened during the struggle. Motivations change in action, as 'often civil wars politicize innocuous or non-violent prewar cleavages' (Kalyvas 2006, 79). As Kalyvas observed:

> Almost every macrohistorical account of civil war points to the impor-
> tance of preexisting popular allegiances for the war's outcome, yet almost
> every microhistorical account points to a host of endogenous mechanisms,
> whereby allegiances and identities tend to result from the war or are radically
> transformed by it.
>
> *(ibid., 3)*

Violence therefore acquires a logic of its own, producing the very same polarization that then fuels it. In Kalyvas' words:

> The advent of war transforms individual preferences, choices, behaviour,
> and identities – and the main way in which civil war exercises its transforma-
> tive function is through violence. . . . Collective and individual preferences,
> strategies, values and identities are continuously shaped and reshaped in the
> course of the war.
>
> *(ibid., 389)*

The conflict thus produces exclusive identities.[2]

Norms are also transformed in action. During civil wars, political violence tends
to take on a dynamic of its own as it is 'feeding on the victimization it created'
(Beissinger 2002, 305). If during violent turmoil 'what was once understood as
normal is no longer recognizable', this is also because 'once initiated, violence
exercised its own independent effect on subsequent events, altering cultural identities' (ibid., 273). In fact, violent nationalism is even more difficult to predict than
nonviolent, as 'nationalist violence unfolds out of conflict and is contingent and
dependent on what takes place within conflictual situations' (ibid., 281). So, in
compressed moments, existing social norms are disrupted and violence becomes
normal (ibid., 294).

We expect radicalization processes leading to civil wars to create and re-create
the conditions of their own development.

From struggle for democracy to civil wars: the research

This book addresses a specific path to civil war: a path started with intense mobilization for democracy. Within a relational approach, della Porta (2014) has singled
out different paths of democratization, with weak states and weak civil society
bringing about the most troubling outcomes. In particular, she identified *eventful democratization* as defining cases in which authoritarian regimes break down
following – often short but intense – waves of protest. While protests in eventful democratization develop from the interaction between growing resources of
contestation and closed opportunities, social movements are not irrelevant players
in the other two paths. First of all, when opportunities open up because of elites'
realignment, *participated pacts* might ensue from the encounters of reformers in
institutions and moderates among social movement organizations. Although rarely

used, protest is also important here, as a resource to use as a threat at the negotiating table. If participated pacts see a relatively strong civil society that meets emerging opportunities, more *troubled* democratization paths develop in very repressive regimes that block the development of autonomous associations. In these cases, an escalation of violence often follows from the interaction of a suddenly mobilized opposition with a brutally repressive regime. Especially when there are divisions in and defections from security apparatuses, skills and resources for military action fuel coups d'état and civil war dynamics. While participated pacts and eventful democratization remain mainly peaceful, violence erupts in situations in which civil society is weaker and repression stronger. Together with brutal repression, escalation is fuelled in these cases by divisions in the repressive apparatuses that, through defections from armies and the police, provide the opposition with arms and military skills. Often, foreign actors contribute to this militarization and related radicalization. The type of regime as well as the type of transition affect the chances for consolidation:

> Transitions from below have better chances of installing a new government which has fewer nondemocratic elements because fewer, if any, promises have to be made to the authoritarian regime to get it to exit, allowing the new democracy more leeway to introduce reform.
>
> *(Casper and Taylor 1996, 10)*

In an implicit comparison with cases of non-radicalization into civil wars, which are more systematically addressed in other work (della Porta 2014; 2016), our research provides an in-depth descriptions of four cases of the trajectory from social movement for democratization into civil war: Syria (Chapter 3), Libya (Chapter 4) Yemen (Chapter 5) and the former Yugoslavia (Chapter 6). The four case studies have been chosen as paired comparisons within a most-different research design oriented to single out causal mechanisms rather than necessary and/or sufficient causes.

Our comparative research design is based on a combination of most-similar and most-different cases approaches. First, by looking at the three cases in the Middle East and North Africa (MENA) region – Libya, Syria, and Yemen – we will identify some common mechanisms that set the three apart from the other cases of the Arab Spring in which there was no such development. As other authors have already conducted research on cases such as Egypt and Tunisia, we are quite confident that we can apply this comparative dimension to the 'negative' cases in our analysis. Second, we will develop a most-different research design – aimed at singling out robust mechanisms – by moving through space and time in addressing the former Yugoslavia as a control case.

With a focus on the first moments of escalation into civil wars, however, we will also consider its activation and reproduction. Following McAdam, Tarrow, and Tilly's (2001) path-breaking approach to contentious politics, we aim to map out similar paths of relations. Using a most-different research design, our aim will be to highlight some existing similarities in the path from social movements to civil wars.

From the empirical point of view, the reported results stem from part of a research project on Mobilizing for Democracy, financed by an ERC Advanced Scholar grant. While other parts of the research have looked at the successful mobilizations as well as at their long-term legacies and memories, this part focuses instead on the particular trajectory from peaceful mobilization to violent civil wars. Fieldwork as well as desk top research will be presented on these cases. For each of the cases analysed, we surveyed existing studies in order to understand the functioning of the causal mechanisms we single out in Chapter 2. Further, when possible, we conducted in-depth expert interviews, as detailed in the presentation of the four case studies.

The structure of the book

In what follows, we will start with a map of causal mechanisms, followed by an analysis of Syria, Libya, Yemen, and then Yugoslavia.

Chapter 2 maps out the causal mechanisms that are mobilized in civil wars. Building upon causal mechanisms that were identified in research on clandestine political violence (della Porta 2013), the chapter addresses such factors at the onset of civil wars, focusing in particular on political destabilization, brutal policing, and social fragmentation. It then proceeds to single out activating mechanisms, such as the fluidification of borders and economic deterioration. It finally highlights the mechanisms of civil wars' reproduction at the relational level (the activation of military networks), the emotional level (spiralling revenge), and the cognitive level (sectarian identification). These mechanisms will be discussed in the following four chapters, each devoted to a case study.

Chapter 3, 'Beyond Syria: Civil society in failed episodes of democratization', explores the development of the Syrian democracy movement and how it related to the peaceful uprising, as well as to its subsequent descent into civil war. The chapter traces the (re)emergence of a movement for democracy in March 2011, with quickly spreading protests demanding 'change' and 'freedom'. It then moves on to narrate its development in the following five years, with the situation steadily turning into a civil war in which multiple groups, supported by a variety of international actors, are fighting – or defending – the regime of Bashar al-Assad and each other. These developments leave the original movement for democratization struggling to survive.

The first section examines the (historically contingent) conditional factors present at the onset of the uprising. On one hand, it addresses the weakness of Syrian civil society due to decades of harsh repression of any type of independent social activism. On the other, it singles out the weakness of the Syrian state, due to its lack of legitimacy among large sections of Syrian society. Taking these conditional factors as a starting point, the second section analyses the processes of fragmentation, radicalization, and the turn to civil war in the Syrian uprising, singling out some of its underlying causal mechanisms. Particular attention is given to how state repression instigated a radicalization within the movement for democracy, and how this radicalization then legitimized further repression in the period between 2011 and 2012. Subsequently, the chapter analyses how a process of upward scale shift – with the Syrian conflict increasingly intertwining with broader conflicts in the region and beyond – intersected with the uprising, turning increasingly violent, sectarian, and fragmented with the increasing influence of foreign actors.

Chapter 4 focuses on 'The failure of the Libyan political transition and the descent into civil war'. The anti-Qaddafi protests reached a critical juncture on 17 February 2011, initiating a string of institutional transformative and disintegrating processes addressed in this chapter. Some of the important factors that are central to the eruption of the popular revolt in Libya are the weakening regime, dysfunctional state institutions, disgruntled tribal allies, deeply dissatisfied urban populations, and the international military intervention on behalf of the opposition. In addition, media outlets and non-governmental organizations have contributed to a massive and temporary democratic output through which the public feels that it is participating in a meaningful debate over its collective future. Such developments were quickly reversed due to the failure of the political elites and numerous militias to agree on a long-term strategy to handle the post-Qaddafi transition. The disagreement then became increasingly violent, erupting into a fully-fledged civil war in the aftermath of the country's first parliamentary elections in July 2012. The chapter will single out some of the causal mechanisms bringing about the escalation, with particular focus on the fragmentation of civil society as well as the spread of military skills and resources. The largest and most powerful militias quickly allied themselves with the prominent and influential political allies, a process that crystallized two major competing political and military forces in Libya, both of which created governing structures.

The emergence of Islamic State (IS) militants and the spread of their control over several Libyan cities adds to the conflict's complexity and subsequently to the prospect of conflict resolution. Besides the endemic insecurity posed by militias, some of which joined IS (indicating the development of radical subcultures with distinctive repertoires of action), there is another challenge. The Libyan state's institutional weaknesses, including a weak civil society, represent potentially insurmountable challenges for the political elites to overcome – despite their recent signing of a peace agreement. The chapter addresses the impact of pre-existing socio-political cleavages in the form of competing tribes, regions, and ethnic groups, but also of tension between urban and rural settlements, on collective identification for both political elites and various militia groups. The religio-ideological framing of violence is then presented as the primary marker of increasing numbers of militants in Libya (ideological encapsulation). IS, among other prominent radical groups, is being increasingly forced (by other powerful militias allied to the mainstream political elites) to consolidate in limited urban spaces, becoming targets for the two competing government forces as well as international actors (the United States, France, the United Kingdom, Egypt, Emirates, and so on).

Chapter 5, entitled 'Yemen's failed transition: From peaceful protests to war of "all against all"', traces the dynamics and evolution of contentious politics in Yemen since 2011. This peripheral country of the Arabian Peninsula has often been perceived through the lens of terrorism, conjuring up images of poverty, unruly tribes, and a traditional society whose members are preoccupied mostly with chewing *qat*. When the first protests were organized in Sana'a in January 2011 at the start of the 'Arab Spring', Yemen's President Ali Abdullah Saleh dismissed the idea of a revolution, calmly stating, 'Yemen is not Tunisia.' Many observers seemed to believe this too, arguing that Yemen's population – highly divided, largely rural, illiterate and lacking access to the Internet – could not be compared to more 'modern' nations like Tunisia, Syria or Egypt, and thus mobilization for radical change was unlikely. Against the narrative of Yemen's exceptionalism, and in line with the theoretical framework of this book, this chapter examines Yemen's popular uprising and scrutinizes the mechanisms of violent radicalization that were put in motion as what began as civil resistance turned into civil war. By so doing, it tells the story of how a popular democratization project that united divergent actors with the common goal of toppling the regime was gradually hijacked by warring elite factions and self-interested regional powers. The chapter reveals how, among other things, economic destitution, social fragmentation, and sectarian identifications have been exploited by entrepreneurs of violence, tearing apart Yemeni society, and fuelling further conflict.

Chapter 6 addresses 'Yugoslavia: From social movement to state movement to civil war'. In line with the rest of this volume, this chapter seeks to uncover Yugoslavia's path from social movement to civil war. To do so, the chapter first depicts the structural context of the country in the later Cold War period. It then retells the story of how the peaceful, strike-based movement that sought nonviolently to remedy economic concerns was hijacked by Slobodan Milošević and used to serve his political objectives, which resonated with the concern of ethnic Serbs. The Yugoslav transition to democracy is perhaps the most complex of all the Eastern European cases, and certainly the most violent one. In fact, no other former socialist country transitioned to democracy through the path of civil war. The country's transition process is therefore puzzling for several reasons. It can be argued that Yugoslavia enjoyed the most favourable initial conditions of any country in the region: the regime was relatively liberal, there was an indigenous, vibrant civil society in place, an economic crisis had put politicians on the defensive, and the country was not overly tied to either Western or Eastern influence. Had these structural conditions told the full story, Yugoslavia might have been able to dissolve without the most heinous conflict Europe had experienced since World War II. However, one major factor came to trump all others: nationalism. As a federation consisting of six republics and two autonomous provinces, imposed on its citizens by the communists that came to power after World War II, only communism could hold the country together. Once that ideological glue was removed, Yugoslavia collapsed on itself. The chapter thus emphasizes, in line with the theoretical framework of the book at large, how social movements may be a force not only for democratization, but also for nationalist objectives that run the risk of degenerating into political violence on a massive scale.

The concluding chapter summarizes the empirical results, pointing to the main contributions to the social science literature on civil war, democratization, nonviolent rebellions, and social movements. In particular, taking as a point of departure causal mechanisms that have been singled out in research on clandestine political violence, our case studies point to some common mechanisms of radicalization into political violence in general, but also to the need to specify them when looking at the development of civil wars. The concluding chapter will close by acknowledging the limitations of the research and indicating future moves.

Notes

1 According to Boix (2008, 216):

> In economies where wealth is either mobile or hard to tax or confiscate, sustained political violence to grab those assets does not pay off since their owners either can leave in response to the threat of confiscation or are indispensable to the optimal exploitation of assets.

2 Brubaker (2004) noted that coding a conflict as ethnic depends on the prevailing framing developed through in-group policing, deliberate staging of violence, and ethnic outbidding, either to mobilize or demobilize the population.

References

Aminzade, Ron, and McAdam, Doug. 2001. 'Emotions and contentious politics', in Ronald Aminzade, Jack Goldstone, Doug McAdam, Elizabeth Perry, William H. Sewell Jr., Sidney Tarrow, and Charles Tilly (eds), Silence and Voice in the Study of Contentious Politics. Cambridge: Cambridge University Press, pp. 51–88.

Baker, Gideon. 1999. 'The taming idea of civil society'. Democratization 6(3): 1–29.

Beissinger, Mark R. 2002. Nationalist Mobilization and the Collapse of the Soviet State. Cambridge: Cambridge University Press.

Blimes, Randall. 2006. 'The indirect effect of ethnic heterogeneity on the likelihood of civil war onset'. Journal of Conflict Resolution 50(4): 536–47.

Boix, Carles. 2008. 'Civil war and the guerrilla warfare in the contemporary world', in Stathis Kalyvas, Ian Shapiro, and Tarek Masoud (eds), Order, Conflict and Violence. Cambridge: Cambridge University Press, pp. 197–218.

Bratton, Michael, and van de Walle, Nicolas. 1997. Democratic Experiments in Africa: Regime Transition in Comparative Perspective. Cambridge: Cambridge University Press.

Brubaker, Rogers. 2004. Ethnicity Without Groups. Cambridge, MA: Harvard University Press.

Casper, Gretchen, and Taylor, Michelle M. 1996. Negotiating Democracy: Transitions from Authoritarian Rule. Pittsburgh, PA: University of Pittsburgh Press.

Chenoweth, Erica, and Stephan, Maria. 2011. Why Civil Resistance Works. New York: Columbia University Press.

Collier, Paul, Eliot, V.L., Hegre, Havard, Hoeffler, Anke, Reynal-Querol, Martha, and Sambanis, Nicholas. 2003. Breaking the Conflict Trap. Civil War and Development Policy. Washington, DC: World Bank and New York: Oxford University Press.

Collier, Paul, and Hoeffler, Anke. 2004. 'Greed and grievances in civil wars'. *Oxford Economic* Papers 56(4): 563–95.

Collier, Ruth Berins. 1999. Paths toward Democracy: The Working Class and Elites in Western Europe and South America. New York: Cambridge University Press.

della Porta, Donatella. 1995. Social Movements, Political Violence and the State. Cambridge: Cambridge University Press.

della Porta, Donatella. 2013. *Clandestine Political Violence*. Cambridge: Cambridge University Press.

della Porta, Donatella. 2014. *Mobilizing for Democracy*. Oxford: Oxford University Press.

della Porta, Donatella. 2016. *Where Did the Revolution Go?* Cambridge: Cambridge University Press.

della Porta, Donatella, Andretta, Massimiliano, Fernandes, Tiago, Romanos, Eduardo, and Vogiatzoglou, Markos. 2017. *Memories in Movements*. Submitted to Oxford University Press.

della Porta, Donatella, and Diani, Mario. 2006. Social Movements: An Introduction. Oxford: Blackwell.

della Porta, Donatella, and Reiter, Herbert. 2004. *Polizia e Protesta*. Bologna: Il Mulino.

Elbadawi, Ibrahim, and Sambanis, Nicholas. 2002. 'How much war will we see? Explaining the prevalence of civil war.' *Journal of Conflict Resolution* 46(3): 307–34.

Evans, Graham, and Newman, Jeffrey. 1998. *Dictionary of International Relations*. Madison, WI: University of Wisconsin Press.

Eyerman, Ron. 2005. 'How social movements move: emotions and social movements', in Helena Flam, and Debra King (eds), Emotions and Social Movements. London: Routledge, pp. 41–57.

Fearon, James, and Laitin, David. 2003. 'Ethnicity, insurgency, and civil war'. *American Political Science Review* 97(1): 75–90.

Flam, Helena. 1994. 'Political responses to the anti-nuclear challenge', in Helena Flam (ed.), States and Antinuclear Movements. Edinburgh: Edinburgh University Press, pp. 329–54.

Flam, Helena. 2005. 'Emotions' map: a research agenda', in Helena Flam, and Debra King (eds), Emotions and Social Movements. London: Routledge, pp. 19–41.

Gamson, William. 1990. *The Strategy of Social Protest*. Belmont, CA: Wadsworth.

Glenn, John K. 2003. 'Contentious politics and democratization: comparing the impact of social movements on the fall of Communism in Eastern Europe'. Political Studies 51: 103–20.

Goodwin, Jeff. 2004. 'Review essays: what must we explain to explain terrorism?' *Social Movement Studies* 3: 259–65.

Goodwin, Jeff, Jasper, James M., and Polletta, Francesca (eds). 2001. Passionate Politics: Emotions and Social Movements. Chicago: University of Chicago Press.

Gunning, Jeroen. 2008. *Hamas in Politics*. New York: Columbia University Press.

Gurr, Ted R. 1970. *Why Men Rebel*. Princeton, NJ: Princeton University Press.

Henderson, Errol, and Singer, J. David. 2000. 'Civil war in the post-colonial world, 1946–92'. *Journal of Peace Research* 37(3): 275–99.

Herbst, Jeffrey I. 2000. *States and Power in Africa: Comparative Lessons in Authority and Control*. Princeton, NJ: Princeton University Press.

Huntington, Samuel. 1991. 'How countries democratize'. Political Science Quarterly 106(4): 579–616.

Huntington, Samuel. 1993. 'The clash of civilizations'. *Foreign Affairs* 72: 22–49.

Jasper, James M. 2004. 'A strategic approach to collective action: looking for agency in social movement choices'. *Mobilization: An International Journal* 9: 1–16.

Jasper, James M. 2006. *Getting Your Way: Using Strategy in Everyday Life.* Chicago: University of Chicago Press.

Jasper, James M., and Duyvendak, Jan-Willem (eds). 2015. *Players and Arena.* Amsterdam: Amsterdam University Press.

Jelin, Elizabeth (ed.). 1987. *Movimientos Sociales y Democracía Emergente,* 2 vols. Buenos Aires: Centro Editor de América Latina.

Kaldor, Mary. 1999. *New and Old Wars.* Cambridge: Polity Press.

Kalyvas, Stathis N. 2006. *The Logic of Violence in Civil War.* Cambridge: Cambridge University Press.

Kalyvas, Stathis N. 2008. 'Promises and pitfalls of an emergent research program: the microdynamics of civil war', in Stathis Kalyvas, Ian Shapiro, and Tarek Masoud (eds), *Order, Conflict and Violence.* Cambridge: Cambridge University Press, pp. 397–421.

Karagiannis, Immanuel. 2011. *Political Islam in Central Asia. The Challenge of Itzb Ut-Tahrir.* London: Routledge.

Kogan Iasnyi, Victor, and Zissernan-Brodsky, Diana. 1998. 'Chechen separatism', in Metta Spencer (ed.), *Separatism.* Lanham, MD: Rowman and Littlefield.

Lake, Anthony, and Rothchild, Donald. 1998. 'Spreading fear: the genesis of transnational ethnic conflict', in Anthony Lake, and Donald Rothchild, *The International Spread of Ethnic Conflict.* Princeton, NJ: Princeton University Press.

Linz, Juan, and Stepan, Alfred. 1996. Problems of Democratic Transition and Consolidation: Southern Europe, South America, and Post-Communist Europe. Baltimore, MD: The Johns Hopkins University Press.

Lipsky, Michael. 1965. *Protest and City Politics.* Chicago: Rand McNally.

Malesevic, Sinisa. 2010. *The Sociology of War and Violence.* Cambridge: Cambridge University Press.

Malthaner, Stefan. 2010. *Mobilizing the Faithful.* Frankfurt am Main: Campus Verlag.

Mann, Michael. 2012. *The Sources of Social Power.* Vol. 1. Cambridge: Cambridge University Press.

McAdam, Doug, Tarrow, Sidney, and Tilly, Charles. 2001. Dynamics of Contention. New York: Cambridge University Press.

Nepstad, Sharon Erickson. 2011. *Nonviolent Revolutions: Civil Resistance in the Late 20th Century.* New York: Oxford University Press.

Olson Lounsbery, Marie, and Pearson, Frederic. 2009. *Civil Wars: Internal Struggles, Global Consequences.* Toronto: University of Toronto Press.

Piven, Frances F., and Cloward, Richard. 1977. *Poor People's Movements.* New York: Pantheon.

Pizzorno, Alessandro (ed.). 1993. Le Radici della Politica Assoluta e Altri Saggi. Milan: Feltrinelli.

Przeworski, Adam. 1991. Democracy and the Market: Political and Economic Reforms in Eastern Europe and Latin America. Cambridge: Cambridge University Press.

Reiter, Herbert. 1998. 'Police and public order in Italy, 1944–1948; the case of Florence', in Donatella della Porta, and Herbert Reiter (eds), *Policing Protest: The Control of Mass Demonstrations in Western Democracies.* Minneapolis, MN: The University of Minnesota Press, pp. 143–65.

Ritter, Daniel P. 2015. *The Iron Cage of Liberalism: International Politics and Unarmed Revolutions in the Middle East and North Africa.* Oxford: Oxford University Press.

Salehyan, Idean. 2009. *Rebels Without Borders.* Ithaca, NY: Cornell University Press.

Sambanis, Nicholas. 2001. 'Do ethnic and non-ethnic civil wars have the same causes?' *Journal of Conflict Resolution* 45(3): 259–82.

Sambanis, Nicholas. 2003. 'Using case studies to expand economic models of civil war'. CPR Working Paper no. 5.

Sambanis, Nicholas. 2004. 'What is civil war? Conceptual and empirical complexities of an operational definition'. *Journal of Conflict Resolution* 48: 814–58.

Schock, Kurt. 2005. *Unarmed Insurrections. People Power Movements in Nondemocracies.* Minneapolis, MN: The University of Minnesota Press.

Snow, David A., Rochford, E. Burke, Worden, Steven K. Jr., and Benford, Robert D. 1986. 'Frame alignment processes, micromobilization, and movement participation'. American Sociological Review 51: 464–81.

Tarrow, Sidney. 1995. 'Mass mobilization and regime change: pacts, reform and popular power in Italy (1918–1922) and Spain (1975–1978)', in Richard Gunther, Nikiforos Diamandouros, and Hans-Jürgen Puhle (eds), Democratic Consolidation in Southern Europe. Baltimore, MD: The Johns Hopkins University Press, pp. 204–30.

Taylor, Max, and Horgan, John. 2012. 'A conceptual framework for addressing psychological process in the development of the terrorists', in John Horgan and Kurt Braddock (eds), *Terrorism Studies: A Reader.* London: Routledge, pp. 130–44.

Teorell, Jan. 2010. *Determinants of Democratization: Explaining Regime Change in the World, 1972–2006.* Cambridge: Cambridge University Press.

Tilly, Charles. 1978. *From Mobilization to Revolution.* Reading, MA: Addison Wesley.

Tilly, Charles. 1986. *The Contentious French.* Cambridge, MA: Harvard University Press.

Tilly, Charles. 1993. *Coercion, Capital and European States, A.D. 990–1992.* London: Blackwell.

Tilly, Charles. 2003. *The Politics of Collective Violence.* Cambridge: Cambridge University Press.

Ulfelder, Jay. 2005. 'Contentious collective action and the breakdown of authoritarian regimes'. *International Political Science Review* 26(3), 311–34.

Weinstein, Jeremy. 2007. *Inside Rebellion: The Politics of Insurgent Violence.* Cambridge: Cambridge University Press.

Wieviorka, Michel. 1993. *The Making of Terrorism.* Chicago: The University of Chicago Press.

Wiktorowicz, Quintan. 2004. 'Islamic activism in social movement theory'. in Quintan Wiktorowicz (ed.), *Islamic Activism: A Social Movement Theory Approach.* Bloomington, IN: Indiana University Press, pp. 1–33.

Wilkinson, Steven I. 2008. 'Which group identities lead to most violence? Evidence from India', in Stathis Kalyvas, Ian Shapiro, and Tarek Masoud (eds), *Order, Conflict and Violence.* Cambridge: Cambridge University Press, pp. 271–300.

Wood, Elisabeth Jean. 2000. *Forging Democracy from Below: Insurgent Transitions in South Africa and El Salvador.* Cambridge: Cambridge University Press.

Wood, Elisabeth Jean. 2015. 'Social mobilization and violence in civil war and their social legacies', in Donatella della Porta, and Mario Diani (eds), *Oxford Handbook of Social Movements.* Oxford: Oxford University Press.

2

CAUSAL MECHANISMS IN CIVIL WARS

A sensitizing map

Donatella della Porta

A dynamic approach to civil wars: an introduction

Research on civil wars has developed chiefly through large-N studies, oriented to single out the causal determinants of the phenomenon, and through single case studies oriented mainly to thick description. In contrast, the search for causal mechanisms has been largely absent in this field of study. This is why, when looking for inspiration for potential mechanisms, we referred to cognate fields of study, focusing on different forms of political violence. In particular, in her research on clandestine political violence, della Porta (2013) suggested an explanatory model linking the contextual, organizational, and interpersonal perspectives – in other words, environmental conditions, group dynamics, and individual motivations. Although radicalization processes, as a political phenomenon, are certainly influenced by the conditions of the political system in which they emerge, they involve fairly small organizations whose internal dynamics inevitably influence their very development. Moreover, like other forms of deviant behaviour, political violence generates changes in individuals' value systems and perceptions of external reality that in turn affect the organization as a whole. In the social movement field, this attention to causal mechanisms linking different analytic levels entered the agenda with the turn towards contentious politics (McAdam, Tarrow, and Tilly 2001), bridging research on social movements with work on revolutions, civil wars, and so on. After looking at the mechanisms proposed by della Porta in her research on clandestine political violence, we will propose parallel ones related to existing research on civil wars.

Causal mechanisms in research on clandestine political violence

Throughout her research, della Porta (2013) has explored causal mechanisms as initiating chains of interaction. We examine similar chains as contributing to the

onset, the persistence, and the demise of radicalization processes. Escalating policing, competitive escalation during protest cycles, and the activation of militant
networks were present at the *onset*. The *persistence* of radical organizations, but also
their transformation, were linked to mechanisms of organizational compartmentalization, action militarization, and ideological encapsulation at the organizational
level, as well as militant enclosure at the interpersonal level. Finally, the *exit* from
radicalization processes was characterized by the activation of mechanisms of de-
escalating policing, moderation of repertoires of protest, organizational demise,
deactivation of militant networks, and affective and cognitive openings.

At the onset of clandestine political violence, during intense political and
social conflicts, forms of action escalate through internal competition as well as
encounters with the state. *Competitive escalation* is the term used to indicate a causal
mechanism that links the radicalization of action forms to the interactions within
and between social movement organizations, social movements, social movement
families, and social movement sectors. Violence is used in part to outbid the com-
petitor, and in part as an unplanned consequence of experimentation with new
tactics during frequent interactions that include physical fights. Activists are thus
slowly socialized to the use of radical means of action. Protest – by challenging
the public order – often brings about encounters between protestors and police,
which tend to become the most visible face of the state. Through *escalating policing*, violence then develops as a reaction to hard and indiscriminate repression,
considered by the challengers as brutal and deeply unjust. In processes of reciprocal
tactical adaptation, violence and counter-violence spiral on each other (della Porta
and Tarrow 2012). Transformative events of increased brutality not only create
martyrs and myths, but also push forward the development of structures and norms
that reproduce violence, building pathways into radical political violence. The
activation of militant networks is the mechanism that forces pathways towards radical
forms of violence. Affective and cognitive dynamics lie at the basis of recruitment
processes within close networks of friends-comrades. They also then support the
maintenance of commitments in the underground.

After the onset, certain mechanisms explain the development and persistence
of underground organizations. In particular, the research points to organizational compartmentalization, action militarization, and ideological encapsulation.
Organizational structures vary in their clandestine extent, in an unequal mix
of hierarchical and network-like components. Radical groups try to adapt to a
more or less hostile environment, often attempting a precarious balance of structures open to sympathizers and more secretive organizations. A mechanism of
organizational compartmentalization tends, however, to push the groups towards
increasing isolation. As state repression produces arrests and deaths among their
ranks, and support shrinks, the radical groups tend to opt for more and more
compartmentalized, isolated structures. A similar mechanism is visible in the evolution of the action strategy of these organizations. While violence is initially
used sporadically, and low-intensity forms tend to prevail, over time a mechanism
of *action militarization* emerges, with a preference for spectacular and deadly

repertoires. The more isolated the groups, the more they in fact lose hope of persuading potential supporters through political propaganda, and the more they use (often indiscriminate) killing and assassinations, engaging in a sort of war with the state. In parallel to these transformations, the narratives developed by the radical organizations change as well. A mechanism of *ideological encapsulation* defines the evolution towards an increasingly elitist definition of the self, a Manichean vision of those outside of the organization as absolute evil, and an essentialization of violence.

Contextual and organizational mechanisms affect individuals through the development of *freedom-fighter identities*. In particular, the activation of militant networks sustains high-risk activism and, once in the underground, a militant enclosure. If grievances and motivations surely count in the sequences of individual choices towards joining the underground, these choices are rarely made by isolated militants. Rather, grievances and motifs are nurtured within special milieus, and recruitment happens in blocks. Through a mechanism of *militant enclosure*, militants enter deeper and deeper into a closed ghetto. As relations outside of the organizations become – logistically and psychologically – increasingly limited, the radical organization remains the only target of *affective focusing*. While the affective life focuses on the other members of the radical group, imprisoned or slain fellow militants become particular motivations for revenge and emulation. At the same time, a *cognitive closure* towards the outside discourages the acknowledgement of defeats and mistakes, and the perception of alternative methods.

However, escalation is neither unavoidable nor endless: mechanisms of escalation are – eventually – reversed. The moderation of repertoires of protest, de-escalating policing, organizational demise, deactivation of militant networks, affective and cognitive openings are all mechanisms that, even if accompanied by tensions and difficulties, still lead to micro, meso, and macro processes of disengagement from violence.

From research on clandestine political violence to research on civil wars

Our empirical research on the path from nonviolent resistance to civil war takes these mechanisms as points of departure, assessing the extent to which they either hold or need revision when looking at a type of political violence which, in a different way from clandestine political violence, implies a contested claim on territorial control. In fact, our case studies point to some common mechanisms of radicalization into political violence in general, but also to the need to specify them when looking at the development of civil wars.

The main difference between civil war and clandestine political violence is seen not only in the number of deaths and the size of the groups involved in perpetrating violence, but also in the degree to which violence disrupts the life of citizens, creating a pursuit for security. While emerging in a context marked by the weakness of both civil society and the state, issues of legitimating violence and reconstituting order often emerge for challengers as they are related to the need to establish (at least partial) territorial control. At the macro level, with economic collapse and political destabilization, threats dominate over opportunities, while social fragmentation triggers calls for the reconstitution of communities and institutions. Brutal and indiscriminate policing increases fear but also outrage, and escalation is triggered by the presence of violent entrepreneurs who organize military groups, as insecurity (also fuelled by economic impoverishment) brings about the search for patrons with access to economic resources and means of violence. The activation of militant networks involves the high presence of military skills and resources, even including the creation of militias. Justifying frameworks and motivations emerge in action, as more and more brutal attacks bring about calls for revenge. Through cyclically recurring processes, various forms of violence, from civil wars to genocide, politicides, massacres, and coups d'états are linked to each other. In fact, 'Once a rebellion has started, a society risks being caught in a conflict trap. Ending a conflict is difficult, and even if it ends, the risk that it will start again is high' (Collier *et al.* 2003, 91).

Against a traditional static vision of the causes and consequences of civil wars, in what follows we shall single out some main mechanisms that trigger and sustain civil wars (see Figure 2.1). At the onset, we will in particular mention political destabilization, indiscriminate policing and social fragmentation and violence justifying framing. Activating mechanisms ensue, including the fluidification of borders and security deterioration. Mechanisms of reproduction are then singled out in the activation of military networks, the spiralling feelings of revenge and the sectarian identification.

Mechanisms at the onset	Activating mechanisms	Mechanisms of reproduction
Political destabilization	Fluidification of borders	Activation of military networks
Indiscriminate repression	Security deterioration	(relational)
Social fragmentation		Spiralling revenge
		(emotional)
		Sectarian identification
		(cognitive)

FIGURE 2.1 Causal mechanisms in civil wars

Political destabilization

In times of political instability, the onset of civil war is triggered by indiscriminate and also partial forms of repression. We focus attention upon specific paths of descent into civil wars: those starting from failed episodes of democratization. Research on civil wars has often looked at political regimes. In particular, intermediate levels of authoritarianism have been associated with a higher probability of civil war. Institutional theories mention that partial democracy fuels instability, even if not automatically but rather through the role of leaders as well as state discrimination. Semi-democracy is associated with the probability of civil war, especially in militarized post-colonial states with relatively low economic development. This is because 'neither the potential for resolving conflicts peacefully nor the threat of repression is sufficient to prevent insurgency' (Henderson and Singer 2000, 279). Therefore, Hegre and Sambanis (2006, 508) have listed the following robust results, relating the onset of civil wars to 'large population and low income levels, low rates of economic growth, recent political instability and inconsistent democratic institutions, small military establishments and rough terrain, and war-prone and undemocratic neighbors'.

All of these preconditions are especially relevant under conditions of pre-existing instability. A history of political instability has been considered a precondition for civil war (for a survey of the literature, see Wood 2015). Large-N studies have revealed that democracy is negatively correlated with civil war only when it is consolidated, but failed democratic transitions can increase the risk of political violence. In the same vein, partial democracy has been seen to tend towards instability (Goldstone *et al.* 2010). The opportunities (as chance of success) for change that need to be present in order for challengers to take up arms (Most and Starr 1989) are present in particular when there is a power vacuum, either during the search for succession (Blainey 1988) or when leaders have had precarious control since the very beginning. In times of a power vacuum, violent groups can find safe havens for training and socialization into violence.

This is all the more so when precarious equilibriums are unsettled, even in episodes of democratization. Notwithstanding the advantages of democracy for non-violent conflicts, democratization processes may in fact facilitate violence as they are volatile moments (Snyder 2000). Literature on civil wars has indeed considered democratization processes as potentially at risk of turning into civil wars, as volatile moments produce instability. It has in fact been noted that

> States rarely transition quickly and effectively from an autocratic regime to one that is solidly democratic . . . Transitions to democracy inevitably mean a loosening of the control leaders once had. Accountability becomes an issue and repression a less acceptable tool for dealing with dissent.
>
> *(Olson Lounsbery and Pearson 2009, 59)*

In fact, 'Although democracy ideally stipulates conflict regulation through norms and institutions, it also induces conflict via increased contestation and polarization' (ibid., 29), as competition for votes increases radical rhetoric and struggles for power.

In cases of persistent conflicts, tension also emerges between strategies of peacebuilding, which is oriented to short-term aims, and democratization, which requires long-term efficacy and legitimacy. Particularly problematic are transitions for newly independent states burdened by a legacy of colonial rule (ibid.). Failed democratic transitions may increase the risk of political violence, especially in regions where a previous special status has been revoked or demands for self-determination increase. This situation is more likely where large minority groups are territorially concentrated and ethnic networks are strong (ibid.). This strengthens the risks of majority rule, and particularly the risk of violence in the first election, as 'Not only may the move to democratization fail; in addition, democratization can exacerbate violent conflict' (Jarstad 2008, 29).

In addition, episodes of democratization might prompt international interventions that might increase instability. Destabilization can be fuelled by international interventions. Blockages in international relations have been mentioned as pushing superpowers to fuel violence as surrogate wars. During the Cold War, for example, clandestine attacks as well as civil wars were defined as 'proxy wars' between the two superpowers, which they fuelled but also controlled. Conditions of occupation by foreign powers have also been said to trigger the temptation to use clandestine violence as a (relatively cheap) form of opposition, when it is impossible to address and mobilize large groups of the population. In a politically relevant international environment, third parties might increase instability. As Balch-Lindsay and Enterline (2000, 615) noted, 'Extremely long civil wars correspond to the equitable distribution of third party interventions – stalemates prolong wars . . . Separatist civil wars and ongoing civil wars in states proximate to the civil war state result in civil wars of longer duration.' As third parties – mainly neighbourhoods and major regional powers – often intervene to react to other third party interventions, the extent and duration of violent conflicts increase. In particular, the technology of the rebellion is affected by international intervention, with a decline of irregular wars in the post-Cold War period which increased the military capacity of rebels in proxy wars (Kalyvas and Balcells 2010). Unarmed protests seem more likely to descend into civil wars in countries that have not been integrated into the democratic global community (Ritter 2015).

In sum, failed episodes of democratization might increase instability, through the intensification of internal domestic conflicts as well as interventions by third parties.

Indiscriminate repression

While protests weaken the government and the regime, repression closes the spaces for democratic processes, activating spirals of reciprocal retribution. Repression tends to be more brutal in authoritarian than in democratic regimes (e.g. Uysal 2005, on Turkey), varying however in the degree of toleration for some actors and forms of protest, as well as in the forms of policing (Boudreau 2004; Ritter 2015). In some cases, repression transforms protest into escalated violence (Gurr 2000), as 'government repression increases opposition and, if repression is incomplete, it can lead to violence' (Sambanis 2003, 34).

At the onset of civil wars, we find high levels of repression by a regime (often corrupt) that exercises control, however uneven that control is, over its territory. In fact, a general political precondition identified in explaining high levels of political violence is the weakness of the state in terms of repressive capacity and even territorial control. In particular, the weakness of central governments in terms of financial, organizational, and political resources facilitates insurgency (Fearon and Laitin 2003).

This is especially the case with indiscriminate repression, perceived as deeply unfair and thus producing anger. Escalation is more likely when indiscriminate state violence triggers moral outrage, thus legitimizing a turn to violence (Wood 2003). Indiscriminate repression then interacts with limited control within the micro-dynamics of conflict. Influentially, Kalyvas has observed that information that allows for selective violence is costly, and decisions to engage in repression are usually delegated to local units. This in turn leads to inaccurate news, which means repression tends to be indiscriminate. In particular, 'malicious denunciation is closely related to interpersonal conflict in the context of "organic" solidarity: small-scale, face-to-face social settings, where people develop dense interpersonal interactions, living and working together in daily mutual dependence, rivalry and love' (Kalyvas 2006, 351). Territorial control that is linked to information as coercion

> must be highly targeted (or selective) to be effective, i.e., it must target individuals on the basis of their actions, very much like law enforcement. In contrast, non-selective (or indiscriminate) violence, i.e., violence targeting individuals on the basis of collective profiling (such as their ethnic or religious identity or the place they live), will tend to be counterproductive, leading civilians to seek protection from the rival group, provided this option is available.
>
> *(Kalyvas 2012, 660)*

Since civilians might use civil war to settle personal disputes, national cleavages are not necessarily reflected at the periphery (ibid.). In time, indiscriminate violence often has the opposite of the desired effect as it is perceived as deeply unfair, producing anger rather than fear. Thus,

> indiscriminate violence is inversely related to the level of territorial control (i.e., it is more likely where the armed group that resorts to it enjoys very low levels of territorial control), whereas selective violence is most likely where the level of territorial control exercised by an armed group is predominant but not absolute.
>
> *(ibid., 661)*

Indiscriminate policing resulting in incomplete monopoly of force by the state is therefore often seen at the onset of civil wars, especially as some transformative events of increased brutality are taken to represent the unfairness of the regime.

Social fragmentation

Fragmented oppositional networks fuel escalation around resource control. When episodes of democratization escalate into civil wars, at the onset, deep territorial cleavages are present and the opposition cleaves along ethnic or religious lines. States that exclude specific (mainly ethnic) groups are at higher risk of violent conflicts, as political institutions affect whether ethnicity erupts into conflict (Wucherpfenning *et al.* 2012). In fact, within a dyadic relationship,

> both government leaders and nonstate challengers can capitalize on the ascriptive nature of ethnicity. Although states can benefit from politicizing ethnic relations by selectively providing political or economic goods for parts of the population while excluding others, once violent conflict breaks out, such policies may backfire on the government and induce severe consequences. In particular, past discriminatory policies make it less likely that incumbent governments will be able or willing to accept settlements that could terminate conflicts. Past policies of ethnic exclusion also operate to the benefit of rebel organizations fighting the government, since members of politically excluded ethnic groups harbor grievances that increase collective group solidarity and render individual fighters more cost tolerant. This, in turn, facilitates the durability of rebel organizations.
>
> *(ibid., 80)*

While states with ethnic minority leaders do not show a higher risk of civil war (Fearon *et al.* 2007), states tend to support the ethnic majority, both in their appeal to nation building and to ensure border controls (Fearon and Laitin 2011). In fact, the likelihood of conflict increases with the exclusion of powerful ethnic minorities (Buhaug, Cedarman, and Rød 2008). In addition, the power distribution among ethnic groups affects levels of violence in civil wars as, in particular, as the size of the ruling coalition decreases,

> The severity of civil conflicts will increase because government leaders are less constrained in their ability to use force and members of the ruling cohort are more likely to go along with campaigns of repression. When political leaders draw support from a narrow segment of society, the private benefits received by each supporter are likely to be large, providing powerful incentives for privileged groups to stay in power at all costs and support the leader's efforts to crush political opponents.
>
> *(Heger and Salehyan 2007, 386)*

Ethno-nationalist conflict is thus seen as linked to a specific path of nation-state formation, in which elites did not integrate the population in the building of a national project. Especially where civil society organizations are weak, ethnic clientelism tends to be used to mobilize political support, with ensuing exclusion of citizens from other ethnic backgrounds from power and public goods.

Ethnic exclusions have been linked in particular to the development of modern nation-states in low-income areas, as the state is ruled in the name of the ethnically defined people, which tend to be defined as majorities. So, civil wars in Sub-Saharan Africa have been explained through the commitment problem in personalist regimes between elites with joint access to the state's coercive apparatus:

> Elites have much to gain by parceling out the state and working together to maintain their hold on power. But they also have a lot to lose if any faction defects from this bargain and conspires to usurp power. Without assurances otherwise, each side maneuvers to protect its share and safeguard against others' first-strike capabilities. Reciprocal maneuvering, however, reinforces suspicion within the regime, often triggering an internal security dilemma that destroys trust and makes eliminating one's rival a vital imperative. Amidst this escalating internal conflict, rulers employ an exclusive strategy to neutralize the existential threat posed by those inside their regime and to secure their grip on power. But the cost of such a strategy, especially when carried out along ethnic lines, is that it forfeits the central government's societal control, leaving it vulnerable to civil war. In short, given the high immediate costs of the coup d'état versus the threat of ethnoregional rebellion in the distant future, the ruler chooses a political strategy that substitutes civil war risk for coup risk . . . Ethnic exclusion significantly reduces the likelihood that members of a group will successfully execute a coup, but at the cost of increasing the risk of societal rebellion and civil war.
>
> *(Roessler 2011, 302)*

Strategic interactions between elites increase the risks of civil war by excluding former allies (especially strong ethnic groups) from the central government. In particular, post-colonial states are defined as semi-states that often suffer from the security dilemma, as elites need to mobilize ethnic support which others see as threatening.

Violence itself then contributes to this fragmentation at the core but, especially, at the periphery, as intra-community dynamics follow the segmentation of the territory as it is divided into zones controlled by rival actors – along with its fragmentation, as sovereignties overlap (Kalyvas 2008b). In fact,

> The likelihood of violence is a function of control. On the one hand, political actors do not want to use violence where they already enjoy high levels of control (because they do not need it) and where they have no control whatsoever (because it is counterproductive since they are not

likely to have access to the information necessary to make it selective). Instead, they want to use violence in intermediate areas, where they have incomplete control.

(ibid., 407)

In this sense, 'Rather than just politicizing private life, civil war works the other way around as well: it privatizes politics' (ibid., 389). As an effect, social solidarities tend to further break down during the armed conflicts.

Political instability and indiscriminate policing also trigger the onset of civil wars through a social fragmentation of the opposition along different lines.

Fluidification of borders

Moving from the onset into activating mechanisms, the fluidification of borders implies de-structuring but also restructuring along territorial lines. Research on civil wars has in fact considered the emerging dynamics proper to militarized political conflicts, stressing the fluidity of borders between states and non-state armed actors. In civil wars, there is a split territorial control.[1]

As the use of violence risks a loss of legitimacy for rulers in the territory that is controlled by the rebels, there is a need for re-legitimization through the re-establishment of order. As Schlichte (2009) observed, it is not by chance that armed groups often fail due to their lack of capacity to meet organizational requirements and territorial control, as they have to 'face the challenge of transforming the crude form of power they achieve by violent means into legitimate rule' (ibid., 113). As rebels control territories, they need to legitimize their violence, resorting to various types of strategies to gain the support of the population by ensuring welfare goods as well as security. In fact, the politics of armed groups goes beyond military activities, also addressing the financing and reproduction in the war economy – usually characterized by a downward spiral of price increases, shortage, stagnation. Growth in fact implies differentiation, but also the need to organize everyday life on the territory, as 'multiple requirements pull armed groups in all directions and threaten their unity and coherence' (ibid., 144), with the risk of losing capacity for political action. Indeed,

> Violence casts a cloud on social relations that is due to the short time frame it introduces and its psycho-physic effects. Violence cuts short, it interrupts, it inflicts pain, and it has lasting effects. This 'shadow of violence' falls on each single organizational aspect of armed groups. Moreover, violence is power. Insurgents need to turn this power into more stable relations and ultimately into domination.
>
> *(ibid., 19)*

With the above-mentioned focus on the local dimension, Kalyvas (2012) pointed to the relevance of the relations between armed groups and civilians at the local level. As armed groups aim at maximizing their support among the population and minimizing the support for their rivals, they deploy strategies ranging from political persuasion, to the provision of public and private goods up to coercion. In the same vein, Staniland (2012) proposed a typology of political orders amidst civil wars as linked to the distribution of territorial control and cooperation (segmented, when each side controls some territory; fragmented, when both sides have a presence throughout the area). The need to secure dominance pushes groups to build localized order and legitimacy (Metelits 2010).

We can add that many armed conflicts happen at the state borders where, given certain conditions, the construction of alternative orders might be easier. In fact,

> Conflicts located at considerable distance from the main government stronghold, along remote international borders and in regions with valuable minerals last substantially longer . . . the distances an army must travel to project power, rebel fighting capacity, and characteristics of conflict region affect how a civil war is fought and who will prevail.
>
> *(Buhaug et al. 2009, 544)*

So, the probability of conflict is found to grow with the relative demographic size of the excluded group; the distance between the excluded group and the capital; and the roughness of the terrain in the settlement area of the excluded group.

The importance of borders is particularly stressed in the analysis of a 'son of the soil' path to civil wars. Indeed, Fearon and Laitin (2011) observed that about half of the civil wars between 1945 and 2008 were ethnic ones and, in one-third of them, the conflict opposed members of a regional ethnic group that defined itself as indigenous 'sons of the soil' versus migrants from a dominant ethnic group recently arrived from other parts of the country.

> [Here,] the spark for the war is violence between members of a regional ethnic group that considers itself to be the indigenous 'sons of the soil' and recent migrants from other parts of the country. The migrants are typically members of the dominant ethnic group who have come in search of land or government jobs. In many cases the state actively supports this migration with economic incentives and development schemes (occasionally funded by the World Bank or other international development agencies).
>
> *(ibid., 199)[2]*

The unsettling of borders is also related to the increasing need for former bystanders to take sides. In this regard, Kalyvas (2006) has stressed the importance of micro-dynamics at the local level, as 'irrespective of their sympathies (and everything else being equal), most people prefer to collaborate with the political actor that best guarantees their survival rather than defect by helping their rival actor' (ibid., 12). Nonparticipation in civil war is not costless; rather, 'faced with a mix of selective violence and protection on one side and indiscriminate violence on the other, most civilians are likely to join the rebels' (Kalyvas and Kocher 2007, 190).[3]

Borders also become fluid through international dynamics, as it is noted that states experiencing civil wars are much more likely to be involved in a militarized conflict with other states (Gleditsch *et al.* 2008). These are directly tied to the issues at stake in the civil wars, as

> the increased risk of interstate conflict associated with civil wars is primarily driven by states' efforts to affect the outcome of the civil war through strategies of intervention and externalization and not by an increase in conflicts over unrelated issues.
>
> *(ibid., 19)*

In fact,

> External states may threaten or use military force in support of rebels to affect the outcome of civil wars. States experiencing civil war may externalize the conflict, directing military force outward to retaliate against others for supporting rebels and/or to conduct cross-border counterinsurgency operations. In addition, the fighting associated with civil wars can create unintended security spillovers that give rise to interstate tension.
>
> *(ibid., 29)*

Therefore, states might intervene to weaken international rivals, remove hostile regimes, protect ethnic kings, attract separatists, or take revenge. Thus, emergent dynamics at the domestic and international levels further reshuffle the definition of borders by challenging existing ones and constituting new ones.

Security deterioration

While borders become fluid, the activation of civil wars is also triggered by spirals of insecurity. Economic variables have often been mentioned as among the preconditions of political violence. The relationship between inequality and discontent is said to be curvilinear, and changes in wealth are related to instability (Nagel 1974). Most significant are the horizontal inequalities between groups – that is, inequalities that coincide with identity-based cleavages – as 'horizontal inequalities may enhance both grievances and group cohesion among the relatively deprived and thus facilitate mobilization for conflict' (Ostby 2008, 143).

Violence, in turn, also activates spirals of impoverishment, with related growth in insecurity that can then fuel civil wars. The analysis of civil war economies as economic processes interacting with political violence allows a move beyond the mere assessment of structural conditions (such as poverty and/or deprivation) (Keen 2001). Impoverishment is triggered by the costs of civil wars, which include declining GDP per capita, displacement, loss of social capital, declining investment, loss of civilians, capital flight, AIDS and epidemics, also increasing probabilities of other wars. Civil wars also have effects on neighbours, among others through the spread of AIDS, malaria, and refugees (Collier *et al.* 2003). Moreover, they have global effects, increasing drug production and trafficking as well as international terrorism (ibid.).

As guerrillas need assets, political and criminal elements tend to merge, but their insatiability creates tensions within the population (Gutiérrez Sanín 2008). Civil wars can also degenerate into organized crime (Sambanis 2003). From an economic point of view, rebellion is in fact sustained through the looting of national resources, extortion of the local population, and/or financial support from ethnic diasporas.[4] War economies have distinctive features, as

> They involve the destruction or circumvention of the formal economy and the growth of informal and black markets, effectively blurring the lines between the formal, informal, and criminal sectors and activities. Pillage, predation, extortion, and deliberate violence against civilians [are] used by combatants to acquire control over lucrative assets, capture trade networks and diaspora remittances, and exploit labour; War economies are highly decentralised and privatised, both in the means of coercion and in the means of production and exchange; Combatants increasingly rely on the licit or illicit exploitation of/trade in lucrative natural resources where these assets obtain; They thrive on cross-border trading networks, regional kin and ethnic groups, arms traffickers and mercenaries, as well as legally operating commercial entities, each of which may have a vested interest in the continuation of conflict and instability.
>
> *(Ballentine and Nitzschke 2005, 2)*

So, endogenously, civil wars can create economic groups that have a vested interest in the continuation of the conflict itself. 'Conflict can become even more difficult to resolve when warring parties become entrenched in the society. This is a particularly tricky aspect to overcome when elites begin to benefit financially from the war' (Olson Lounsbery and Pearson 2009, 133).

In sum, civil wars develop especially in the context of inequalities, but they also fuel insecurity by creating economic impoverishment and uncertainty within informal (and even criminal) economies.

Activation of military networks

Civil wars are fuelled by reproductive mechanisms at the relational, emotional, and cognitive levels. Relational mechanisms include the activation of military networks. Aiming to bridge social movements with civil war approaches, scholars like Elisabeth Wood (2003) and Joselyn Viterna (2013) have focused on the meso level, looking at civil wars as escalations of social and political conflicts with effects on the organizational infrastructure of the conflicts. The activation of militant networks involves a high presence of military skills and resources, even the creation of militias. Violence is fuelled by the creation and recreation of violent entrepreneurs, as insecurity brings about the search for patrons.

The shift from peaceful oppositional groups into armed militias is fuelled by the presence of military skills and equipment. In particular, when the military splits, as those who defect from the regime army bring arms and military skills to the opposition, civil wars are promoted by organizations that look more and more like armies, recruiting young and uneducated males who are often looking for safety (Collier *et al.* 2003). Additionally, risk acceptance leaders tend to protract the conflict (Bueno de Mesquita 2000, 255). Armed groups are defined as 'figurations, that is smaller social settings, groups and less structured collectives, and as ensembles of interdependent individuals. These individuals are linked by asymmetric power balances as they exchange favors or commodities' (Schlichte 2009, 17). They crystallize around some events, developing their own codes but still keeping fuzzy boundaries.

At the onset of armed groups, there are shared experiences of political battles, dense networks, as well as some degree of military expertise. The different characteristics of these networks explain different forms and degrees of violence during civil wars. Jeremy Weinstein (2007) has explained variations in violence against civilians by armed groups' initial endowments, suggesting that those rich in economic resources attract opportunistic recruits who tend to be difficult to discipline, while those that are not attract recruits more loyal to the groups' aims.

The geographical location is important in distinguishing loot-seeking versus justice-seeking rebels (Gates 2002). Natural resources have been considered a potential source of incentives for combatants. Civil wars have been said to be more frequent in countries with high inequality and immobile wealth (Boix 2008). This is all the more the case because, since the end of the Cold War, civil wars tend to be more self-financed:

> In addition to the traditional means of pillage and plunder, the trade in lucrative natural resources, diaspora remittances, and the capture of foreign aid have become increasingly important sources of combatant self-financing. Facilitated by weakly regulated globalisation and weak states in the developing world, combatants benefit from business deals with criminal networks, arms traffickers, and unscrupulous corporate entities, reaching well beyond the war zones to the world's commodity markets and major financial centres.
>
> *(Ballentine and Nitzschke 2005, 2)*

Greed has been considered particularly relevant when the rebels' leaders need to motivate soldiers, through selective incentives of various types (Regan and Norton 2005). Lootable resources (gemstones, narcotic crops, timber) then become important to control for the insurgents (Ballentine and Nitzschke 2005), as well as for fuelling expectations about post-conflict rewards (Collier and Hoeffler 1998). Scholars who talk of greed tend to see military networks as an industry generating profits from looting, as the insurgents are presented as indistinguishable from bandits or pirates and, like them, motivated by greed (Grossman 1999, 269), with economic interests, including contraband and protection rackets (Vargas 2009). The supply of rebels has been seen as a function of poverty (Elbadawi and Sambanis 2002) as recruitment in the rebel army provides selective benefits, at both the material and nonmaterial levels.

The role of militias tends to increase during the conflict, so that civil wars are not 'a war of all against all and neighbor against neighbor – a condition in which pretty much everyone in one ethnic group becomes the ardent, dedicated, and murderous enemy of everyone in another group – ethnic war essentially does not exist' (Mueller 2000, 42). Rather, civil wars are

> waged by small groups of combatants, groups that purport to fight and kill in the name of some larger entity. Often, in fact, 'ethnic war' is substantially a condition in which a mass of essentially mild, ordinary people can unwillingly and in considerable bewilderment come under the vicious and arbitrary control of small groups of armed thugs.
>
> *(ibid., 42)*

Faced with challenges to internal discipline coming from rebels motivated by the desire for personal enrichment, groups with stronger (non-corrupted) institutions are more capable of imposing internal discipline (Wood 2009) and groups with political wings are better able to exert restraints on the use of violence (Stanton 2016). So, for instance, the spread of rape as revenge, or forced impregnation for ethnic cleansing, depends on collective norms among rebels but also on the capacity to enforce orders within the rebel army (Wood 2008).

In sum, civil wars are reproduced through relational mechanisms that bring about more and more militarized structures. As splits in the military take military skills and equipment to the opposition, military networks are activated and follow their own logic.

Spiralling revenge

Emotions constitute powerful mechanisms for the reproduction of civil wars. Fear spreads with the turmoil, pushing civilians to look for protection, but outrage can also fuel feelings of hate and revenge. A group's action to increase its own security might reduce others' security, which can then reduce the security for the first group (Rose 2000). The perception of insecurity feeds different emotions, each of which has specific consequences: fear predicts violence against the most threatening group, hatred against traditional enemies, resentment against higher-status and vulnerable groups, incoherent target selection (Petersen 2002; see also Kaufman 2001).

As violence needs justification (Malesevic 2010), collective memory and trauma following mass killings from the past can mobilize in the present during wars. Violence is then legitimated as self-defence, revenge against distressing feelings of having been dishonoured, or anger that follows shame and humiliation. In order to overcome fear, rituals can enforce warriors' habit centred on social honour (Schlichte 2009).

The brutality of forms of action in civil wars tends to rapidly spiral under emotional pressure. As Mark Beissinger observed about ethnic violence during the collapse of the Soviet Union:

> Usually, at the beginning of waves of mobilized nationalist violence, specific chains of events crystallized widely shared moods of fear, revenge, outrage, and self-assertion which, when combined with a sense of license gained from supportive cues sent by state authority, erupted into violence. In other cases, the state itself directly initially mobilized violence in ethnic groups or ethnicized segments of the Soviet state as part of attempts to control challenges to its territoriality. Thus, within the context of 'thickened' history social norms proscribing nonstate violence between segments of a single state were set aside, and violent action came to be considered permissible and even moral by large numbers of people.
>
> *(2002, 318)*

Violence is justified by narratives of revenge. For instance, the genocide in Rwanda developed both top-down, in a planned manner, and chaotically, in a horizontal way, led at the local level by well-educated administrative officers with participation by young, aggressive, unemployed party members. As the killing of Tutsi became a sort of new law, those who did not participate perceived risks of in-group sanctions (Strauss 2008).

However, civil wars can also be fuelled by positive emotions of empowerment. Hyper-exploitation, together with repression, especially indiscriminate against peasants, fuelled guerrillas in El Salvador as motivations emerged in action.[5] As Wood noted:

> Because participating in the organizations also meant participating in a greater movement, the experience of collective agency against the landlords and the state appealed to many activists: it undermined any self-perception that the disdain of the landlords had a basis in fact.
>
> *(2000, 50)*

In those struggles, 'The emphasis on redistribution and democratic reform in the rhetoric of the insurgents proved a powerful mobilizing force' (ibid., 197).

So, civil wars are reproduced endogenously, as increasing insecurity fuels fear but also the desire for revenge, while participation in the conflict also triggers sentiments of empowerment.

Sectarian identification

Emotional mechanisms are intertwined with cognitive ones. A stream of research on civil wars has considered ideological motivation, distinguishing identity (ethnic/ religious) civil wars from revolutionary (ideological) ones (Sambanis 2001). In particular, Gutiérrez Sanín and Wood suggested that ideology is fundamental for the internal life of armed groups:

> Organized violence is about ideas as well as power. Like any other public undertaking . . . armed conflict has to adopt the rhetoric of collective interest and public good. No significant rebellion has been mute; violence is seldom a substitute for voice . . . ideology is also fundamental for the internal life of armed groups. Rebels generally spend significant time and resources producing, transmitting, and discussing ideas. They divide and fight around ideas. And they use ideas when taking literally life and death decisions
>
> *(2014, 213)*

In a weak version,

> [Ideology is] a more or less systematic set of ideas that includes the identification of a referent group (a class, ethnic, or other social group), an enunciation of the grievances or challenges that the group confronts, the identification of objectives on behalf of that group (political change – or defense against its threat), and a (perhaps vaguely defined) program of action.
>
> *(ibid., 214)*

In a stronger version,

> Ideologies also prescribe – to widely varying extent, from no particular blueprint to very specific instructions – distinct institutions and strategies as the means to attain group goals. There are of course other sources of variation in institutions and strategy; ideology comprises an important but often neglected source of such variation bloom.
>
> *(ibid., 215)*

Ideology works as a cognitive device that helps to identify friends and foes, but it also deepens cohesion. Chosen by founders, it remains sticky, as some join for normative reasons. It also increases hierarchical control and thus the normative constraints on strategies and tactics.

Cognitive mechanisms fuel identification processes. Rebellion is influenced by the presence of communal identity, group incentives, and capacity for action (Gurr 2000). At a cognitive level, civil wars need group identification, which is strengthened by a search for safety in (large) numbers (Olson Lounsbery and Pearson 2009). Recruitment in civil war is facilitated by identification processes, activating a participatory identity that makes participation a source of pride for 'people like me' (Viterna 2013, 50–1). Research has therefore looked at the capacity of the groups themselves to socialize their members (Wood 2003) as well as at the different paths of recruitment (Viterna 2006).

Exclusive identification might ensue from the dynamics of the civil war itself. As a strong identity provider, ethnicity (defined as a familiar group of people sharing culture, origins, or language) might be mobilized in ethno-nationalist movements, often steered by mass media, political office holders, and the political rhetoric of charismatic leaders (Bozik 1999). Civil wars in fact require intellectuals, as, together with the spread of charismatic ideas, there is often a revision of history with historical experiences read as characterized by national liberation, social emancipation, democracy, and human rights (Schlichte 2009). Especially in the case of ethnic (exclusive) nationalism, political leaders try to create loyalty through cultural attachments (the other two types he calls revolutionary or counterrevolutionary) (Snyder 2000).

During civil wars, with group splintering and competition, the increasing importance of security concerns might push towards sectarian identification. Identification is especially likely when group survival appears in danger (Kaufman 2001), as well as when there are only weak cross-cutting allegiances. Emotional narratives tend to present violence as righteous rather than radical, aimed at mobilizing specific identities (Viterna 2013, 54). Also during civil wars, cognitive processes construct identities through perceptions (Hirshleifer 2001), sectarian tales, and use of symbols by the elites (Kaufman 2001), as inciting sectarian killings as a way to address political problems (Valentino 2004). Violence has powerful effects in terms of the politicization of ethnicity (Fearon 2008), as identity shifts can be promoted by incumbent political actors (Kalyvas 2008a).

Cognitive mechanisms might therefore reproduce civil wars, through ideological moves towards sectarian identification processes.

Conclusion

In sum, understanding civil wars implies moving from a causal to an emergent and processual approach. In social movement studies, this approach developed within attention to eventful protests as capable of changing relations through the activation of cognitive, affective, and relational processes (della Porta 2016). In civil war studies, as well, it is sometimes noted that insurgency proceeds through trial and error. Addressing the debate on new wars, Kalyvas (2001) opposed the idea of new civil wars as criminal, depoliticized, private, and predatory, as opposed to old wars seen as ideological, political, collective, noble – pointing at a constant mix of motive and support by the population.

Some specific tipping points represent tests in action. Thus, interactions during the mobilization influenced the nationalist frames that emerged from the protest events as, in Beissinger's words, 'Thickened history had provided the context for a fundamental transformation of identities which, in "quieter" times, were once believed to be fixed and immutable' (2002, 148). While in quiet times, nationalist entrepreneurs indeed aim at building some structural advantages, these advantages are then put to work in noisy times, when 'the constraining parameters of politics undergo fundamental challenges, leading to rapidly shifting assumptions about the limits of the possible' (ibid., 151).

The developments of civil wars are therefore hard to predict, as the relative strengths and weaknesses emerge in action. As Cunningham *et al.* (2009, 570) suggested, within a dyadic perspective,

> [S]trong rebels, who pose a military challenge to the government, are likely to lead to short wars and concessions. Conflicts where rebels seem weak can become prolonged if rebels can operate in the periphery so as to defy a government victory yet are not strong enough to extract concessions.

However, strength is usually built in action, as

> Rebel groups typically start off weak relative to the state, and launch a rebellion with the expectation that they will be able to mobilize a sufficient military threat to achieve their objectives. If rebels are not defeated at the beginning of the conflict but able to survive the initial period of vulnerability, the prospects for a government victory become increasingly poor. Rebels that succeed in mobilizing large forces and are strong in the sense of being able to effectively target the government militarily can potentially undermine the state by either winning directly, or by creating threats to unseat the government from challengers questioning its competence . . . rebels that are able to mobilize rapidly and gain a significant offensive advantage are more likely to win decisive victories. By extension, weak opposition groups that do not have much hope of successful military mobilization should be unlikely to rebel. At the outset, however, there is often considerable uncertainty as to how strong the rebels will become at some point in the future.
>
> *(ibid.)*

These emergent dynamics are clearly visible in the case studies presented in the chapters to follow.

Notes

1 Brutalization has been found to be particularly strong in areas in which territorial control is split and contested; so, for instance,

> selective violence by the Vietcong was much more common in hamlets that were predominantly, but not fully, controlled by them than it was in hamlets that were fully under Vietcong control, hamlets that were contested between the rival sides, or hamlets under predominant or full government control . . . government bombing and shelling most heavily affected hamlets that were under total Vietcong control.

> The two types of violence . . . happened in different places; furthermore, they did not occur in the most contested territory, the type of place that most resembles the front line of a conventional war.
>
> *(Kalyvas and Kocher 2009, 336)*

2 Sons-of-the-soil conflicts are typically long (Fearon 2004). Most common in the larger countries of Asia, these conflicts have similar dynamics:

> The violence often begins with attacks between gangs of young men from each side, or in pogroms or riots following on rumors of abuse (rapes, thefts, insults) or protests by indigenous against the migrants. State forces then intervene, often siding with the migrants, and often being indiscriminate in retribution and repression against members of the indigenous group. In a few cases, the state intervenes on the side of the indigenous minority.
>
> *(Fearon and Laitin 2004, 199)*

3 In fact,

> Rebel organizations do not always maximize recruitment. It is often forgotten that military success is not simply a function of manpower. With limited logistic means, few weapons, and low capacity to support troops, many rebel organizations prefer to recruit and train a small number of full-time fighters and channel their sympathizers into large civilian networks of support. This is why the absence of a collective action problem on the rebel side does not automatically translate into larger (or more successful) rebel armies.
>
> *(ibid., 212)*

4 Many of these effects last after the civil war has ended.
5 As a peasant stated, violence is justified by lack of a perceived alternative: 'We were seen as animals, working from 4:00 and without even enough to put the kids in school. This is the origin of the war: there was no alternative. The only alternative was the madness of desperation' (Wood 2000, 48).

References

Balch-Lindsay, Dylan, and Enterline, Andrew J. 2000. 'Killing time: the world politics of civil war duration, 1820–1992'. *International Studies Quarterly* 44(4): 615–42. doi:10.1111/0020–8833.00174.

Ballentine, Karen, and Nitschke, Heiko. 2005. *The Political Economy of Civil War and Conflict Transformation.* Berlin: Berghof Research Center for Constructive Conflict Management.

Beissinger, Mark R. 2002. Nationalist Mobilization and the Collapse of the Soviet State. Cambridge: Cambridge University Press.

Blainey, Geoffrey. 1988. *The Causes of Wars.* New York: Free Press.

Boix. Carles. 2008. 'Civil war and the guerrilla warfare in the contemporary world', in Stathis Kalyvas, Ian Shapiro, and Tarek Masoud (eds), *Order, Conflict and Violence.* Cambridge: Cambridge University Press, pp. 197–218.

Boudreau, Vincent. 2004. *Resisting Dictatorship: Repression and Protest in Southeast Asia.* Cambridge: Cambridge University Press.

Bozik, Agneza. 1999. 'Democratization and ethnopolitics in Yougoslavia', in Karl Cordell (ed.), *Ethnicity and Democratisation in the New Europe.* London: Routledge, pp. 117–30.

Bueno de Mesquita, Bruce. 2000. *Principles of International Politics*. Washington, DC: Congressional Quarterly Press.

Buhaug, Halvard, Cederman, Lars-Erik, and Rød, Jan Ketil. 2008. 'Disaggregating ethnonationalist civil wars: a dyadic test of exclusion theory'. *International Organization* 62: 531–51.

Buhaug, Halvard, Gates, Scott, and Lujala, Päivi. 2009. 'Geography, rebel capability, and the duration of civil conflict'. *Journal of Conflict Resolution* 53(4): 544–69. doi:10.1177/0022002709336457.

Collier, Paul, Eliot, V.L., Hegre, Håvard, Hoeffler, Anke, Reynal-Querol, Martha, and Sambanis, Nicholas. 2003. *Breaking the Conflict Trap: Civil War and Development Policy*. Washington, DC: World Bank and Oxford University Press.

Collier, Paul, and Hoeffler, Anke. 1998. 'On economic causes of civil war'. *Oxford Economic Papers* 50(4): 563–73.

Cunningham, D.E., Gleditsch, K.S., and Salehyan, I. 2009. 'It takes two: a dyadic analysis of civil war duration and outcome'. *Journal of Conflict Resolution* 53(4): 570–97. doi:10.1177/0022002709336458.

della Porta, Donatella. 2013. *Clandestine Political Violence*. Cambridge: Cambridge University Press.

della Porta, Donatella. 2016. *Where Did the Revolution Go?* Cambridge: Cambridge University Press.

della Porta, Donatella, and Tarrow, Sidney. 2012. 'Double diffusion: police and protestors in transnational contention'. *Comparative Political Studies* 20: 1–34.

Elbadawi, Ibrahim, and Sambanis, Nicholas. 2002. 'How much war will we see? Explaining the prevalence of civil war'. *Journal of Conflict Resolution* 46(3): 307–34.

Fearon, James D. 2004. 'Why do some civil wars last so much longer than others?' *Journal of Peace Research* 41(3): 275–301. doi:10.1177/0022343304043770.

Fearon, James D. 2008. 'Ethnic mobilization and ethnic violence', in Barry R. Weingast and Donald A. Wittman (eds), *The Oxford Handbook of Political Economy*. Oxford: Oxford University Press, pp. 852–69.

Fearon, James D., Kasara, Kimuli, and Laitin, David D. 2007. 'Ethnic minority rule and civil war onset'. *American Political Science Review* 101(1): 187. doi:10.1017/S0003055407070219.

Fearon, James D., and Laitin, David D. 2003. 'Ethnicity, insurgency, and civil war'. *American Political Science Review* 97(1): 75–90.

Fearon, James D., and Laitin, David D. 2011. 'Sons of the soil, migrants, and civil war'. *World Development* 39(2): 199–211. doi:10.1016/j.worlddev.2009.11.031.

Gates, Scott. 2002. 'Recruitment and allegiance: the microfoundations of rebellion'. *Journal of Conflict Resolution* 46(1): 111–30. doi:10.1177/0022002702046001007.

Gleditsch, K.S., Salehyan, I., and Schultz, K. 2008. 'Fighting at home, fighting abroad: how civil wars lead to international disputes'. *Journal of Conflict Resolution* 52(4): 479–506. doi:10.1177/0022002707313305.

Goldstone, Jack A., Bates, Robert H. Epstein, David L. Gurr, Ted, Lustik, Robert Michael B., Marshall, Monty G., Ulfelder, Jay, and Woodward, Mark, 2010, 'Global model for forecasting political instability'. *American Journal of Political Science* 54(1): 190–208.

Grossman, H.I. 1999, 'Kleptocracy and revolution'. *Oxford Economic Papers* 51: 267–83.

Gurr, Ted. 2000. *Peoples Versus States*. Washington, DC: US Institute of Peace Press.

Gutiérrez Sanín, Francisco. 2008. 'Clausewitz vindicated? Economic and politics on the Colombian war'. In Stathis Kalyvas, Ian Shapiro, and Tarek Masoud (eds), *Order, Conflict and Violence*. Cambridge: Cambridge University Press, pp. 219–41.

Gutiérrez Sanín, Francisco, and Wood, Elisabeth Jean. 2014. 'Ideology in civil war: instrumental adoption and beyond'. *Journal of Peace Research* 51(2): 213–26.

Heger, Lindsay, and Salehyan, Idean. 2007. 'Ruthless rulers: coalition size and the severity of civil conflict'. *International Studies Quarterly* 51(2): 385–403. doi:10.1111/j.1468-2478.2007.00456.x.

Hegre, Håvard, and Sambanis, Nicholas. 2006. 'Sensitivity analysis of empirical results on civil war onset'. *Journal of Conflict Resolution* 50(4): 508–35.

Henderson, Errol, and Singer, J. David. 2000. 'Civil war in the post-colonial world, 1946–92'. *Journal of Peace Research* 37(3): 275–99.

Hirshleifer, Jack. 2001. *The Dark Side of the Force: Economic Foundations of Conflict Theory.* New York: Cambridge University Press.

Jarstad, Anna K. 2008. 'Dilemmas of war to democracy transition'. In Anna K. Jarstad, and Timothy D. Sisk (eds), *From War to Democracy: Dilemmas of Peace Building.* Cambridge: Cambridge University Press, pp. 17–36.

Kalyvas, Stathis N. 2001. '"New" and "old" civil wars: a valid distinction?' *World Politics* 54(1): 99–118. doi:10.1353/wp.2001.0022.

Kalyvas, Stathis N. 2006. *The Logic of Violence in Civil War.* Cambridge: Cambridge University Press.

Kalyvas, Stathis N. 2008a. 'Ethnic defection in civil war', *Comparative Political Studies* 41(8): 1043–68.

Kalyvas, Stathis N. 2008b. 'Promises and pitfalls of an emergent research program: the microdynamics of civil war'. In Stathis Kalyvas, Ian Shapiro, and Tarek Masoud (eds), *Order, Conflict and Violence.* Cambridge: Cambridge University Press, pp. 397–421.

Kalyvas, Stathis N. 2012. 'Micro-level studies of violence in civil war: refining and extending the control-collaboration model'. *Terrorism and Political Violence* 24(4): 658–68.

Kalyvas, Stathis N., and Balcells, Laila. 2010. 'International system and technologies of rebellion: how the end of the cold war shaped internal conflict'. *American Political Science Review* 104(3): 415–29.

Kalyvas, Stathis N., and Kocher, Matthew Adam. 2007. 'How "free" is free riding in civil wars?: Violence, insurgency, and the collective action problem'. *World Politics* 59(2): 177–216.

Kalyvas, Stathis N., and Kocher, Matthew Adam. 2009. 'The dynamics of violence in Vietnam: An analysis of the Hamlet evaluation'. *Journal of Peace Research* 46(3): 335–55.

Kaufman, Stuart J. 2001 *Modern Hatred: The Symbolic Politics of Ethnic War.* Ithaca, NY: Cornell University Press.

Keen, David. 2001. 'War and peace: what's the difference?' In Adekeye Adebajo, and Chandra Lekha Sriram (eds), *Managing Armed Conflict in the 21st Century.* London: Frank Cass, pp. 1–22.

Malesevic, Sinisa. 2010. *The Sociology of War and Violence.* Cambridge: Cambridge University Press.

McAdam, Doug, Tarrow, Sidney and Tilly, Charles. 2001. *The Politics of Contention.* Cambridge: Cambridge University Press.

Metelits, Claire. 2010. *Inside Insurgencies. Violence, Civilians, and Revolutionary Group Behavior.* New York: New York University Press.

Most, Benjamin, and Starr, Harvey. 1989. *Inquiry, Logic and International Politics.* Columbia, SC: University of South Carolina Press.

Mueller, John. 2000. 'The banality of "ethnic war"'. *International Security* 25(1): 42–70. doi:10.1162/016228800560381.

Nagel, Jack. 1974. 'Inequality and discontent: a nonlinear hypothesis'. *World Politics* 26(4): 453–72.

Olson Lounsbery, Marie, and Pearson, Frederic. 2009. *Civil Wars. Internal Struggles, Global Consequences.* Toronto: University of Toronto Press.

Ostby, Gudrun. 2008. 'Polarization, horizontal inequalities and violent civil conflict'. *Journal of Peace Research* 45(2): 143–62. doi:10.1177/0022343307087169.

Petersen, Roger D. 2002. *Understanding Ethnic Violence: Fear, Hatred, and Resentment in Twentieth-Century Eastern Europe.* Cambridge: Cambridge University Press.

Regan, Patrick, and Norton, Daniel. 2005. 'Greed, grievance, and mobilization in civil war'. *Journal of Conflict Resolution* 49(3): 319–36.

Ritter, Daniel P. 2015. *The Iron Cage of Liberalism: International Politics and Unarmed Revolutions in the Middle East and North Africa.* Oxford: Oxford University Press.

Roessler, Philip. 2011. 'The enemy within: personal rule, coups, and civil war in Africa'. *World Politics* 63(2): 300–46. doi:10.1017/S0043887111000049.

Rose, William. 2000. 'The security dilemma and ethnic conflict: some new hypotheses', *Security Studies* 9(4): 1–51.

Sambanis, Nicholas. 2001. 'Do ethnic and non-ethnic civil wars have the same causes?' *Journal of Conflict Resolution* 45(3): 259–82.

Sambanis, Nicholas. 2003. 'Using case studies to expand economic models of civil war'. CPR Working Paper no. 5.

Schlichte, Klaus. 2009. *In the Shadow of Violence. The Politics of Armed Groups.* New York: Campus.

Snyder, Jack. 2000. *From Voting to Violence: Democratization and Nationalist Conflicts.* New York: W.W. Norton.

Staniland, Paul. 2012. 'States, insurgents, and wartime political orders'. *Perspectives on Politics* 10(2): 243–64.

Stanton, Jessica A. 2016. *Violence and Restraint in Civil War.* Cambridge: Cambridge University Press.

Strauss, Scott. 2008. 'Order in disorder: a micro-comparative study of genocidal dynamics in Rwanda'. In Stathis Kalyvas, Ian Shapiro, and Tarek Masoud (eds), *Order, Conflict and Violence.* Cambridge: Cambridge University Press, pp. 301–20.

Uysal, Ayshen. 2005. 'Organisation du maintien de l'ordre et répression policière en Turquie', in Donatella della Porta and Olivier Fillieule (eds), *Maintien de l'ordre et police des foules.* Paris: Presses de Science Po.

Valentino, B.A. (2004) *Final Solutions: Mass Killing and Genocide in the Twentieth Century.* Ithaca, NY: Cornell University Press.

Vargas, Gonzalo. 2009. 'Urban irregular warfare and violence against civilians: evidence from a Colombian city'. *Terrorism and Political Violence* 21(1): 110–32.

Viterna, Jocelyn. 2006. 'Pulled, pushed, and persuaded: explaining women's mobilization into the Salvadoran Guerrilla Army'. *American Journal of Sociology* 112(1): 1–45.

Viterna, Jocelyn. 2013. *Women in War: The Micro-Processes of Mobilization in El Salvador.* Oxford: Oxford University Press.

Weinstein, Jeremy. 2007. *Inside Rebellion: The Politics of Insurgent Violence.* Cambridge: Cambridge University Press.

Wood, Elisabeth Jean. 2000. *Forging Democracy from Below: Insurgent Transitions in South Africa and El Salvador.* Cambridge: Cambridge University Press.

Wood, Elisabeth Jean. 2003. *Insurgent Collective Action and Civil War in El Salvador.* Cambridge: Cambridge University Press.

Wood, Elisabeth Jean. 2008. 'Sexual violence during war: towards understanding of variation'. In Stathis Kalyvas, Ian Shapiro, and Tarek Masoud (eds), *Order, Conflict and Violence*. Cambridge: Cambridge University Press, pp. 321–51.

Wood, Elisabeth Jean. 2009. 'Armed groups and sexual violence: when is wartime rape rare?' *Politics and Society* 37: 131–61.

Wood, Elisabeth. 2015. 'Social mobilization and violence in civil war and their social legacies'. In Donatella della Porta and Mario Diani (eds). *The Oxford Handbook of Social Movements*, Oxford: Oxford University Press.

Wucherpfennig, Julian, Metternich, Nils W., Cederman, Lars-Erik, and Gleditsch, Kristian Skrede. 2012. 'Ethnicity, the state, and the duration of civil war'. *World Politics* 64(1): 79–115. doi:10.1017/S004388711100030X.

3

BEYOND SYRIA

Civil society in failed episodes of democratization

Teije Hidde Donker

Introduction

In March 2011, the unthinkable happened: Syrians started protesting, demanding political reforms. The country was thought to be immune to public shows of discontent due to its repressive regime and effective intelligence services. But in a matter of weeks, protests demanding 'change' and 'freedom' spread across the country. Tens of thousands would participate in protests demanding democratic change and, soon after, the fall of the Syrian autocratic regime. Though these two words and initial demands still resonate profoundly among Syrians today, the country soon descended into a civil war in which multiple groups, supported by a variety of international actors, are fighting the Syrian regime and each other, culminating in the emergence of the Islamic State organization (ISIS, in Arabic abbreviated as *daesh*). These developments have left the original movement for democratization struggling to survive.

The Syrian case is an interesting one in the context of this book, because activists were well aware of the structural context at the onset of mobilization and the challenges it implied for protests. Following the start of the protests, they attempted to adapt to a quickly changing context, but they were still overtaken by the escalation and polarization of the ensuing conflict. As such, the Syrian case shows how a democracy movement can kick-start a process that it does not control, is subsequently overtaken by events, and ends up struggling to survive. The gradual nature of this transformation – it took about a year and a half for the uprising to fully transform into a civil war – render it, however painful, a perfect case to analyse the constituent mechanisms of this process.

As with the other case studies, this chapter seeks to understand how and why the initial uprising turned into civil war. It pinpoints three country-specific issues – increasing sectarian polarization, security (rather than accountability) as the source of political legitimacy, and an unstable international context – that influenced mechanisms in the process of turning the Syrian uprising into a civil war. This chapter, then, aims to relate the specificities of the Syrian uprising to the general process of mobilization to civil war as central to the topic of this book. The chapter is structured as follows. It starts with a brief discussion of the main case-specific issues and related mechanisms in the Syrian uprising. This is followed by a historical overview of the emergence of the Syrian regime and a brief description of its structural characteristics. Subsequently we narrate the emergence of the Syrian uprising, the escalation of mobilization repertoires, and the descent of mobilization into civil war, all the while observing what mechanisms were at work at different stages of this process. Finally, we explore how the above influenced and was reflected in the emergence of ISIS.

Syria in the balance

In public debates on the Syrian uprising, the ethnic and religious cleavages in the country, and the specific position of Bashar al-Assad in these divisions, have been discussed at length (van Dam 1996; 2011; Ziadeh 2011). The same holds for the authoritarian nature of the regime and the influence of the international context (Brownlee 2013; Human Rights Watch 2009; Perthes 2001; Ziadeh 2010). Additionally, a string of reports has provided micro-level analyses of particular actors in the uprising (Bunzel 2015; Ilina Angelova 2014). In line with the focus of this book, this particular chapter provides a meso-level analysis that stands at the intersection of more structural and micro-level analyses among these studies. We will show how a limited set of particular mechanisms, as described in Chapter 2 of this book, constituted a Syrian process of mobilization turned civil war. These mechanisms, and their interrelations, emerge around three key issues that stand at the basis of the failure of the democracy movement and the turn to civil war in the Syrian case.

The first issue relates to how political actors – including but not limited to the Syrian regime – gain popular legitimacy. There is a choice, and a struggle, between gaining legitimacy through the provision of security (the strongman logic) or through some type of political representation (a logic of accountability). It is a struggle that is at the heart of the democracy movement. Despite their aim to alter the basis of political legitimacy in Syria, Syrian democracy movements have only partially achieved this – not only in their failure to topple the Assad regime, but also in their inability to remain a dominant force among other opposition groups. Tendencies that prefer strongmen (or groups) among opposition movements have grown more pronounced over the years, giving outsize legitimacy to movements with the largest military capabilities – which are not necessarily those that hold promise for a democratic Syrian future.

The second issue relates to the general failure of the international community to hold the Syrian political regime effectively accountable for its actions against the Syrian population. Though to some extent associated with the US/EU and

Russia/Iran dichotomy, it relates more to the overall failure to take seriously the interests of various countries (including Turkey, the Gulf Countries, and so on) and work for an international context that would facilitate stability in Syria. This failure left many Syrians with the impression that an armed uprising was the only available option both to ensure security and to extort some form of accountability from the regime.

The third issue relates to the fragmentation of Syrian society. Increasing polarization between the Syrian regime, its opponents, between opposition groups themselves and the emergence of the Islamic State had an immense impact on Syria's social fabric. Most Syrians will passionately argue for the unity of the country, while at the same time using a depressingly polarized ethnic-cleansing-type language. As these divisions are ever more polarized, it begs the question of what type of unified democratic system can be built on top of such polarized social divisions.

In this chapter we will observe that these three issues directly relate to the characteristics of initial mobilization in the uprising (when the very fact of being able to come out in numbers drew more protestors out on the streets, despite quickly escalating and fragmented policing strategies); its escalation phase (when mobilization started to split along social lines, and with it sectarian polarization increased while militant groups started to emerge); and civil war (with increasing foreign involvement and the uprising itself transgressing Syrian borders). These issues were therefore reflected in the transformation of popular mobilization to a civil war in Syria.

The emergence of contemporary Syria

Most dynamics of the ongoing Syrian uprising have their historical roots in the emergence of the current regime in the late 1960s and early 1970s. Hafez al-Assad (b. 1930–d. 2000), father of the current president Bashar al-Assad, emerged as ruler of Syria in 1970. At the start of his rule, Hafez al-Assad's power was built on an extremely small popular base – coming as he did from an Alawi (minority Shiite religious sect) rural background (Perthes 1992). To stabilize his control over the army and key security positions, he was overtly dependent on informal relations (or *asabiya*) to his own tribe and family (Hinnebusch 2001). In the 1980s, the important names in Syria were the brother of the president and chief of the *siraya al-difa'* (Defence Forces), Rifa'at al-Assad; chairman of the Presidential Intelligence Committee and Chief of Air Intelligence, Muhammad al-Khawli; and the head of military intelligence, 'Ali Dubah. All these individuals are Alawis and from Assad's tribe (Batatu 1982). Thus, to understand the power structures of the Syrian regime, the 'normal' state institutions do matter (a president, a government, the People's Assembly, security services and the army) – but mostly as part of an informal power structure forming the basis of the authoritarian regime (Zisser 1998). For instance, the main security services (political, military, air force, and general) and their various branches act almost completely independently from the judicial system and also operate prisons independently (International Crisis Group 2004, fn. 10).

In an attempt to overcome the sectarian backlash all of the above might involve, Hafez al-Assad took pains to placate and involve various minorities, and the Sunni majority, in the regime. A number of Christians, Ismaelis, and Sunnis were given high – but non-influential – positions within the army and political bodies (Kelidar 1974, 17). Additionally, the Sunni elite classes – now sidelined from real political influence – were economically tied to the new regime, for instance, by leaving control of the Chamber of Commerce in their hands (Batatu 1982; Hinnebusch 2001). Rural villages, previously largely non-politicized, were unionized from above along a corporatist logic implemented through the organization of the ruling Ba'ath Party.

In this context, the army, intelligence services, and Ba'ath Party organizations became an instrument for institutionalized corruption in which powerful patrons secured support from lower-ranking members via a highly developed clientelist system (Perthes 1997). *Wasta* (having connections) became the prime vehicle for achieving economic and political success (Hinnebusch 1995, 314–15). Lacking effective oversight of these institutions, stories of corruption within security forces have existed since the early days of the regime (Batatu 1982). An extreme example of state-institutionalized corruption was the apparent drug cartels in the late 1970s which, in return for (both financial and armed) support for the regime, were tacitly allowed to form semi-militias and run drug businesses between Lebanon and Syria. The story goes that they were soon called '*shabiha*' or 'ghosts' due to their clandestine nature (Salih 2014).

These strategies seemed effective, and Syria under Hafez was reasonably stable. In the mid-1970s, though, the country was hit by a severe economic recession (Perthes 1997, 23–36) and the Syrian state reacted with economic *infitah* (liberalization) policies in which companies were privatized and a new commercial bourgeoisie was created (ibid., 50–8). Individuals close to the regime used their advantageous political positions to capitalize on these new *infitah* policies. Through their relations, they gained near monopolies in specific economic fields and created an elitist economic position for themselves and their families (Perthes 1992, 124). As a result, economic disparities within society widened.

In the 1970s, resistance to the regime emerged. Although from the outset opposition to the Hafez regime was a unified structure of various parties and (urban) labour unions, soon the most prominent movement was the Islamic one:[1] the religious frame had great resonance within Syrian society, in addition to mosques and religious institutions providing a well developed institutional structure for the emergence of a broad-based movement. The Syrian Muslim Brotherhood would be its main embodiment, but many other movements were also present – though strict boundaries among these were often hard to discern (abd-Allah 1982). As these movements evolved, they started to frame their conflict with Hafez and the Ba'ath Party increasingly as a fight against an Alawi minority rule. By focusing their framing attempts on the Alawi sect, leaders hoped to galvanize support. Instead, they ended up estranging themselves from other religious minority and secular groups (Lobmayer 1995, 199). The uprising climaxed in February 1982 in the city of Hama. Mujahedeen (Islamist fighters) provoked the army, although accounts differ, into a violent response. The army ended up shelling civilian quarters and shooting whole families, even after the town was pacified (Seale 1988, 333). Not much later, the Islamic uprising in Syria was crushed (Lobmayer 1995, 325–7, fn. 152). Islamic political movements within the country itself were destroyed and seemingly ceased to exist (see also Ziadeh 2008).[2] As a result, Syrian Islamists found themselves chased out of their home country and scattered across the Arab world and Europe.[3] Those non-Islamist opposition groups that had been at the inception of the uprising – mainly the urban-based unions – were pacified and incorporated into a national Ba'thist union structure (Hinnebusch 1993).

Throughout the three decades of his rule, Hafez al-Assad's regional politics were marked by a combination of strategic pragmatism and often antagonistic relations with direct neighbouring countries. Concerning Israel, he tried to achieve military parity through Soviet military assistance, aiming to pressure Israel into returning the Golan Heights, lost in 1967. He changed his strategy when the Soviet Union collapsed, engaging with Israel through US-led negotiations without result before his death in 2000. Syria remained formally at war with Israel, did not recognize the country, and hosted most Palestinian resistance movements, including Hamas, the PLO, and PFLP-GC, thus strengthening its importance (and position) as a negotiation partner in a possible Palestinian-Israeli peace deal (Seale 1988).

Concerning Lebanon, Syria sent troops to the country in 1976 within the framework of an Arab 'peacekeeping' army during the then recently started Lebanese civil war. They never left, and Syria became an increasingly important player in Lebanese politics. Lebanon's fragmented political structure and close national and cultural linkages to Syria made it an ideal context for symbiotic political and economic relationships between elites in both countries – with Syria, the more powerful party. When the Lebanese civil war ended in 1990 and the Lebanese construction tycoon Rafiq Hariri returned from Saudi Arabia to Lebanon, Syria supported his presidency, as he proved an ideal actor to open up corrupt construction deals: the reconstruction of war-ravaged Lebanon proved to be a hugely lucrative market. At the same time, Syria supported Hezbollah – shipping Iranian weapons to southern Lebanon and thereby further increasing their importance as a negotiation partner to Israel and gaining legitimacy as one of the last Arab countries continuing armed opposition to Israel (Leenders 2012b).

The rule of Bashar al-Assad

In June 2000, Bashar al-Assad became the Syrian president following the death of his father and president Hafez. Bashar embodied a promise of a new era. In the first year of his rule, a relative liberalization of the political sphere took place, and initial changes in the government seemed to imply a focus on technocrats that could support regime reforms (Perthes 2004). The immediate effect was a short-lived period in 2001 – dubbed the 'Damascus Spring' – in which more civil and political freedoms seemed to lie in store. When opposition figures started to demand substantial political reforms, the regime backtracked on its liberalizations and had many activists jailed (International Crisis Group 2004).

The 'Damascus Spring' would prove to be only the first episode of a relatively unstable period in the country: in the next ten years, Syria would go from one crisis to the next. In 2003, the United States invaded Iraq. Afterwards, Syria was accused by the United States and its allies of aiding Jihadi insurgent groups in their opposition to the US occupation. In March 2004, an uprising spread across the Kurdish regions, following a soccer match where the opposing team (from Deir Ezzor) held up posters of Saddam Hussein. Dozens were killed in the subsequent regime crackdown. A year later, the Syrian regime was sent into turmoil with the murder of the former Lebanese president Rafiq Hariri in 2005. International political isolation was the result. Increasingly, the Syrian regime sought to strengthen relations with Russia and Iran in the search for necessary (political and economic) foreign support. Throughout the last years before the 2011 uprising, Syrian international isolation decreased somewhat. This was especially true after French president Nicolas Sarkozy invited Bashar al-Assad to join his newly initiated (and soon to be forgotten) Union for the Mediterranean in July 2008 (Syrian Arab News Agency 2008).

Despite these crises and new leadership, the authoritarian regime itself changed little. At the end of the day, most individuals at the upper political echelons had been replaced since the rule of Hafez; but the ways in which key individuals gained and exercised their positions remained the same (Perthes 2004, 9). The synthesis of political and economic spheres that had emerged under Hafez remained – despite calls for battling it, corruption thrived under Bashar's tenure – with children of key actors taking over the positions of their parents from the mid-1990 onwards. All of these actors had vested (economic) interests in the maintenance of the regime. The structural context before the uprising can thus be summarized as follows:

• The country was marked by religious and ethnic divisions, with around 16 different sects present. There was a large Kurdish minority in the north of the country. Although the state and its institutions were explicitly national, the spread of political power was unevenly distributed along sectarian and clan lines, favouring the Alawi sect of the President and, to a certain extent, other minorities.
• The Syrian regime effectively co-opted or repressed independent civil society actors, to the extent that none seemed to be present. During the Damascus Spring of 2001, some activists emerged, but they were swiftly and effectively silenced after demanding political reforms.
• An informal structure of regime power was built on family and tribal links, and institutionally focused around the army and the intelligence services. Any dissent, especially Islamic, was harshly and effectively repressed. There was a close integration between (informal) political power and economic power. Those at the top of the political regime profited greatly from *infitah* policies. Therefore, a clear disconnect between political-economic elites and the rest of society emerged.

- The country has always had an influence on various conflicts in the region. This is true of the Israeli-Arab conflict, but particularly the US-Iraq conflict and internal Lebanese affairs.

All of these structural factors would influence the dynamics of the 2011 uprising.

Mobilization

After the exit of Tunisia's autocrat Ben Ali in January 2011, some in Syria also attempted to organize protests in Syria. These attempts were initially unsuccessful. For instance, there was a call for a Syrian 'day of rage' on 1 February 2011, but crowds failed to materialize (*The New York Times* 2011a).[4] What was needed was a spark, a specific transformative event that would mobilize the larger parts of society. The following section describes the event, taking place in the southern town of Dara' on 6 March 2011, that would prove to be the transformative spark needed for the uprising to emerge. In the rest of the section, we will observe how the uprising developed afterwards: from attempts at institutionalization to pre-existing movements attempting to join the mobilization. At this stage the very fact of being able to mobilize a large number of protestors incited more protests – and therefore kept the uprising going. We also see how the Syrian regime initially reacted: with harsh but uneven repression. Protestors, and quite a few innocent civilians, were incarcerated, wounded, tortured, or killed. In short, we will show how the initial phase of the Syrian uprising was shaped by the interplay between the mechanisms of *escalating policing* and *motivating in action*.

Dara's spontaneous protests

On 6 March 2011, a group of youngsters wrote '*As-sha'ab yurid isqat an-nizam*' (the people want the fall of the regime) on a wall in *Dara'* (Macleod 2011). For copying what they had seen on television about Tunisia and Egypt, they were arrested and tortured. None of the perpetrators was older than 15. The story goes that when the local governor was asked about their whereabouts and release, he replied that if they missed their children so much they should give him their wives – he would make them some new ones. True or not, in a region where clan ties are strong, and family honour an important part of the social reality, the families and the town were enraged by the story. Relatives first took to the streets on 11 March 2011, marching to the governor's house to demand their children's release. They were met by bullets. They returned to the streets on 15 March, and again the next Friday, 18 March, after Friday prayers. An estimated 3,000–4.000 people joined the protests that day to demand the release of the boys and express their anger at the security services. Facing bullets yet again, four were killed. Their funerals the next day turned into even larger protests (Leenders and Heydemann 2012).

Dara' provided the transformative event that mobilized a large cross-section of the country in what would become a wave of non-institutionalized nationwide protests. Lacking pre-institutionalization, initially it drew on a mixture of (new) social media and pre-existing social (and religious) institutions to mobilize people. Calls went out over Facebook, YouTube, Twitter and other websites – and soon on TV stations such as al-Jazeera – but it was only on the basis of traditional family, clan, and religious ties that large-scale protests could be organized. Friday prayers, the only event where it was possible to gather large groups of people, were used as springboards for protests (France 24 2011b).

Demands were aimed mainly against the (power of) the security services and corruption, and for political liberalization (ibid.). In the initial phases, demands remained relatively underdeveloped and could be placed under the general banner of 'change' and 'freedom'. Some protests were more explicit, for instance, demanding an end to corruption, tyranny, the accumulation of wealth of the Syrian regime, and often also calling explicitly for democratization (France 24 2011a). But due to the highly decentralized nature of the uprising, a well-developed overarching set of demands was absent. What did happen, however, was that these general demands were tied to more direct grievances ranging from income and the price of bread, to the release of (particular) prisoners (All4Syria 2011) and particular regime elites. Rami Makhlouf, a business tycoon and a relative of the president, was an early verbal target for the protestors in Dara' – as was the local governor of the city (al-Khalidi 2011).

Often religion was invoked, but specific claims for Islamic rule or the creation of an Islamic State were absent. So we see, for instance, that on 15 March 2011, during the very first protests in Damascus, people chanted *Allah, Suriye, huriye uw bess* (God, Syria, freedom and that's it'), in addition to repeating the slogan 'the people want the fall of the regime' (France 24 2011b). In other protests during the first weeks these chants were often repeated, in addition to *La ilahi ila allah* ('There is no God but God') (Misbar Syria 2016). In all these instances, religion was invoked as a tool to delegitimize Bashar's rule by implying that true sovereignty lies only with God – not with Bashar al-Assad and his regime. Actual demands made by protestors were explicitly non-religious and non-sectarian.

The number of people on the streets during the first Friday was limited in many places, but over the next few weeks the amount and size of the protests grew rapidly. On the second and third Fridays (25 March and 1 April), protestors in Homs, Dara', and Banyas numbered from hundreds to a few thousand (France 24 2011c). Protests also emerged in Latakya, Deir Ez-Zor, and Damascus. The initial protests, although largely peaceful, were met with deadly repression. On 25 March, 19 were killed; on the next Friday, 29.[5] Every time, funerals would turn into protests and further escalate the uprising.[6]

Institutionalization: the local coordination committees

Despite, or maybe because of, harsh repression, protests quickly spread throughout the country (*The New York Times* 2011b). With increasing size came coordination and organizational initiatives. Within the first two weeks, coordination committees and dedicated Facebook pages emerged. (The Facebook page for 'the Revolution Against Bashar al-Assad' was particularly popular.[7]) These were often founded by people who had met at rallies and formed a social bond through their experience of regime repression. Many did not know each other before the uprising (Leenders 2012a). Increasingly institutionalized, these groups came to be known as the *local coordination committees (LCCs)*. Organized at the neighbourhood level, these committees met practical needs associated with collective mobilization: organizing protests, gathering, disseminating information and providing first aid care – as protestors would often face arrest when taken to regular hospitals (Shadid 2011b; Zoepf 2011).[8] In time, they became the institutional backbone of peaceful protests throughout the country.

Emboldened by the seeming early successes in overwhelming the regime, these committees became increasingly active. They borrowed from the mobilization repertoire of protestors in other (Arab) countries: soon placards, petitions, songs, Facebook pages, and YouTube videos were used in anti-regime protests. At the start, repertoires differed between cities and their coordination committees. In Hama, protestors attempted to occupy the central square, while in Duma (a Damascus suburb) a campaign of civil disobedience was attempted (Shadid 2011b). Every committee charted its own course. But within weeks, coordination between committees increased. The fact that weekly Friday protests began to be 'themed' is a good example of this: see, for instance, the Friday of Dignity (25 March 2011), Perseverance (8 April 2011), Defiance (6 May 2011) and The Free Children (27 May 2011).[9] While the initial protests had varying demands related to political change and reform, all of these later protests demanded the fall of the regime.

In response to ever increasing protests, the Syrian authorities retreated from various cities around the country (most notably Homs and Hama) in an apparent attempt at focusing repression on the two main cities of Aleppo and Damascus and their suburbs. Protests only expanded as a result (Shadid 2011a). On 8 April 2011, hundreds of thousands of Syrians reportedly took to the streets (though the number is probably an overestimation) in various Syrian cities on the 'Friday of Steadfastness' (*sumud*) – 73 were killed.[10] A week later – on the 'Friday of Insistence' – between thousands and tens of thousands of protestors (compare France 24 2011d; with As-Sharq al-Awsat 2011a) were reported in various cities across the country. 'Only' 11 people were killed on that day.[11]

The actual implementation of repression was marked by stark differences between different army divisions and intelligence services. With formal state institutions subservient to informal allocations of power, some intelligence services and army divisions are near states-within-states. Some have immense resources – for instance, the Fourth Division under Bashar's brother, Maher – while the regular army has very little. The initial campaign against Homs (in May 2011, see further below) was carried out by the Fourth Division led by Maher al-Assad and marked by its professionalism, while in other campaigns more 'regular' army divisions were used and repression was seemingly random. With the emergence of Alawi-dominated militias or '*shabiha*', these differences were exacerbated as the latter were often accused of perpetrating the most random and deadly acts of violence (Landis 2012a). To what extent these acts were orchestrated by political elites or not remained unclear: The president would claim ignorance (Slackman 2011), but all of the above fed the perception that the regime had a survival logic of its own and could not be negotiated with.

Pre-existing movements: struggling to join

Even though popular mobilization had been effectively repressed before the uprising, a number of pre-existing Syrian movements did exist. All of these movements would attempt, with varying degrees of success, to mobilize within the suddenly newly emerging Syrian Movements for democratization. The first movement is constituted by the 'Damascus Declaration' opposition. These are the opposition parties, groups and individuals that signed the October 2005 'Damascus Declaration' calling for the 'establishment of a democratic national regime' as the basic approach to political reform. They stated that this reform had to be 'peaceful, gradual, founded on accord, and based on dialogue' (ibid.). The signatories included a few Kurdish parties (see below) in addition to the Committees for the Revival of Civil Society, an organization that emerged from the 2001 'Damascus Spring' period. In addition, a number of 'elite opposition figures' signed the petition: Riad Saif (former MP and businessman and founder of the Forum for National Dialogue), Michel Kilo (Christian and long-time opposition figure and publicist), Jawdat Said (Shaykh and Islamic scholar from Quneitra near the Golan Heights), and Haitham al-Maleh (former judge and human rights activist) are a few of the most well-known names (Damascus Declaration, 16 October 2005). Most of the actors above played a role, albeit not a pivotal one, in the uprising. Haitham al-Maleh was one of the first to attempt to establish a foreign council to represent the Syrian uprising – but failed. Riad Saif became a senior member of the National Coalition in November 2012. They are seen by many to be the traditional elite opposition that is rather disconnected from the general Syrian population.

In addition to this, there are the Kurdish movements. The Kurdish minority in (Northern) Syria has traditionally been highly politicized. As result, there are numerous parties and movements: two examples are the Kurdish Future Movement of the late Mashaal Tammo and the Democratic Union Party (PYD, which has close connections with the Kurdish PKK) (Arango 2012). Many of these parties are at odds with each other over their relationships with other Kurdish parties in Iraq and/or Turkey, their positions vis-à-vis the Bashar regime, and so on. Splits are common: for example, after the assassination of Mashaal Tammo in October 2011 (Shadid 2011c), a leadership crisis developed (Carnegie Endowment 2011). The PYD is a strong proponent of far-reaching autonomy for Kurdish Syria. In the context of the foundation of the Syrian National Council (SNC) in October 2011, the Kurdish National Council (KNC) was also founded through the direct mediation of the Kurdish Iraqi president Barzani. With the exception of the PYD, these parties favour a Kurdish role within a future unified Syria. As we will see further below, as the uprising continued, and especially with the emergence of ISIS, the PYD emerged as the most powerful Kurdish movement, declaring its own Kurdish autonomous region in 2015.

In addition to this, there is the Syrian Muslim Brotherhood (SMB). Although it remains the only Islamist political party with a history in Syrian politics, it has not been able to recreate an effective structure inside the country following the repression of the 1980s. After the start of the uprising, the Brotherhood quickly became active in foreign-based umbrella organizations. The Syrian National Council (SNC, see below) is one example in which the SMB quickly gained a dominant position. The organization was criticized early on by opposition figures from all ideologies and backgrounds for its authoritarian tendencies within the SNC.

Two groups that are often at the forefront of collective mobilization have remained largely absent from the Syrian one: The first is the Syrian Labour movement. Due to the historical development of labour unions, the Syrian regime was able to effectively pacify unionism in the country. In the 1960s, they emerged in the Syrian periphery as corporate Ba'athist structures. After the 1979–82 uprising, even the urban labour unions (those that predated Ba'athist rule) were co-opted into a national Ba'athist organization and rendered ineffective as regime opposition. As such, labour organizations at both the local and the national levels have been effectively tied to the regime (Hinnebusch 1993). In previous episodes of mobilization, as in the current uprising, they played no significant role.[12] The same holds for organized politicized student movements. These are largely absent in Syria, as their institutional structures, together with general unionism in the country, have historically been effectively co-opted by the Ba'athist regime. This does not mean that students have not been active in the uprising, or that universities have not been a breeding ground for mobilization: University dorms have become infamous as centres of protests (France 24 2011e). As the uprising emerged, specific student coordination committees emerged at various universities. But these groups did not build on pre-existing organizational structures or collective identities.

Escalation

The authoritarian corporatist characteristics of the Syrian regime, in combination with a multi-sectarian society, had a particular influence on how the uprising developed. Having previously incorporated all nationwide social organizations in a successful attempt at pacifying regime opposition (for instance, in case of the labour and student movements), it created a situation in which independent activism was only permitted to emerge within separate social, ethnic, and religious groups. As such, the argument that without regime tutelage competing ethnic and religious groups would find themselves in a devastating conflict held some currency. From the first days of the uprising, regime supporters would use this logic – the regime provides social stability and security – to legitimize regime actions in the face of massive shows of opposition. Inadvertently this meant that protestors were, from day one of the uprising, implied to be Sunni extremists supported by outside forces that were out to repress Syrian minorities (Leenders and Heydemann 2012).

The approach proved successful. Despite internal feuds, the idea that the fall of the regime would mean their annihilation kept minority groups largely supporting the regime. The idea that a change in status quo would be detrimental to their interests also kept other elite (Sunni trader) groups on the regime's side. As a result, traditionally operationalized political opportunity structures (for instance, regarding party alliances, divisions in the political elites, emergence of potential allies within the political sphere, and contested elections) remained closed throughout the uprising. This meant that the democracy movement was faced with a regime that facilitated social fragmentation and sectarian identification within its opposition ranks, all the while repressing protests with deadly force – resulting in increasing calls for drawing from more violent protest repertoires. As we will see in the following section, despite attempts to counter these tendencies, it was exactly these mechanisms that would constitute the main elements of escalation in the Syrian uprising.

Safeguarding unity

As a strategic response to the regime's description of the protests as sectarian and foreign-based, protestors often called for the unity of the Syrian nation. They accentuated their Syrian nationalistic outlook and thereby explicitly called for the strengthening of an independent Syrian civil society. We see, for instance, that in addition to calls for freedom, change, and the fall of the regime, a recurrent chant was *Wahd, wahd, wahd, al-Shab al-Suri wahd* ('One, one one, the people of Syria are one') (Misbar Syria 2016). In addition, on the Syrian Revolution against Bashar al-Assad Facebook page, a statement against sectarianism was posted for the first time on 21 March 2011 and re-posted multiple times over the following years.[13]

At the same time, the strong nationalist message of the coordination committees could not obscure the fact that Sunnis were overrepresented in popular mobilization. Although protests and committees were explicitly non-sectarian, some biases within the make-up of the committees were soon apparent: it was overtly Sunnis from smaller cities that joined the uprising. Minorities and 'elite' Sunnis remained largely on the sidelines (Kodmani 2011). In the Idlib region, a foreign-based Syrian Sunni *shaykh*, Adnan al-Arour, incited protests for many months.[14] Additionally, in the Kurdish Northeast of the country, specifically Kurdish LCCs had emerged (KurdWatch 2011). In July 2011, Sunni and Alawis clashed in Homs, only to be (relatively) contained through the intervention of local *shaykhs*, social leaders, and committees (Landis 2011c). As such, the LCC umbrella organization could not hide the fact that certain tendencies – for the use of violence and sectarian identification within the uprising – had grown stronger (Shadid 2011b).

In the following weeks and months, a deadlock in the uprising emerged: The regime's use of live ammunition was not able to completely suppress protests, but activists were unable to enlarge protests (or seriously endanger the regime) due to repression. This situation, in which protestors persisted in the face of live ammunition, occasional shelling, and mass arrests, marked much of the following year. Though there was a natural tendency to use violence in response to regime repression, this was actively resisted by co-ordination committees at the time, which persisted in their call for the sole use of a non-violent protest repertoire. The question, though, was how long they would be able to maintain this position.

Violence begets violence

From the start of the uprising, protestors debated the use of violence. The general opinion among activists was that it would only invite more regime violence. At the same time, though, in reaction to regime repression, there were instances of spontaneous uses of live fire by small groups of protestors from March 2011 onwards (Slackman and Stack 2011). An early example was explored by Joshua Landis, Director of the Center for Middle East Studies at the University of Oklahoma: in April 2011, an apparent case of defecting soldiers being shot by their commander in Banyas turned out to be an ambush by armed protestors. Nine soldiers were killed (Landis 2011e). An activist from Saraqib (Idlib region) told one of the authors that youngsters in his village had, at the start of the uprising, used antique rifles to shoot at a car carrying security personnel as they entered the city to arrest protestors. Many other examples of local youths taking up guns by themselves were mentioned in interviews.[15] However, it should be stated again that the use of violent repertoires was, at the start of the uprising, a very spontaneous and localized affair.

What happened on 6 June 2011 in Jisr as-Shurugh, a town southwest of Aleppo and close to the border of Turkey, is noteworthy in this respect. What was initially described as a mass defection followed by intra-army clashes (Stack 2011) was probably one of the first successful attempts by local residents to ambush the army and subsequently ransack and attack all the town's government buildings (Landis 2011b). The town's inhabitants quickly declared it to be 'liberated'. The reaction from the regime was meant to send a message: the town was surrounded, shelled relentlessly, and retaken a week later by the army (the Fourth Division under the command of Maher al-Assad) after heavy fighting. It was the first time that clashes between the opposition and the army were reported on this scale (As-Sharq al-Awsat 2011b). Despite the apparent failure of the exploit, Jisr as-Shurugh would prove an example for other regions and cities. Where violence had previously been sporadic, it became more widespread after this event.

In June–July 2011, small militias aimed at 'protecting the people' began to emerge in various parts of the country. Their organizational structure was fundamentally different from those of the LCCs: where the latter attempted to organize as representatively as possible, militias had to organize secretively and as insular entities. They therefore often emerged around small groups of people within a neighbourhood, a mosque, or a village. On 29 July 2011, the formation of the Free Syrian Army (FSA) was announced:[16] It was an attempt to provide a nationwide structure for militias and an apparent acknowledgement of the emergence of violent repertoires among protestors. Founded by seven officers, it aimed to promote desertions from the Syrian army and protect civilians from government repression (Landis 2011d). The existence of violent repertoires was therefore theoretically legitimized by their purely 'defensive' application, at the same time safeguarding the peaceful nature of the popular uprising. The FSA was thus meant to be the umbrella organization for all local militias in the country. In practice, it never lived up to this role. The legitimacy of the FSA remained limited, distrust was endemic, and the FSA brand was eventually primarily used as a common denominator for the outside world.

Protestors had seen Ramadan (August) 2011 as an opportunity to enlarge protests and increase defections. What happened instead was a pure 'security solution' to protests on the part of the regime: with the goal of rendering protest impossible, the regime dealt with it as a direct security threat. This meant that various branches of the regular army were ordered to bomb and attack civilians with full force as they protested. On the first day of Ramadan, 138 people were killed.[17] Hama and Deir ez-Zor were surrounded, shelled, and then invaded (both around 5 August 2011, see Bakri and Shadid 2011), and Idlib and Latakya would suffer the same fate in the days leading up to Ramadan. Yet, despite increasing repression, no meaningful schism between the army, security services, and the political regime appeared. Defections never threatened the integrity of core parts of the army or the regime: The large majority of defectors were Sunni, and among the higher ranks, solely Sunni. This meant that the most powerful sections of the army and intelligence services – positions filled by Alawis – remained fully under the control of the regime.[18] To many protestors, this showed the ineffectiveness of non-violent protest repertoires in the Syrian context.

The real turning point came through an example from a fellow Arab country. On 20 August 2011 (during Ramadan), a broad coalition of Libyan rebel forces successfully attacked Tripoli, the capital of their country. The success of this operation sent shock waves through the Syrian opposition. With the successful attack of Libyan rebel forces in Tripoli, discussions started to tilt in favour of the use of arms.[19] Militias became more numerous and active throughout the country. Like the FSA, they were officially formed to 'protect the people' but were often much more offensive in practice. In the following year (August 2011–July 2012), they became increasingly larger, more organized and well trained. Examples of powerful militias at the time were the Liwa al-Tawhid in Aleppo and the Farouk Brigade in Homs. These militias payed lip service to the FSA, but were in reality highly autonomous.

From massacres to all out war

In the year that followed the formation of the FSA and the emergence of rebel militias, a gruesome deadlock of escalating violence took hold of the uprising. Syrians continued to protest, the army continued to repress, but increasingly the newly formed militias (more or less under the banner of the 'FSA') would fight back. Neighbourhoods, towns, and cities were invaded by the Syrian army, but it often proved unable to fully retain control of the area after their initial 'pacification'. Dara' (April 2011) and Hama (August 2011) were early examples of the regime's retaking control of a city, but Homs (November 2011–March 2012) would be the first example where militias actively – and for a long time effectively – opposed regime incursions. Other examples were the Jebel al-Zawiyah area (January/ February 2012) and the suburbs of Damascus (Macfarquhar 2012a; Shadid 2011d). In all these cases, residents became increasingly well-armed, trained, and organized in resisting violent Syrian repression. Increasingly, non-violent protests began to follow the dynamic of the violent conflict (for example, on the 'Friday of the Free Army' of 14 October 2011) rather than the other way around.

The emergence of militias alongside the FSA also laid the basis for an Islamization of the uprising. As the uprising militarized, Islamist movements became more numerous and powerful (Barry 2012). Protestors increasingly followed Salafist *shaykhs*, called for a Jihad against Bashar al-Assad and – sometimes – demanded some form of Islamic rule (Rosen 2012). Even in the process of online voting to name the Friday protests, the struggle between more Islamic-minded and secularminded protestors became more pronounced (Al-Jazeera English 2012a). Many of these Salafi-style groups proved adept at securing (financial and armed) support from private backers in mostly conservative Gulf countries.

With increasing Islamization came increasing polarization along sectarian lines. A string of massacres – of which the Houla (25 May 2012) and Qubeir (6 June 2012) are possibly the most well known – brought ethnic cleansing ever closer to reality (MacFarquhar 2012b). In both examples, dozens of people were killed by Syrian government forces and *shabiha*. Though both were linked to regular military operations (Landis 2012b), the killings were perpetrated, and placed, within an explicit sectarian framework: Many civilians had been executed, seemingly because they were Sunni Muslims.

At the same time, the extent of mobilization differed greatly across the country. The region encompassing Idlib, Homs, and Hama proved the most active: It is a conservative Sunni majority region in which *shaykhs* such as Adnan al-Arour were very effective in stirring up mobilization and supporting armed insurrection (Rosen 2012). The Kurdish regions were to some extent mobilized, especially after the assassination of the opposition figure Machaal Tammo. Dara' and the South had been effectively silenced for the time being. The largest two cities – Aleppo and Damascus – remained mostly quiet. In Damascus, it was impossible to rise up due to the dense presence of security forces, while in Aleppo inhabitants were generally wary of mobilizing due to their (economic) interests in maintaining the political regime.

On 18 July 2012, this all changed with a successful bomb attack on elite regime leaders in Damascus. It killed Asef Shawkat, the minister of defence, and three other elite security leaders. Responsibility was claimed by the FSA and a previously unknown Jihadist group: Liwa al-Islam (Brigade of Islam). The attack electrified the opposition by showing the vulnerability of those at the very top of the Syrian regime. Immediately afterwards, an attack on various neighbourhoods in Damascus was launched. Rebels in the North followed the example and attacked Aleppo. Within days, they had succeeded in securing large parts of the city. Most of the newer rebel groups involved in these attacks had an explicit Islamic character and were built on the idea of fighting an Islamic Jihad against Bashar al-Assad. Examples are Suqour al-Sham (Levant Falcons Brigade),[20] Ahrar al-Sham (The Freemen of the Levant), and Jabhat al-Nusra li Ahl al-Sham (the Support Front for the People of the Levant) (Lund 2012). In the South, Jaysh al-Islam ('The Army of Islam' of the late Zahran Aloush) became one of the major players. All of these movements first emerged at the beginning of 2012 and became more prominent throughout that year (Ignatius 2012).

Civil war

The 18 July 2012 attack proved to be the starting signal for an opposition offensive on both Aleppo and Damascus. It meant that, by July 2012, the uprising had escalated and moved to a full-scale civil war. In the months and years after, fortunes shifted repeatedly for all parties involved. At the beginning of 2013, rebels were still gaining ground: In March 2013, they conquered Raqqa and opposition groups gained control over the eastern oil fields in the same month. But as spring turned into summer, the picture became increasingly dire (Gordon and Landler 2013). From a phase in which an uprising tended towards violence and escalated, we arrive now at a situation in which civil war has taken hold of the country and evolves into a fragmented war of attrition.

Spurred on by the increasing sectarianism of the conflict, the use of violence became ever more indiscriminate and deadly throughout 2012 and 2013. This spiralling revenge and brutalization was linked to the increasing pervasiveness of frames justifying violence among the actors involved; revolving around doomsday scenarios and ethnic cleansing-type language. All this was facilitated by an increasing influence of foreign powers in the Syrian conflict, concurrent with a breakdown and fragmentation of governance within the country. The latter meant that not only were front lines flexible and contested, but competencies within areas controlled by rebels were often ambiguous and disputed. These three mechanisms – fluidification of borders, spiralling revenge, and sectarian identification – were key in the final stages of the uprising's transformation to civil war.

Transgressing borders

Throughout Syrian history, multiple foreign groups have found refuge inside the country. During the uprising, many of these organizations took specific positions within the conflict and, as the strength of the regime decreased, their roles became more pronounced. One example is Hamas: they chose to remain relatively uninvolved, distancing themselves from the regime while retaining ties to Iran by quietly leaving Syria during the first year of the uprising (Farrell 2012). On the other side, a Palestinian fringe party (the Popular Front for the Liberation of Palestine-General Command, or PFLP-GC) continued to support the regime – and actively aided the repression of Palestinians living in those Syrian camps that came out to support the uprising (Kershner 2011). This resulted in an intra-Palestinian conflict, which escalated as Damascus was attacked in July and November 2012 (MacFarquhar 2012c). Hezbollah also chose to support the Syrian regime, as it felt it needed its Syrian ally to continue its fight against Israel. Early stories that Hezbollah fighters were supporting the Syrian army proved correct when Hezbollah began acknowledging that fighters were killed inside Syria from April 2012 onward (Barnard 2012).

Concerning the Kurds, relations with and their presence in the conflict of foreign Kurdish parties (mainly the PKK and the Iraqi KDP) became increasingly pronounced as Syrian troops withdrew from Kurdish areas. This created the situation in which the Syrian conflict intersected with conflicts over Kurdish independence in Turkey and Iraq. Finally, as mentioned above, as the conflict became more violent and militias emerged, conservative Islamic groups also became more pronounced among the Syrian opposition. In this context, foreign jihadists increasingly began to see Syria as a battleground against an apostate regime – and began travelling to the country (MacFarquhar and Saad 2012). Many within the opposition were opposed to their involvement as it provided the regime with the opportunity to describe the uprising as extremist, but they often felt they had no other choice, as few foreign countries had come to the aid of the uprising in any military sense.

It was not just pre-existing groups that became entangled in the ongoing conflict. Foreign actors also became ever more active participants as the uprising turned into civil war. For instance, whereas in 2012 it was mainly Hezbollah fighters fighting alongside regular regime forces (*Enab Baladi* 2014c), in 2013, more and more Iranian and Iraqi (Shiite) forces were observed in the battlefields supporting the Syrian regime. Concurrently, the regime has become ever more dependent on foreign donors to keep its economy running. Questions have surfaced regarding the level of sovereignty of the Syrian regime, some describing Bashar increasingly as a puppet of Iran and/or Russia. This has fed perceptions that the Syrian opposition is fighting the Syrian regime, and that Iran has shaped the way that the uprising has subsequently been framed by opposition forces: not only against a Syrian regime, but also against a 'Shiite' Iranian one.

The increasing dependence on foreign aid applies not only to the Syrian regime: The same holds for rebel groups. Syrian Salafist groups, including Ahrar al-Sham, are often supported by Saudi Arabia. The Muslim Brotherhood is supported by Turkey and (initially) Qatar. More secular groups are generally backed by the United States and Europe. The extent of support from these countries was directly related to the position of their patrons in the international political arena. Whereas Qatar was quick to support the Muslim Brotherhood across the region in 2011 and 2012, in an attempt to bolster its power abroad, this support sharply declined when Saudi Arabia became more assertive. With this change, the Muslim Brotherhood saw its political opportunities plummet. At the same time, it meant that throughout 2014 and the beginning of 2015, Ahrar al-Sham started receiving more aid and became more powerful. Conservative Islamic and Salafi groups proved successful in securing support from (non-state) actors in the Gulf. This support helped strengthen the perception that Islamist actors had a decisive advantage over secular opposition figures – thereby automatically 'Islamizing' the opposition. Overall, foreign support facilitated the fragmentation of the Syrian opposition, as opportunities for foreign aid differed sharply between groups and changed over time.

Additionally, Syrian and foreign groups are interlinked at more informal levels. Personal and cultural linkages have always crossed Syrian borders, with extended families often split between countries. Though most extreme in the case of Lebanon – to the extent that Lebanon is perceived as part of Syria by some Syrians – this is also true of communities in the Antakya region in Turkey and at the borders with Jordan and Iraq. Antakya (which borders Syria in the northwest) is a mostly Alawi region, and many of its inhabitants side with the Syrian regime. As more and more Sunni Syrians – and specifically Sunni rebels – flooded the region, tensions arose, though they were effectively contained by Turkey (Gettleman 2012). In Lebanon, these tensions were more pronounced (Wood 2011) due to the sectarian nature of the Lebanese political system and its close connections with the Syrian polity. Hezbollah (pro-Syrian regime) is politically powerful, but the Sunni groups of Sa'ad Hariri (anti-Syrian regime) have been emboldened by the ongoing uprising against Bashar. As a result, political and sectarian divisions polarized. In the northern Lebanese city of Tripoli,[21] sectarian tensions came to a head in June 2012 when Sunni and Alawi communities clashed. Dozens died (Saad 2012).

Lastly, there is the influence of the international political community. The international community attempted to resolve the ever-escalating conflict, but diverging views on the need for regime change frustrated any coherent international response. International attempts at finding a resolution have been marked by the lack of consensus within the United Nations Security Council (UNSC), where Russia has vetoed any (US, French, and British) attempts at formulating a binding resolution against the Syrian regime. There have been a string of other initiatives: the Arab League peace plans (2011–12), the Friend of Syria initiative (February 2012), and the Geneva I, II, and III meetings (2012, 2014, and 2016) are but a few examples. The most that these initiatives have been able to achieve to date are temporary and limited ceasefires (Al-Jazeera English 2012b).

Justifying violence

Concurrent with the increasing brutality and fluidity of borders in the conflict came an increasing sectarian tone. Despite continuing efforts to call out the regime on its strategy of claiming legitimacy as an indispensable strongman in the face of a

Sunni onslaught (Dinya *et al.* 2011), the descent into armed conflict exacerbated sectarian tensions, exemplified in the previously mentioned string of sectarian massacres. Soon, voices of Alawi dissent against this sectarian strongman logic were drowned out by those warning of an imminent Christian and Alawi annihilation. In a context of societal disintegration (Amr 2014), apocalyptic prophecies flourished on both sides, generally legitimizing the collective punishment – and killing – of other social groups. All this meant that the Syrian uprising was increasingly framed in the larger context of an Islamic Jihad. Foreign elements became more pronounced as Jihadists started to flood the Syrian battlefield (Rosen 2012).[22]

Attempts at rebel governance

The shift to civil war also meant that the Syrian regime lost control over some regions in the country which, in the areas controlled by the opposition, resulted in the emergence of new governance initiatives. These initiatives proved highly fragmented. An important one was the Syrian Interim Government (SIG), which was formed in March 2013 as an outgrowth of the National Coalition for Opposition Forces (SOC), founded in November 2012, which aimed to represent the Syrian opposition abroad.[23] The SIG was created to provide an opposition-led governance structure as the practical institutionalization of a democratic Syrian polity. It was thereby meant to show that an accountable and representative Syrian polity was possible. The formation of the SIG kick-started the creation of local and regional councils throughout opposition-held areas. These councils emerged alongside pre-existing local coordination committees but were primarily meant as attempts at creating governance bodies – not coordination of protests or relief work.

On top of this, Islamist rebel groups across liberated areas instituted Islamic Governance Boards. Most of these appeared in late 2012, then spreading quickly throughout the opposition-held territories. Though often presented as court-like structures in which religious and civil law is used to mediate and judge disputes, these boards have also been an institutional centrepiece in early attempts to build a style of 'Islamic governance' in opposition-held territories (AFP 2013). As was the case with the Islamist militias, these boards were far from unified. First, they were fragmented geographically, with many boards being locally organized. Second, a struggle emerged among these governance boards on the extent to which they were being controlled by dogmatic Salafist movements – often with links to Jabha al-Nusra. The result was the founding of the more Sufi-inclined Syrian Islamic Council in April 2014, for which a number of local governance boards immediately expressed their support (*Enab Baladi* 2014b). But whether more Sufi- or Salafi-inclined, in their attempts to articulate a practical implementation of Islamic governance, these boards are a direct challenge to the legitimacy and governance attempts of the civil-defined local councils.

Soon, questions arose about the struggles over governance in the liberated areas, and especially the role religious-based institutions would have in them (Abuzeid 2013). The question about the extent that a future Syria should be (Sunni) Islamic – and to what extent this could be combined with a democratic state – took a central role in framing the democracy movement. Even among Islamist movements, positions differed markedly. Consider, for instance, Suqour al-Sham (SaS), Ahrar al-Sham (AaS), and Jabhat al-Nusra (JaN): SaS has been the most pragmatic of the groups mentioned here, with a willingness to show an Islamist bent and working together with a range of Islamist groups – including the al-Qaeda-related JaN – while at the same time coordinating action with other FSA brigades. AaS has stated and been shown to support a future civil Syria, while at the same time speaking of an ideal Islamic State that they saw for its future (Barnard 2013). JaN publicly stated – throughout 2012 and 2013 – that they aimed to support the Syrian people as jihadists in their battle against Bashar, but that they would not get involved in the day-to-day management of the liberated areas nor in the pragmatics of forming a future Syria. This was a popular position among Syrians who appreciated their fighting power, while accepting the seeming disinterest in a civil or religious future for the Syrian nation-state.

These positions altered over time. As the dynamics of the uprising shifted – and support seemed to arrive mostly from conservative Islamic Gulf actors, active within informal networks built on religious credentials – public statements from AaS and SaS swung more to the use of Islamic States and waging Jihad, thereby increasingly mimicking JaN (International Crisis Group 2012; Sinjab 2012). Currently, as the United States is increasing its support and Saudi Arabia is increasingly controlling private money flows to Syria, the language has shifted back towards arguing for the fall of Bashar and the strengthening of accountable governance structures in opposition-held territories. As a result, governance in opposition-held territories never stabilized and remained fragmented among various rebel groups.

To make matters more complicated, Kurdish groups have also increasingly institutionalized their attempts at self-governance. In the evolving conflict, the armed wing of the Kurdish PYD proved to be the only Kurdish group able to provide security to Kurdish communities in the face of attacks by the ISIS (see the next section), Jabhat al-Nusra, and other opposition movements (Lund 2014). The practical outcome was that the PYD took effective control over large parts of Northern Syria. In November 2013, the party declared the foundation of Rojava (Western Kurdistan), a largely autonomous Kurdish region in Northern Syria. Three months later it announced the formation of a provisional Kurdish government for the area (Reuters 2014a). The group stated that it strove for a pluralistic democratic federal Syria (with extensive autonomy for the Kurdish regions) – although Kurds in the currently PYD-administered areas have complained of its authoritarian tendencies. Despite the formal election of local authorities, all authorities and bureaucratic personnel are appointed or controlled by the PYD and any type of popular protest against their rule is repressed.

We thus arrive at a situation in which Syria has been effectively split in three by different warring parties: the regime, the opposition, and Kurdish forces. The war has become deeply embedded in international conflicts and inside the country itself, governance is fragmented and incomplete. At the same time, sectarian tensions have been exacerbated to such an extent that different groups were literally out for each other's annihilation and the war became a rallying cry for Jihadists across the globe. Meanwhile, the international community was incapable of creating a more stable regional context in which a resolution to the conflict might have been possible. At this stage it seemed that the Syrian conflict could not get much worse.

ISIS

This was when, in April 2013, the Islamic State in Iraq (ISI) extended into Syria and ISIS, or *daesh*, was founded. The emergence of ISIS, and the foundation of its 'Islamic State' in June 2014 (Bunzel 2015), caused a fundamental shift in the Syrian conflict. Where the Syrian civil war before had mainly revolved around a fight between opposition and regime forces – with the Kurds relatively quietly working towards their own goals – it turned into a four-way fight as the Kurds became more assertive and ISIS fought both regime and opposition forces (The Associated Press 2014b). The latter found themselves hemmed in between ISIS, on the one side, and the regime, Hezbollah, and eventually Russia, on the other. Through this shift, many of the earlier discussed mechanisms were amplified.

Sectarian identification

With its military successes in early 2014, ISIS saw an opportunity to further institutionalize and formally declare the foundation of its Caliphate. This was an attempt to create a state structure fully based on Islamic authority and identity: It was built on Islamic authority (any type of laws were legitimated on the basis of religion, there were no elections as public authority was seen to rest with God) and Islamic collective identity (any Muslim was automatically seen to be a citizen of the Islamic State, due to his or her religious identity). These attempts thereby also meant that this state turned explicitly hostile to any other secular nation-state, other religious groups (especially Shia Muslims), and anyone else who did not recognize their claim to representing Islam – including but not limited to the large majority of Sunni Muslims in the world. Despite, or possibly because of, its openly belligerent attitude thousands of Muslims from around the world answered the call to come and live under a governance structure fully, and solely, legitimized by its reference to religion. In effect, the creation of an Islamic State built on, and exacerbated, existing sectarian and ethnic polarization.

Spiralling revenge

Within this context of sectarian polarization, the Syrian civil war descended to new levels of brutality. While ISIS caught the world's attention through its own use of 'shock and awe' – killing foreigners as gruesomely as possible and posting clips of their murders online – it also showed its brutality to the local population and any opposition to its rule. Following the executions of popular activists at the hands of ISIS, in late 2013 – before the international intervention – a broad coalition of Syrian opposition forces attacked the group. Though initially successful (*Enab Baladi* 2014a; Reuters 2014b), following surprise gains by ISIS in Northern Iraq and acquiring massive amounts of (mostly American-made) weapons, the group turned around to use them on the Syrian battlefield. Syrian militias did not stand a chance. Following their victory, ISIS wanted to make a point: hundreds of opponents were executed and some tribes in North and East Syria were almost wiped out (The Associated Press 2014a).

To make matters worse, the Syrian regime's fight against 'terrorists' gained legitimacy through the rise of ISIS. The emergence of ISIS thereby provided the regime with an opportunity to escalate repression even further on opposition-held territory, most of which was outside ISIS control, and to terrorize citizens in Northern Syria with a relentless campaign of random barrel bombs. The regime steadily increased its repression, with around 200 strikes counted in 36 hours around 21 October 2014 (Reuters 2014c). Eventually, Russia would enter the war with a bombing campaign aimed at sustaining the Syrian regime, but legitimized through a fight against 'terrorism'.

Fluidification of borders

In September 2014, the United States, in collaboration with other Gulf and European countries, decided to attack ISIS. This international coalition explicitly focused on ISIS alone (as a threat to its own stability and as an actor that lacks international recognition), leaving the Syrian army untouched due to international constraints. What followed in the subsequent years were a number of shifts in fortunes, all related directly to shifts in foreign support to the various sides in the Syrian uprising. In late 2014 and early 2015, for instance, the United States (wary of strengthening the Syrian regime through its strikes on ISIS) and Saudi Arabia (wary of the increased Iranian influence after a possible defeat of opposition forces) started supporting rebel forces more actively (Hisab 2015). This shift led to initial gains by the Syrian opposition, which in turn convinced Russia in September 2015 to intervene more actively. The Russian support turned the fortunes back to the Syrian regime, with the regime slowly but steadily regaining control over Syrian territory after destructive bombardments on opposition-held territories. But the physical destruction of cities such as Homs and Aleppo after years of fighting and relentless bombing, and the continued reliance on foreign actors to keep the Syrian army and state functioning, beg the question to what extent the Syrian regime will be able to control its territory effectively in the future.

Conclusion

This chapter has explored how and why the initial uprising in Syria turned into a civil war. In the introduction it pinpointed three country-specific issues – increasing sectarian polarization, provision of group security as a source of political legitimacy, and an unstable international context – that returned throughout the narrative on Syria's descent into civil war. The chapter showed how activists were well aware of the structural context in which they started to mobilize, but were still overtaken by the escalation and polarization of the ensuing conflict. As such, the Syrian case shows how a democracy movement can kick-start a process that is out of its control, and how it is overtaken by subsequent events. This process has left the initial democracy movement struggling to survive.

The gradual transformation provided the opportunity to tease out the sequence of events that led to the civil war in great detail. However painful, it shows that Syria is a perfect case to analyse the constituent mechanisms of the process towards civil war. We observed, for instance, how in the initial phase a combination of escalating policing and ongoing mobilization resulted in a standoff that provided an incubator for the emergence of militant networks, social fragmentation, and increasing sectarian identification among activists and rebels. The combination of sectarian identification at the micro-level and the emergence of militant groups set the stage for the ever-more-brutal nature of the conflict and the endemic ethnic cleansing-type language among the different warring groups. In this context, increasing foreign involvement, increasing Kurdish activism, and fragmentation among opposition groups led to a situation in which territorial control for all parties involved was questionable at best. It was at this stage that a civil war had properly developed in Syria, and it was this situation that provided the opportunity for an organization such as ISIS to emerge.

An epilogue to Syrian democracy movements

As uprising turned into civil war, peaceful protests were sidelined. Despite the dire circumstances, a social movement for democracy – at the basis of the initial uprising – still persisted. For instance, just after Raqqa was 'liberated' by an amalgam of rebel Islamist movements in early 2013, protests erupted against Jabhat al-Nusra because of how they were managing the city. Many complained that the first thing the group had done after taking over the city was to appropriate all the money stored at Raqqa's central bank, leaving the city in chaos. There were also complaints about the treatment of defected soldiers, the increasing policing of social mores in public life, and seemingly random arrests. Most of these protests took the form of sit-ins in front of Jabhat al-Nusra's headquarters at the former governor's building, while holding placards and shouting slogans such as *ya haram, ya haram, bidu la'ba bi ism Islam* ('How dare you, how dare you: what you wish to do in name of Islam') (*Enab Baladi* 2013).[24] After ISIS took over Raqqa a few months later, any type of public opposition was harshly repressed. Still activists continued: A campaign was founded called *ar-Raqqa tadhbah bi-samt* ('Raqqa is being slaughtered silently').[25] It aimed at documenting and disseminating news about actions by ISIS in Raqqa, in absolute secrecy but with significant resonance both inside and outside Syria.

Other examples abound from across Syria: In February 2014, there were protests describing the new leadership of the FSA as dictators, and in the same month people declaring that the earlier rebel retreat from Homs was necessitated by their internal corruption. Another example in this respect is the *wa-Itisamu* ('and we persevere'): It was a Facebook initiative[26] that called for unity within the opposition ranks and unification of the civil and military wings of the opposition movement. Started in August 2014, it proved popular, and relatively successful, to the extent that a council was formed in which various military groups and civil activists were represented. Another example came from the Damascus suburb of Daraya, where a related initiative started in November 2014. On the fourth anniversary of the revolution, in March 2015, various protests were organized, all with the aim of showing that the revolution was still alive. A town that must be mentioned in this regard is Kafranbel in the Idlib governorate, where a group of activists continued to organize protests throughout the years – often not more than a few dozen protestors at a time – with humorous protest posters reminding both Syrian and foreign observers that the Syrian protest movement is still alive and kicking.[27]

Notes

1 For an exhaustive account of the 1979–82 uprising, see Abd-allah (1982), Lobmayer (1995), and Ziadeh (2008).
2 This was not just true for the Muslim Brotherhood; Salafists and Hizb al-Tahrir were also repressed and exiled. In addition, any religious institutes that had supported the uprising – or whose students had supported it – were subject to dismantling: examples are the Abi Dharr and Jama't Midan groups and the Zayd movement (Pierret 2009, 3). Hundreds of *shayks* and *'ulama* (religious scholars) were exiled.
3 For their own view of this process, see the five volumes of Adnan Sa'ad ad-Din, *The Syrian Muslim Brotherhood: Memos and Memoirs (Arabic)*, 2006, Dar Ammar (Amman).
4 Two weeks later, a small demonstration appeared in Damascus; see Landis (2011a).
5 Following the numbers provided by: http://syrianshuhada.com. These numbers tend to overestimate the number of casualties by about 10 per cent.
6 Protestors were mostly male, but women also took to the streets. Though less visible following increasing regime repression, they do play an active role in supporting protests. See Stack and Zoepf (2011).
7 See www.facebook.com/Syrian.Revolution
8 See also www.lccsyria.org/about
9 For a list of named Fridays in the uprising, see http://ar.wikipedia.org: 'التسلسل الزمني للأزمة السورية'
10 See http://syrianshuhada.com/default.asp?a=st&st=3
11 Ibid.
12 See the website of the national Syrian union: http://wu-sy.org/c/
13 See also a dedicated Facebook page to the document: www.facebook.com/%D9%85%D9%8A%D8%AB%D8%A7%D9%82-%D8%B4%D8%B1%D9%81-%D8%B6%D8%AF-%D8%A7%D9%84%D8%B7%D8%A7%D8%A6%D9%81%D9%8A%D8%A9-152999281426499/
14 See his YouTube channel at: www.youtube.com/user/adnanalarour
15 For instance: interview with group of Syrian opposition youngsters, 29 August 2011, Istanbul.
16 The statement can still be viewed on YouTube: www.youtube.com/watch?v=SZcCbIPM37w

17 According to http://syrianshuhada.com
18 For an enlightening interactive overview of diplomatic defections, see: www.aljazeera. com/indepth/interactive/syriadefections/2012730840348158.html
19 Interview with Alawi opposition activist from Damascus, 24 August 2011, Istanbul.
20 See their Facebook page at www.facebook.com/sokor.ehsem
21 Not to be confused with the Libyan capital that bears the same name.
22 See www.rferl.org/contentinfographics/foreign-fighters-syria-iraq-is-isis-isil-infographic/ 26584940.html
23 See their website at: http://en.etilaf.org/acu/about-the-acu.html
24 See a clip of the protests: youtube.com/watch?v=9hOsyH7zasw
25 See their website at: www.raqqa-sl.com/en/
26 See their Facebook page at www.facebook.com/waitasemo?fref=nf
27 See their website at www.occupiedk afranbel.com/

References

Abd-Allah. 1982. *The Islamic Struggle in Syria*. Jakarta: Mizan Press.
Abuzeid, Rania. 2013. 'Syria: how Islamist rebels are ruling a fallen provincial capital'. *World.time.com*, March. Available at: https://goo.gl/W2XS8w
AFP. 2013. 'مجموعات إسلامية مقاتلة تشكل 'هيئة شرعية' في شرق سوريا'. *Alarabiya.net*, 10 March. Available at: https://goo.gl/sIzkyR
Al-Jazeera English. 2012a. 'The battle to name Syria's Friday protests'. Aljazeera.com, 14 April. Available at: www.aljazeera.com/indepth/features/2012/04/201241314026709762.html
Al-Jazeera English. 2012b. 'Interview: Syria peace envoy Lakhdar Brahimi'. *Aljazeera.com*, 20 September. Available at: www.aljazeera.com/news/middleeast/2012/09/2012920731 664541.html
al-Khalidi, Suleiman 2011. 'Syrian forces kill three protestors in southern city'. *Reuters*, 18 March. Available at: www.reuters.com/article/2011/03/18/us-syria-protest-id USTRE72H88M20110318
All4Syria. 2011. 'اعتصام لنسوة يطالبن باطلاق سراح معتقلين قرب بانياس السورية'. all4syria.info, 13 April. Available at: http://all4syria.info/web/archives/3420
Amr, Bilsan. 2014. 'سوء الظن عصمة المجتمع السوري، بين الشك والفطنة'. *Enab Baladi*, 16 March. Available at: www.enabbaladi.org/archives/15881
Arango, Tim. 2012. 'Kurds to pursue more autonomy in a fallen Syria'. *The New York Times*, 28 September. Available at: www.nytimes.com/2012/09/29/world/middleeast/ kurds-to-pursue-more-autonomy-in-a-fallen-syria.htm
As-Sharq al-Awsat. 2011a. 'سورية.. شعار جمعة الإصرار إسقاط النظام'. *As-Sharq Al-Awsat*, 16 April. Available at: www.aawsat.com/details.asp?section=1&issueno=11827&arti cle=617538
As-Sharq al-Awsat. 2011b. 'قوات الأسد تقتحم جسر الشغور مدعومة بالدبابات والهليكوبترات.. والمئات يفرون إلى تركيا'. *As-Sharq Al-Awsat*, 13 June. Available at: www.aawsat.com/details.asp?section= 4&issueno=11885&article=626305&search=%D3%E6%D1%ED%C7&state=true
Bakri, Nada, and Shadid, Anthony. 2011. 'Syria broadcasts scenes of destruction in Hama'. *The New York Times*, 5 August. Available at: www.nytimes.com/2011/08/06/world/ middleeast/06syria.html
Barnard, Anne. 2012. 'Hezbollah's Syria policy puts it at risk'. *The New York Times*, 5 April. Available at: www.nytimes.com/2012/04/06/world/middleeast/hezbollahs-syria-policy-puts-it-at-risk.html
Barnard, Anne. 2013. 'Jihadist leader envisions an Islamic state in Syria'. *The New York Times*, 19 December. Available at: www.nytimes.com/2013/12/20/world/middleeast/ jihadist-leader-envisions-an-islamic-state-in-syria.html

Barry, Ellen. 2012. 'In Syria, kidnapping of Kochneva shows new danger'. *The New York Times*, 20 December. Available at: www.nytimes.com/2012/12/21/world/middleeast/ in-syria-kidnapping-of-kochneva-shows-new-danger.html

Batatu, Hanna. 1982. 'Syria's Muslim brethren'. *Merip Reports* 110: 12–36.

Brownlee, Billie Jeanne. 2013. 'Syria – A decade of lost chances: repression and revolution from Damascus Spring to Arab Spring'. *Mediterranean Politics* 18(1): 138–40.

Bunzel, Cole. 2015. 'From paper state to caliphate: The ideology of the Islamic State'. Analysis Paper no. 19. Washington, DC: The Brookings Institution.

Carnegie Endowment. 2011. 'The Kurdish Future Movement'. *Carnegie Endowment for International Peace*. Available at: http://carnegie-mec.org/publications/?fa=48524

Damascus Declaration. 16 October 2005. 'المجلس الوطني لإعلان دمشق من أجل التغيير الوطني الديمقراطي'. Available at: www.nadyalfikr.com/showthread.php?tid=23678

Dinya, Tawfiq, Nazar Hamoud, Saadallah Maqsoud, and Mi Nabahan. 2011. 'بيان من ابناء الطائفة العلوية للشعب السوري العظيم'. *all4syria.info*. 9 August. Available at: http://all4syria.info/ web/archives/21800

Enab Baladi. 2013. 'اعتصامات للمطالبة بمعتقلين لدى «جبهة النصرة» في الرقة'. *Enab Baladi*, 23 June. Available at: enab-baladi.com/archives/9295

Enab Baladi. 2014a. 'تنظيم «الدولة» ينسحب من اللاذقية وإدلب وتركيا تهدد بالتدخل لحماية أراضيها'. *Enab Baladi*, 16 March. Available at: www.enabbaladi.org/archives/15917

Enab Baladi. 2014b. 'أربعون هيئة إسلامية تعلن تأسيس «المجلس الإسلامي السوري»'. *Enab Baladi*, April 20. Available at: www.enabbaladi.org/archives/16739

Enab Baladi. 2014c. 'تنظيم حزب الله في داريا من جديد'. *Enab Baladi*, 20 April. Available at: www. enabbaladi.org/archives/16754

Farrell, Stephen. 2012. 'Leader of Hamas makes rare trip to Jordan'. *The New York Times*, 29 January. Available at: www.nytimes.com/2012/01/30/world/middleeast/leader-of-hamas-makes-rare-trip-to-jordan.html

France 24. 2011a. 'السوريون في موعد مع 'يوم غضب' ضد الأسد بعد صلاة الجمعة'. *FRANCE 24– Monte Carlo Doualiya*, 4 February. Available at: www.france24.com/ar/20110203-syria-demonstrations-bashar-alassad-day-anger-friday-prayer

France 24. 2011b. 'عشرات السوريين يلبون دعوة للتظاهر من أجل التغيير والحرية'. *FRANCE 24– Monte Carlo Doualiya*, 15 March. Available at: www.france24.com/ar/20110315-syria-demonstrations-change-freedom-bashar-alassad-facebook.

France 24. 2011c. 'مظاهرات في مدن عديدة ومزيد من القتلى رغم إعلان الأسد عن إصلاحات'. *FRANCE 24– Monte Carlo Doualiya*, 25 March. Available at: www.france24.com/ar/20110325-daraa-syria-clashes-fire-demonstration-police-dead

France 24. 2011d. 'الآلاف يتظاهرون في مدن عديدة رغم الإعلان عن حكومة جديدة'. *FRANCE 24 – Monte Carlo Doualiya*, 15 April. www.france24.com/ar/20110415-syria-bashar-alassad-demonstrations-friday-prayer-freedom-human-rights-reforms

France 24. 2011e. 'طالب من جامعة حلب أمام القضاء بتهمة ' الشغب وتحقير رئيس الدول 400 إحالة'. Available at: www.france24.com/ar/20110627-syria-justice-trial-students-accused-demonstraters-kurdish-human-right-statment-critic-against-alassad

Gettleman, Jeffrey. 2012. 'Syria's conflict intrudes on Antakya, Turkey'. *The New York Times*, 28 July. Available at: www.nytimes.com/2012/07/29/world/middleeast/syrias-conflict-intrudes-on-antakya-turkey.html

Gordon, Michael R., and Landler, Mark. 2013. 'As rebels lose ground in Syria, U.S. mulls options'. *The New York Times*, 10 June. www.nytimes.com/2013/06/11/world/middleeast/ as-rebels-lose-ground-in-syria-us-mulls-options.html

Hinnebusch, Raymond A. 1993. 'State and civil society in Syria'. *The Middle East Journal* 47(2): 243–57.

Hinnebusch, Raymond A. 1995. 'The political economy of economic liberalization in Syria'. *International Journal of Middle East Studies* 27(3): 305–20.

Hinnebusch, Raymond A. 2001. *Syria: Revolution from Above*. London: Routledge.

Hisab, Fariz. 2015. 'التركي السعودي و«الدعم» الشامية الجبهة حلّ بين ..حلب تحرير'. *Enab Baladi*, 19 April. Available at: www.enabbaladi.org/archives/31618

Human Rights Watch. 2009. 'Far from justice: Syria's Supreme State Security Court'. Human Rights Watch. Available at: www.hrw.org

Ignatius, David. 2012. 'Al-Qaeda affiliate playing larger role in Syria rebellion'. *Washington Post*, 30 November. Available at: www.washingtonpost.com/blogs/post-partisan/post/al-qaeda-affiliate-playing-larger-role-in-syria-rebellion/2012/11/30/203d06f4–3b2e–11e2–9258-ac7c78d5c680_blog.html

Ilina, Angelova. 2014. 'Governance in rebel-held East Ghouta in the Damascus Province, Syria'. Cambridge: University of Cambridge Centre of Governance and Human Rights.

International Crisis Group. 2004. 'Syria under Bashar (II): domestic policy challenges'. Available at: www.crisisgroup.org/en/regions/middle-east-north-africa/egypt-syria-lebanon/syria/024-syria-under-bashar-2-domestic-policy-challenges.aspx

International Crisis Group. 2012. 'Tentative jihad: Syria's fundamentalist opposition'. 131. (International Crisis Group). Available at: www.crisisgroup.org/en/regions/middle-east-north-africa/egypt-syria-lebanon/syria/131-tentative-jihad-syrias-fundamentalist-opposition.aspx

Kelidar, A.R. 1974. 'Religion and state in Syria'. *Asian Affairs* 5(1): 16–22.

Kershner, Isabel. 2011. 'Fighters shoot protestors at a Palestinian camp in Syria'. *The New York Times*, 7 June. Available at: www.nytimes.com/2011/06/08/world/middleeast/08damascus.html

Kodmani, Bassma. 2011. 'The road to ruin for the Assad regime'. *Financial Times*, 14 June. Available at: www.ft.com/cms/s/0/5bdf4198–96b8–11e0-baca-00144feab49a.html#axzz1PMoNuXKI

KurdWatch. 2011. 'Conflicts with the Kurdish Patriotic Conference lead to division of protest movement'. *KurdWatch.org*, 7 November. Available at: www.kurdwatch.org/index.php?aid=2167&z=en&cure=232

Landis, Joshua. 2011a. 'Demonstration in Damascus'. *Syria Comment*, 18 February. Available at: www.joshualandis.com/blog/?p=8410

Landis, Joshua. 2011b. 'What happened at Jisr Al-Shagour?' *Syria Comment*, 13 June. Available at: www.joshualandis.com/blog/?p=10202

Landis, Joshua. 2011c. 'Syrians scared and angered by sectarian fighting. Little unity among opposition'. *Syria Comment*, 19 July. Available at: www.joshualandis.com/blog/?p=10837

Landis, Joshua. 2011d. 'Free Syrian Army founded by seven officers to fight the Syrian Army'. *Syria Comment*, 29 July. Available at: www.joshualandis.com/blog/?p=11043

Landis, Joshua. 2011e. 'The armed gangs controversy'. *Syria Comment*, 3 August. Available at: www.joshualandis.com/blog/?p=11181

Landis, Joshua. 2012a. 'Military casualties rise; president speech; Houla'. *Syria Comment*, 4 June. Available at: www.joshualandis.com/blog/?p=14859

Landis, Joshua. 2012b. 'Tremseh: a massacre or a fight? Annan's new plan: for and against'. *Syria Comment*, 13 July. Available at: www.joshualandis.com/blog/?p=15378

Leenders, Reinoud. 2012a. 'Collective action and mobilization in Dar'a: an anatomy of the onset of Syria's popular uprising'. *Mobilization: An International Quarterly* 17(4): 419–34.

Leenders, Reinoud. 2012b. *Spoils of Truce: Corruption and State-Building in Postwar Lebanon*. Ithaca, NY: Cornell University Press.

Leenders, Reinoud, and Heydemann, Steven. 2012. 'Popular mobilization in Syria: Opportunity and threat, and the social networks of the early risers'. *Mediterranean Politics* 17(2): 139–59.

Lobmayer, Hans Gunter. 1995. *Opposition und Widerstand in Syrien*. Hamburg: Deutschen Orient-Instituts.

Lund, Aron. 2012. 'UI Brief No 13 – Syrian Jihadism. 2012', 17 September. Available at: www.ui.se/eng/

Lund, Aron. 2014. 'The politics of the Islamic Front, part 5: The Kurds'. *Carnegie Endowment for International Peace*. Available at: www.carnegieendowment.org/syriaincrisis/?fa=54367

MacFarquhar, Neil. 2012a. 'Syrian rebels withdrawing from key enclave in Homs'. *The New York Times*, 1 March. Available at: www.nytimes.com/2012/03/02/world/middleeast/rebels-resisting-onslaught-in-syrian-city-activists-say.html

MacFarquhar, Neil. 2012b. 'Syrian Alawites divided by Assad's response to unrest'. *The New York Times*, 9 June. Available at: www.nytimes.com/2012/06/10/world/middleeast/syrian-alawites-divided-by-assads-response-to-unrest.html

MacFarquhar, Neil. 2012c. 'Syrian rebels claim to kill dozens of soldiers'. *The New York Times*, 5 November. Available at: http://www.nytimes.com/2012/11/06/world/middleeast/Syria.html

MacFarquhar, Neil, and Saad, Hwaida. 2012. 'As Syrian war drags on, jihad gains foothold'. *The New York Times*, 29 July. Available at: www.nytimes.com/2012/07/30/world/middleeast/as-syrian-war-drags-on-jihad-gains-foothold.html

MacLeod, Hugh. 2011. 'Inside Deraa'. *Al-Jazeera*, 19 April. Available at: english.aljazeera.net/indepth/features/2011/04/201141918352728300.html

Misbar Syria. 2016. 'الثورة السورية25 جمعة العزة جامع الرفاعي آذار'. *Youtube.com*. Youtube. Available at: www.youtube.com/watch?v=PcVmPGQsoIM.

Perthes, Volker. 1992. 'The Syrian private industrial and commercial sectors and the state'. *International Journal of Middle East Studies* 24(2): 207–30.

Perthes, Volker. 1997. *The Political Economy of Syria under Asad*. New York: I.B. Tauris.

Perthes, Volker. 2001. 'Syrian regional policy under Bashar Al-Asad: Realignment or economic rationalization?' *Middle East Report*, 31(220): 36–41.

Perthes, Volker. 2004. *Syria under Bashar Al-Asad: Modernisation and the Limits of Change*. London: Routledge.

Pierret, Thomas. 2009. 'Sunni clergy politics in the cities of Ba'thi Syria'. In Fred H. Lawson (ed.), *Demystifying Syria*. London: SOAS.

Reuters. 2014a. 'Kurds solidify autonomy in Syria on eve of peace talks'. *The New York Times*, 21 January. Available at: www.nytimes.com/reuters/2014/01/21/world/europe/21reuters-syria-crisis-kurds.html

Reuters. 2014b. 'Al Qaeda splinter group in Syria leaves two provinces: activists'. *The New York Times*, 14 March. Available at: www.nytimes.com/reuters/2014/03/14/world/middleeast/14reuters-syria-crisis-withdraw.html

Reuters. 2014c. 'Syria Air Force strikes 200 times in 36 hours: monitor'. *The New York Times*, 21 October. Available at: www.nytimes.com/reuters/2014/10/21/world/middleeast/21reuters-mideast-crisis-syria-raids.html

Rosen, Nir. 2012. 'Islamism and the Syrian uprising'. *Foreign Policy*, 8 March. Available at: mideast.foreignpolicy.com/posts/2012/03/08/islamism_and_the_syrian_uprising.

Saad, Hwaida. 2012. 'In Tripoli, Lebanon, a deadly battle over Syrian conflict'. *The New York Times*, 2 June. Available at: www.nytimes.com/2012/06/03/world/middleeast/in-tripoli-lebanon-a-deadly-battle-over-syrian-conflict.html

Salih, Yassin Al-Haj. 2014. 'The Syrian Shabiha and their state – statehood & participation'. Heinrich Böll Stiftung. Available at: https://lb.boell.org/en/2014/03/03/syrian-shabiha-and-their-state-statehood-participation

Seale, Patrick. 1988. *Asad: The Struggle for the Middle East*. Berkeley, CA: University of California Press.

Shadid, Anthony. 2011a. 'Syria pulls armed forces from some cities'. *The New York Times*, 29 June. Available at: www.nytimes.com/2011/06/30/world/middleeast/30syria.html

Shadid, Anthony. 2011b. 'Disparate factions from streets fuel new opposition in Syria'. *The New York Times*, 30 June. Available at: www.nytimes.com/2011/07/01/world/middleeast/01syria.html

Shadid, Anthony. 2011c. 'Activist's killing stokes tensions among Syria's Kurds'. *The New York Times*, 8 October. Available at: www.nytimes.com/2011/10/09/world/middleeast/killing-of-opposition-leader-in-syria-provokes-kurds.html

Shadid, Anthony. 2011d. 'Syria lays siege to a city, Homs, that puts up a fight'. *The New York Times*, 7 November. Available at: www.nytimes.com/2011/11/08/world/middleeast/syrian-city-of-homs-suffers-bloody-assault.html

Sinjab, Lina. 2012. 'Secularism and Islamism compete among Syrian rebels'. *BBC*, 25 October. Available at: www.bbc.co.uk/news/world-middle-east-20079317

Slackman, Michael. 2011. 'Syria tries to ease deep political crisis'. *The New York Times*, 27 March. Available at: www.nytimes.com/2011/03/28/world/middleeast/28syria.html

Slackman, Michael, and Stack, Liam. 2011. 'Syria tense as protestors mourn their dead'. *The New York Times*, 26 March. Available at: www.nytimes.com/2011/03/27/world/middleeast/27syria.html

Stack, Liam. 2011. 'Syria, claiming heavy toll in town, hints at retaliation'. *The New York Times*, 6 June. Available at: www.nytimes.com/2011/06/07/world/middleeast/07syria.html

Stack, Liam, and Zoepf, Katherine. 2011. 'Clashes intensify in Syria as protestors reject Assad's concessions'. *The New York Times*, 18 April. Available at: www.nytimes.com/2011/04/19/world/middleeast/19syria.html

Syrian Arab News Agency. 2008. 'Union for the Mediterranean Summit kicks off with the participation of President Al-Assad'. Available at: http://sana.sy/eng/183/2008/07/13/183894.html

The Associated Press. 2014a. 'Al-Qaida splinter group encircles Syrian city'. *The New York Times*, 11 June. Available at: www.nytimes.com/aponline/2014/06/11/world/middleeast/ap-ml-syria.html

The Associated Press. 2014b. 'Syrian opposition asks for help in 2-front fight'. *The New York Times*, 27 June. Available at: www.nytimes.com/aponline/2014/06/27/world/middleeast/ap-ml-kerry-syria.html

The New York Times. 2011a. '"Day of Rage" protest fails to materialize in Syria'. *The New York Times*, 4 February. Available at: www.nytimes.com/2011/02/05/world/middleeast/05syria.html

The New York Times. 2011b. 'Officers fire on crowd as Syrian protests grow'. *The New York Times*, 20 March. Available at: www.nytimes.com/2011/03/21/world/middleeast/21syria.html

van Dam, Nikolaos. 1996. *The Struggle for Power in Syria: Politics and Society under Asad and the Ba'th Party*. New York: I.B. Tauris.

van Dam, Nikolaos. 2011. 'Syria: The dangerous trap of sectarianism'. *Syria Comment*, 14 April. Available at: www.joshualandis.com/blog/syria-the-dangerous-trap-of-sectarianism-by-nikolaos-van-dam/

Wood, Josh. 2011. 'Syria's unrest seeps into Lebanon'. *The New York Times*, 4 May. www.nytimes.com/2011/05/05/world/middleeast/05iht-M05-SYRIA-REFUGEES.html

Ziadeh, Radwan. 2008. الإسلام السياسي في سوريا *(Political Islam in Syria)*. Abu Dhabi: The Emirates Center for Strategic Studies and Research.

Ziadeh, Radwan. 2010. 'Years of fear: the forcibly disappeared in Syria'. Freedom House. Available at: www.dchrs.org/english/File/Books/YearsOfFearBook.pdf

Ziadeh, Radwan. 2011. 'The Islamist Movement in Syria: historical, political and social struggle'. In Tugrul Keskin (ed.), *The Sociology of Islam: Secularism, Economy and Politics.* Reading, UK: Ithaca Press.

Zisser, Eyal. 1998. 'Appearance and reality: Syria's decisionmaking structure'. *Middle East Review of International Affairs* 2(2): 29–41.

Zoepf, Katherine. 2011. 'Long repressed, a Syrian opposition takes shape'. *The New York Times*, 27 April. Available at: www.nytimes.com/2011/04/28/world/middleeast/28syria.html

4

THE FAILURE OF THE LIBYAN POLITICAL TRANSITION AND THE DESCENT INTO CIVIL WAR

Emin Poljarevic

Introduction

Starting in mid-January 2011, a number of scattered protests in Libya – inspired by the Tunisian and Egyptian mass mobilizations against their authoritarian rulers – seriously disrupted Qaddafi's control of important cities, primarily in the eastern region (Abdel-Baky 2011). The rapid evolution of these demonstrations into an uncontainable mobilization surge and organized violence in mid-February is symptomatic of the socio-political convulsions related to the Libyan state's distinctive arrangement and social order. What had begun as a series of peaceful protests against the regime's administrative misconduct became a full-scale confrontation between frustrated crowds of protestors and ever more violent regime forces and their supporters, all of which revealed deep-seated grievances among a significant part of the population.

The Libyan case illustrates a sequence of events in which the initial mobilization process was premised upon the popular desire to reform the political structure from a totalitarian into a more representative, just, and free system, and which ultimately failed to sustain enough momentum to subvert and control the critical elements of the state and therefore establish full institutional control. This chapter explores how and why the country failed to achieve a peaceful transition, as well as why it descended into civil war. This is done by proposing a string of casual mechanisms that explain the trajectory of failed democratization in Libya. First, it is important to clarify the particularities at the *onset* of the popular uprising. Second, the chapter explicates the process of *activating* the spiral of violence. Finally, we explore the triggers that help in *reproducing* the civil war.

In order to contextualize and thereby link the causal mechanisms together it is important to describe and situate the underlying pretext of the uprisings and some structural elements that help frame the subsequent discussion. Initially, the chapter presents a socio-political and economic context within which the mass protests began in February 2011. It also explains some of the reasons behind the activation of a spiral of violence in light of the mass movement's fragmentation in the immediate aftermath of the regime's implosion. Within this process, we find in the framing of the Qaddafi regime's brutal response to the protests an important contributory factor to the escalating violence on the part of the demonstrators.

It is also important to understand how the local interest groups led by political elites developed self-legitimizing narratives of socio-political separateness to maintain a sense of legitimacy and loyalty within their own social group. The conflict activation process demonstrates how the initially shared goals of the revolutionary protests (namely, dignity, freedom, justice, national unity and, not least, economic prosperity) were transformed in order to fit into the existential narrative of each separate socio-political group, thereby triggering a range of old and incipient military networks that in turn became a part of a set of reproducing mechanisms in the Libyan civil war. This has meant that the fallout of the anti-Qaddafi movement revealed the deeply fragmented civil society, weak state infrastructure, economic instability, and fluidification of internal and external borders – all of which have contributed to the failure of the peaceful political transition and the descent into civil war.

Fragmented state and society

The state structure that had developed during the four decades of Qaddafi's rule had clear sultanistic characteristics (see Linz and Stepan 1996).[1] As such, the regime's repression strategies relied upon cultural and institutional components that were, in turn, directly based upon the existing patron-client networks. Qaddafi used the potential of these networks and institutions to his advantage by making any form of internal opposition highly risky and costly. More concretely, within a traditionally weak state administration, a tribal-based civil society, and a personality cult-based political system, Libyan state structures were unlike those of its regional neighbours. The civil society has traditionally consisted of a loosely bound entity held together through a mixture of traditional religious and cultural practices that have evolved slowly over the past two centuries.

Despite this gradual evolution, the civil society and state administration remained politically and administratively disjointed and underdeveloped for far longer than was the case for its neighbours. There are multiple reasons behind this institutional bankruptcy, ranging from the insufficient improvement of the infrastructure to effectively govern its vast territory in the post-colonial period, to the lack of interest on the part of the Ottoman Empire and the subsequent Italian colonial administrations in developing the institutional foundation upon which to build a state (Ahmida 1994). The administrative and social fissures can also be addressed by highlighting the anachronistic dynamic of politics in Libya, at least when we compare it to some of its immediate neighbours. In sum,

Libyan society has been fractured, and every national institution, including the military, is divided by the cleavages of kinship and region. As opposed to Tunisia and Egypt, Libya has no system of political alliances, network of economic associations, or national organizations of any kind. Thus, what seemed to begin as nonviolent protests similar to those staged in Tunisia and Egypt soon became an all-out secession – or multiple separate secessions – from a failed state.

(Anderson 2011, 6)

This multi-layered fragmentation fuelled the continuation of the civil war. However, it is simplistic to describe the warring parties as tribe-centred adversaries, for the contemporary tribal discourse blends with and is clearly subordinate to a collective patriotism that forms the root of the current national struggle. Since this movement began, Libya's tribes have issued numerous statements about the situation that largely reflected the patriotism that pervades these associations (Bamyeh 2011). Nonetheless, the traditional view is that the country's tribal structure, usually complemented by sub-divided clans, has been a fundamental component of the Libyan state and civil society.[2]

In order to understand this fragmentation, it is important to present an overview of the transformation of state structures, and, partly, the Libyan civil society. After independence in 1951, a largely successful project was undertaken to unite these regions under a unitary rule. From 24 December 1951 to 1 September 1969, the British-appointed King Idris (d. 1983) provided a coherent political authority throughout what we know today as Libya. The National Congress (Parliament), comprised of tribal representatives and supported by the occupying British authorities, selected Idris, a provincial leader of Cyrenaica (the eastern region), and proclaimed him king of a unified Libya. This has also meant that the Senussi religious and political practices became part of a strategy by which to bridge tribal and regional differences and solve disagreements among the various social groups (McGuirk 2007).

The specific features of social fragmentation of the civil society have been considered an impediment to building a unified state since its conception. Recognizing this, the political elites, under the rule of the king, attempted to establish a federally organized constitutional monarchy that recognized the particularities of traditional and internally disparate political cultures. The expectation has always been that the institutional arrangement would allow increasing socio-political coalescence and thereby reduce the inconsistencies in political and economic influence among various tribes and regions.

The discovery of massive oil reserves in 1959 made state building significantly more difficult. One consequence of the increase in economic resources has in fact been the rapid growth of a new urban, economically prosperous, and politically sentient middle class. A political opposition thus resulted from the king's failure to integrate the increasingly independent middle class into the state's decision-making mechanisms. Other important grievances related to the king's failure to distribute the ever-increasing wealth, the growth in administrative corruption, and the inadequate development of public services, all of which undermined the monarch's political authority (Takeyh 2000). It is worth noting that many of the same grievances were echoed during the 2011 mass uprising, when the protestors' main complaints concerned Qaddafi's personality cult, state corruption, and the institutionalized state repression of every form of opposition.

The main result of the 1960s political opposition led by the middle classes was the 1 September 1969 coup d'état under the leadership of Colonel Muamar Qaddafi – together with ca. 70 of his army-officer colleagues, all of whom were members of relatively small and disadvantaged tribes. The coup-makers, the Libyan Free Officers, inspired by the Egyptian 1952 Free Officers' overthrow of a monarch, proclaimed a republican system of governance anchored in Arab nationalism and socialism. Under the strict rule of Qaddafi, however, this political project gradually evolved into a totalitarian-style state characterized by the leadership's popular rhetoric combined with brutal repression and control of all elements of civil and political life.

Subsequently, Qaddafi viewed state institutions as potential hotspots of opposition, leaving them underdeveloped and even abolishing the tribally based parliament. Moreover, the role of the military shifted over time, as power struggles between military officers increasingly threatened Qaddafi's state control. We know of at least four incidents in which army officers were implicated in attempts to overthrow Qaddafi. These and other perceived internal threats caused the regime to purposefully weaken the regular army, instead creating parallel military structures with elite brigades, all of which were funded by and answered directly to the Qaddafi family (Barany 2011, 34).

Qaddafi further responded by strengthening interpersonal networks with the various tribes. These direct interpersonal dealings came to dominate the domestic administrative structures, which in turn, and among other things, allowed arbitrary dispersion of justice, personal favouritism, and unpredictable governmental rule. In practice, this meant that at the higher levels of government, Qaddafi would communicate personally with a limited number of representatives who would then oversee and follow up on the political decisions and their implementation (see Obeidi 2013).

In order to give legitimacy and ideological support to his system of repression, and perhaps in an attempt to create a political model for other countries to emulate, Qaddafi proclaimed a political theory of so-called *Jamahiriyyah* (self-rule of the masses) in 1977.[3] Local popular councils (Popular Social Committees) were created to deal with neighbourhood issues (e.g. arbitration between individuals and land distribution) and to provide a form of representation for communal interests at the regional and national levels of authority. In reality, the new system recognized and strengthened the local elites with already established ties to the regime. The role of the local councils was in fact to strengthen the regime's control over the growing urban populations. In return for overseeing the regime's interests, the local and tribal elites received better housing, building permits, and employment.

The local governing groups and extended interpersonal networks with the regime were organized primarily around tribal allegiances and, sometimes, around Islamist loyalties. This power dynamic developed self-conscious politico-administrative units within which local elites functioned as public information exchange hubs through which informants could pass relevant information on to the *mukhabarat* (state security) and through which the local leaders dispensed relevant information from the regime. This exchange of information and the system of rule represented a point of interaction between the regime and the civil society. Qaddafi's *Jamahiriyyah* project ultimately failed both to live up to, and to deliver, the implementation of people's expectations of self-rule beyond the narrow paths of patrimonial networks between the local political elites and the Qaddafi family. The clientelist nature of local governance eventually backfired as the overwhelming majority of the population came to view it as inefficient, undesirable, and ultimately illegitimate.

This failure amplified the existing grievances, which eventually contributed to the development of the mechanism of *political destabilization*. As we shall see, in the wake of popular protests, a great number of local administrators and political representatives allied themselves with their extended constituencies: tribe, town, city neighbourhood, or region. However, there is more to this background. The primary, and perhaps most viable oppositional framework in Libya, much like in the rest of the region, has been formulated by Islamist groups. Islamist political opposition is important, as it often cuts through the traditional forms of social allegiance. The importance of Islamist opposition will be expanded upon as the chapter discusses the development of *activating mechanisms* and later the *mechanisms of reproduction* of the civil war.

Political destabilization: the erosion of totalitarian control

An Islamic awakening in the 1980s and early 1990s proved the backdrop of the formation of a violent Islamist opposition. During the early 1990s, when many of the Libyan *mujahideen* were returning from the Afghan-Soviet war, the Libyan Islamic Fighting Group (LIFG) was formed and attached itself to a growing violent Islamist trend. The same period saw the rise of violent opposition groups in both Algeria and Egypt. In pursuit of its original goal – to depose the Qaddafi regime and establish an Islamist government – during 1995–98 it waged an intermittent low-intensity insurgency, which also staged several assassination attempts against Qaddafi himself (see Ashour 2012). It is important to remember that the already established Libyan Muslim Brotherhood (LMB) simultaneously developed its own oppositional, grassroots infrastructure through which they never challenged the regime through violent mobilization.

The Qaddafi regime's response to the Islamist opposition and insurgency was initially designed to remove the ideological incentive for the mobilization in the first place. The regime started a series of nationwide Islamization programmes that focused on reforming the education system and a string of social programmes.

These policies included the increase in funding for mosque-run social programmes, including the widening of religious education by boosting a national network of Islamic study circles across the country. At the same time, targeted repression allowed the security forces to arrest, kill, and incapacitate the backbone of the LIFG network. In 1996, during the height of the conflict, a prison riot broke out in Tripoli's Abu Salim prison, known for housing a large number of political (Islamist) prisoners, resulting in the deaths of 1,200 inmates in a single day. The event, later described as a national trauma, has been invoked by anti-regime activists during the 2011 uprising. Given its powerful emotional significance for many families affected by the deaths and torture of inmates, this event triggered a mechanism of *spiralling revenge*.

The regime's repressive measures against the LIFG were successful, so that by 1998 the group's campaign of anti-regime violence had virtually ceased (ibid.). The Islamist network survived, however. The non-violent Islamist opposition in the form of the LMB had seemingly melted into the regime-supported Islamic social networks, where it remained socially active but politically dormant until the 2011 revolt.[4] In the immediate aftermath of the breakdown of the Qaddafi regime in November 2011, in recognition of their long-standing opposition to the regime, some of the surviving leading figures of the LIFG came to be integrated into the National Transition Council (NTC) and later were active in the negotiation process between the warring parties (Ashour 2011; *Euronews* 2015). They were considered a significant asset in terms of their organizational and military capabilities in the ensuing civil war, in particular through a mechanism of the *activation of military networks*.[5]

During the 1990s, the regime's repression and reformation measures stretched beyond its ideological opponents to include Libya's largest tribe, the Warfalla. The animosity between the regime and the tribal leaders grew to the point of a rebellion that posed the greatest threat to the regime's authority since the start of Qaddafi's rule. The main grievance behind the 1993 Warfalla rebellion was the unbalanced distribution of power. Besides assassinating the most unrepentant tribal leaders, the regime's most effective strategy was to incorporate the least critical Warfalla leaders as its tribal representatives into the Qaddafi clientelist governance network. Their participation was later rewarded by increased economic benefits for the majority of tribal members. By the end of the 1990s, the regime's integration of the Warfalla tribe into the governing structure had been successful in deflecting any form of opposition from this important tribe. Warfalla and Maqarha tribal leaders were appointed to a number of the state institutions' top positions, with the exception of any influence in the country's military leadership, which was reserved for Qaddafi's own Sirte-based tribe. In order to secure his unique position of power, Qaddafi had increased his personal control over the security forces by creating the 'People's Guard', an elite military unit composed of select loyalists who were personally dedicated to protecting the dictator and his family, and targeting the potential 'internal enemies' of the state (Mattes 2004).

In order to integrate various repressive measures into a more comprehensive political system (*Jamahiriyya*), Qaddafi designed a 'code of honour' specifically addressing the Libyan tribes. Among other things, the 'code' explains the right of the regime to institute the collective punishment of *any* tribe, family, and/or extended network of *anyone* involved in 'obstructing the people's [i.e. Qaddafi's] authority'. This means that anyone found to be engaged in any form of anti-regime activities with or without 'tribal' implications would be severely punished (UNHCHR 1997). This totalitarian reform implied that any citizen and his/her (tribal or otherwise known) associates were now potential targets, which understandably resulted in widespread public fear and suspicion of anyone outside one's family circle and tribe, even close friends. Many families and even entire tribes of certain detainees were pushed to denounce, disown, and even accuse their relatives who had been arrested for 'plotting' against the state (see Obeidi 2013). The intricate web of state security informants was responsible for identifying potential agents of political dissent, which increased pressure on the economic and religious elites (Black 2011).

This development is clearly indicative of the indiscriminate repression that was instituted well before the 2011 mass uprising. This was also visible in other instances of repression. In the summer of 2000, a spontaneous and brief eruption of anti-regime violence followed a football game in Benghazi. When the Tripoli-based soccer team of Saadi Qaddafi (the leader's third son) made an apparently fraudulent attempt to win a match against the Benghazi-based team of the same name, Al-Ahly, several thousand fans stormed the field, interrupted the game, and later spilled out on the streets shouting anti-Qaddafi slogans (Mittelstaedt 2011). The regime deployed repressive tactics immediately. The Benghazi team's management was imprisoned, some of its leading players and an unknown number of protesting supporters were sentenced to long prison terms, and a few were sentenced to death. These latter sentences were later commuted (ibid.). The fans and their teams have traditionally been a source of violent protest against the repressive regimes in North Africa (Dorsey 2016). It is worth noting that, immediately after the Egyptian uprisings on 25 January 2011, the regime cancelled all the planned soccer matches in the country without further notice. Nonetheless, during the 2011 uprising, some of the fiercest revolutionary units from Benghazi were organized by soccer fans supporting the local team.

Popular discontent also increased against a series of administrative reforms aimed at modernizing the state bureaucracy. In the summer of 2007, Qaddafi decided to lay off more than one-third of the civil servants, a total of 400,000 people (Reuters 2007).[6] In order to soften the ensuing widespread criticism and to allow them time to find alternative jobs and means of survival, he stated that all of them would receive full pay for three years. This radical reform appeared to create additional tensions, given the Libyan demographics during the 2000s, with a population peak in the range of 15–24-year-olds, who made up more than 70 per cent of the unemployed and underemployed in comparison to the total employable numbers of Libyan citizens (ICG 2011b; UNDP 2011; see also Goldstone

2002). More specifically, the regime's failure to meet housing demands was arguably felt most intensely by the young population, who comprised the bulk of the 2011 uprising (Abdel Baky 2011; Reuters 2011b). As a result, the urbanized and young segment of the population created a politically volatile socio-political force that perceived the corruption of local authorities as a direct result of Qaddafi's patrimonial policies. During the same period, the regime had sponsored sending a significant number of university graduates to the EU countries to complete their doctoral studies in exclusively natural science disciplines (e.g., geology, chemistry, and biomedicine).

Even if justified as an attempt to address the public's frustration with the high levels of corruption of the civil administration (Pargeter 2010), administrative reform also allowed Qaddafi to appoint his immediate family members to a number of key positions and thereby to secure the allegiance of a handful of trusted people who had great influence on inter-regional/tribal networks and thereby local governance. The already strict clientelist system became even more tightly knit in the network of relationships between the Qaddafi family members and the leading representatives of various interest groups.

Despite the regime's efforts to maintain a high level of repression, social changes had a long-lasting effect on the public's rising expectations and hopes for greater participation and influence in political, social, and economic sectors of the state, usually dominated and controlled by a select few. The next section discusses some of the effects of the rising subjective anticipation for freedom manifested in the public's objective claims-making, which clearly had a destabilizing effect on the political system's patrimonial balance. This development of the mechanism we call *political destabilization* coincided with the sudden breakdown of Tunisia's and Egypt's authoritarian regimes between December 2010 and February 2011. The immediate effects of these uprisings in the neighbouring countries only added the important moral incitement to the existing anti-regime critique in Libya. The cumulative consequence of the above-mentioned processes of state repression, the mixed results of the regime's reformation efforts, and people's rising expectations was a delegitimization of the Qaddafi family rule.

The onset of mass demonstrations

In January 2011, inspired by the popular uprisings in Tunisia and Egypt, the Libyan protestors initially demanded improved state services and criticized the authorities' economic mismanagement, including what they perceived as rampant administrative corruption (Al Jazeera 2011). Within the days and weeks ahead, however, popular calls for dignity, freedom, and justice rapidly evolved into revolutionary political claims and radical requests to overthrow the entire regime and reform the political system (Michael 2011). The rapid evolution of the grassroots request was facilitated by social media that represented an important 'public' forum for airing demands. The initially low cost of participating in online dissent contributed to the widespread diffusion of protest. The online claims and framing of the street protests, together with images of state authorities' brutality towards the demonstrators, contributed to spreading a critique of indiscriminate repression. This in turn contributed to the militarization of protests, activating a mechanism of *spiralling revenge*. This meant that the gradual transformation of the initial demands and the state responses brought about a radical change in the protestors' collective consciousness, adding a critical mass to the development of the mechanism of *political destabilization*. Furthermore, the absence of the middle-class bureaucrats and professionals in shaping the core of the cycle of the early protests seemed reflected in a rather spontaneous and unstructured process of mobilization (Lacher 2011).

The level of regime violence reached a turning point on 17 February 2011 – the anniversary of Benghazi's anti-regime soccer rally – when oppositional activists called for a 'Day of Rage', modelling their call for regime change after Tunisia and Egypt. The day also contributed to the naming of the uprising as the 17 February Revolution (*The Guardian* 2011a; 2011b; Jacinto 2011). Indeed, it was then that the overwhelmingly peaceful protests began to turn violent, largely as a consequence of and a response to the Qaddafi security forces' brutal repression of political dissent (Amnesty International 2011c).

Anticipating further destabilization from the increased protests, the regime authorities warned all mobile phone users through a text message that the state security would forcibly disperse any 'collective activities that promote public sedition' (see Reporters Without Borders 2011). In line with the long-standing authoritarian tradition, the regime responded by deploying brutal policing tactics, causing an escalation in protestors' violence. So, when groups of protestors in the eastern city of Ajdabiya came out in large numbers to demand the fall of the regime, state authorities deployed snipers from the rooftops surrounding the main demonstration venue (Human Rights Council 2011, 23–6). The widespread availability of Internet connections and information technology devices such as mobile and satellite phones as well as communication radios made communication and information dissemination relatively inexpensive, enabling the coordination of political and military activities among the fragmented opposition groups.

This escalating spiral of violence created a sense of confusion within the vital segments of the ruling structure of the regime. Several high-level (political and military) regime defectors sided with the protestors, adding much-needed political and military management experience. The high-profile defectors coordinated the formation of basic political and military structures that could act as both the envoys of the revolutionaries and the military leaders and trainers of local militias, all of which sped up the political destabilization as well as the creation of military networks.

As a response to their deteriorating control over important parts of the country, the Qaddafi regime targeted key opposition leaders through Internet traffic surveillance. This had been an earlier and well-established strategy by which to target the intellectuals and other identifiable 'high value' individuals they considered a threat to the regime (see Freedom House 2009). One notable incident that demonstrated the regime's repressive strategy in the initial stages of the protests

(January–February 2011) is the case of Jamal al-Hajji, a lawyer and one of the bet-ter-known domestic dissidents, who had also defended political opposition figures in the past. He was arrested after posting anti-regime statements online and became a recognizable symbol of the arbitrary nature of judicial processes in Libya (Amnesty International 2011a; 2011b). However, the sheer number of critical posts, streams, and private forum discussions overwhelmed the state security's capacity to oversee, follow up, and act upon the perceived anti-regime activities online.

Another instance of the regime's brutal tactics was the murder of the famous amateur journalist Muhammed Nabbous, who, together with a number of his colleagues, had reported on the atrocities committed by the regime forces in the early days of the uprising. They had posted a large amount of video/audio material on his Internet-TV channel *Al Hurra* (Freedom), which showed various clips of authorities' assaults on demonstrators and other civilians.[7] Their work was arguably one of the contributing factors behind the UN's requests for a ceasefire after Qad-dafi's troops started storming Benghazi (*Media Spy* 2011). Nabbous was killed by a sniper on 19 March 2011, while reporting on the temporary ceasefire between the regime and the revolutionary groups in the East (Wells 2011).

Despite Qaddafi's efforts, Internet communication remained vital to the coordi-nation of the opposition's progressively more complex operations and their efforts to maintain its logistical connections in opposition-controlled ares. It also appears that the regime did not possess the necessary software to trace the vast amount of frequent Skype-based communications between the revolutionary groups in the East and West of the country. The (often live) reports on the regime's indiscriminate repression could thus reach both domestic and foreign audiences instantaneously.

At the same time, the bulk of Libya's economic sector turned against the regime, strengthening the opposition's position. As early as March 2011, the Arabian Gulf Oil Company, the second-largest state-owned oil company in Libya, announced plans to use oil funds to support the anti-Qaddafi forces. Joined by a number of important Islamic religious leaders and clerics (notably the Network of Free Ulema–Libya), the key Warfalla, Tuareg, and Magarha tribes announced their sup-port for the protestors. For example, the Zuwayya tribe, in eastern Libya, threat-ened to cut off oil exports from the region's fields if the regime's security forces continued to attack demonstrators. Such defections by economic and civil society functionaries severely harmed the regime, adding to the success of the uprising (ICG 2011; Small Arms Survey 2012).

Besides the large number of disillusioned and frustrated urban young men, important parts of the Qaddafi opposition consisted of previously exiled political opponents based mainly in the European Union and the United States; the domes-tic political opposition that grew rapidly in the early days of the protests, consist-ing of domestic political elites; and a significant number of women who became increasingly involved in organizing the logistics of support for the evolving urban militias.

The anti-Qaddafi activists in exile, who had actively protested for years in both the European Union and the United States, played an important role in the early stages of the popular uprising (see Ahmida 2012), building up information hubs for the domestic opposition. Several of them had lived in the United States since the 1980s, where they created the National Front for the Salvation of Libya under the guidance of Ibrahim Sahad. The majority of the organized opposition, including Sahad, were former Libyan diplomats and government and military officials. Right from the beginning, the Front worked closely with the NTC to establish independent communication networks in order to coordinate the revolutionaries' anti-regime actions (Elkin 2012).

Internal regime-opponents included high-profile defectors such as Mustafa Abdul Jalil (former Minister of Justice), Abdul-Fattah Yunis (Minister of Interior), Mahmoud Jibril (former head of the National Planning Council of Libya, an intergovernmental body set up by Saif al-Qaddafi to introduce a neo-liberal economic system), Ali Essawi (former Deputy Foreign Minister), and Abdel-Salam Jalloud (a late defector and Qaddafi's close aide). These and other prominent political leaders made up the bulk of the NTC members – among them well-educated émigré opposition figures and traditional tribe representatives – all of whom played a role in the initial stages of the uprising (Bell *et al.* 2011). Later, the NTC functioned as a *de facto* government by organizing the country's first ever democratic elections (see Reuters 2011c).

Another important segment of the protest participants was women. The fact that the intermingling of the sexes was limited during the protests made the women a distinguishable group among the crowds (see OECD 2009). Their collective demands, especially in Benghazi, concerned the relatives killed in the Abu Salim massacre in 1996, as well as the freeing of the thousands of political prisoners still held in the regime's prisons. During the increasingly violent clashes between the regime and opposition forces, women organized the medical support and food distribution to the armed anti-regime groups (ICG 2011b). Due to a deep-rooted culture of gender-based honour, women seem to have been frequent regime targets during the initial phase of the conflict (Wueger 2012). This clearly further antagonized the activists and increased the impact of the mechanism of spiralling revenge.

The militarization of the conflict

At the onset of the uprising, the Qaddafi regime initiated a media campaign to discredit the activists and deployed a significant number of Tuaregh mercenaries, considered a viable alternative to those army brigades that had defected to the camp of demonstrators-turned-revolutionaries (Amnesty International 2011d). Among other factors, the *fluidification of borders* between Libya and Mali and other neighbours to the south allowed a significant number of mercenaries to be employed by the regime. In addition, the activation and escalation of violence from the regime side in the months after 17 February 2011 make it hard to speak of activist protests in any conventional sense. As a result, the vast majority of demonstrators had begun to organize themselves into urban guerrillas by accumulating military equipment and using militia tactics. The overall security situation in Libya deteriorated significantly thereafter.

It is important to remember that the regime's responses to the uprisings need to be understood in relation to the above-mentioned power networks among the various ruling elites, including government bureaucrats, military officers, state security service personnel, and the economically privileged – all of whom were necessarily entwined with the ruling family (see Dalacoura 2012). When these alliance networks started to disintegrate in the wake of mounting pressure from street protests, the regime started to lose the essential support of the key Libyan tribes and individuals within the government and the army. The traditional power structure imploded, as the growing opposition coalesced and various NATO members and Arab countries intervened militarily under the auspices of the UN Security Council starting on 19 March 2011. Such developments reinforced the fluidification of borders, dividing the country into the 'rebel'-controlled and regime-controlled territories.

The militarization of the uprising spiralled as the European Union and the United States decided to intervene on the rebels' side, supported by United Nations Security Council Resolution 1973, through which the council authorizes its member states 'to take all necessary measures, . . . to protect civilians and civilian populated areas' (UNSC 2011). This resolution justified primarily NATO's systematic bombardment of the regime's forces so that they could not advance on the rebel stronghold of Benghazi and other rebel-held populated areas. The direct military involvement of foreign actors was crucial in the regime's disintegration. The involvement contributed both to the public's polarization between regime supporters and opponents, and to the increased defections from Qaddafi's inner circle. When NATO's bombardment of military infrastructures prompted the regime to rely more heavily upon tribally based allegiances, the support of tribes loyal to the Qaddafi family was not enough to sustain the system.

The UN-approved NATO bombardment of Qaddafi loyalists was crucial in turning the tide of conflict in the rebels' favour, thus activating a broad spectrum of military networks across the country. As the conflict continued during the subsequent months, the UN sanctioned the creation of the UNSMIL (United Nations Mission in Libya) as the primary international body for negotiating the settlement of hostilities between the warring parties.[8] Nevertheless, the bombardment allowed various militias to regroup, to reinforce their supply routes and, subsequently, to advance on key regime bases in Tripoli and Sirte as well as areas in and around the cities of Zuwara and Ajdabiya. The anti-regime forces received much-needed help in terms of communication equipment, training and, above all, military support from a substantial number of countries (among others, Egypt and the United Arab Emirates) as well as several NATO member-states in May 2011.

As the battles unfolded during the summer months of 2011, the opposition advanced towards the capital with constant support from NATO aerial forces. The fall of Tripoli on 20 August, and the killing of Mu'ammar Qaddafi and one of his sons in Sirte on 20 October, made it clear that the opposition had evolved into a political and military force composed of different tribes and ideological groups. The infrastructure for intra-state violence was taking shape, as clashes between numerous local rebel militias in the form of military networks only increased, despite the Qaddafi regime's collapse. The everyday violence between armed militias had activated a mechanism of security deterioration, which came to be reproduced, as we shall see below, because the political elites failed to create a non-violent atmosphere for the political dialogue.

The reproduction of civil war

As outlined above, Qaddafi had a vested interest in maintaining social fragmentation, clientelism, and inter-tribal suspicion in order to maintain control over various potentially threatening socio-political factions within the state. Qaddafi's control strategy over Libyan civil society had an immediate debilitating effect on its capacity to contribute to a political transition from authoritarianism to a plural and inclusive political system. For instance, from the very early days, the NTC found the opposition's military organization and capabilities hard to control. Even before the July 2012 parliamentary elections, the NTC leadership had decided to dismantle Qaddafi's military structure, effectively destabilizing the already brittle security situation. Instead, the hope was that various (armed) revolutionary organizations would be able to maintain order and that the newly installed General National Congress (GNC) with its 200 representatives would be able to agree on a strategy by which to establish the monopoly of violence and social control within the Libyan borders.

This hope was not fulfilled, however. Due to the power vacuum in the various regions of the country, as well as unclear political and military authority due to inter-militia fighting for control over resources, institutions, and territory in the aftermath of the Qaddafi regime collapse, the GNC proved to be inefficient, divided, and ultimately unable to gain control over the already fragile institutions. In fact, some armed groups took up weapons to settle old grudges with 'old' enemies. Others saw an opportunity to reposition themselves and their interests more favourably within the newly elected parliament (BBC News 2011). The ensuing disintegration of national security continued all through 2012 and 2013, despite numerous attempts to form a functioning central government.

The most important point of tension had been the power struggle between the political elites in the eastern versus western regions (Reuters 2011a). This became clear in January 2012, when the NTC drafted a new Constitution. The NTC had agreed to hold the first general elections in June 2012, which had to be postponed to July due to disagreement on the regional representation and distribution of the parliamentary seats (Kjaerum *et al.* 2013). The national public debates in the wake of the first parliamentary elections also revealed some of the regional tensions related to the majoritarian system of voting (ibid.).

The competing political parties' agendas reflected much of the dynamic found in regional and ideological schisms and partisan interests. The largest party was the National Forces Alliance (NFA), which primarily represented the interests of the traditional political elite and that of Cyrenaica (see Lacher 2013). The majority of the elected parliamentarians were in fact Islamists, including the Justice and Construction Party (JCP), readily recognized as the Libyan version of the Muslim Brotherhood, together with a large number of independent, non-party-affiliated Islamists and Salafi-oriented Members of Parliament (Ashour 2012; Lacher 2013, 10ff). The NFA was a broad-spectrum alliance of a wide variety of regional and tribal networks that had few common goals besides political and economic stability. Some common features included populist nationalist agendas and liberal-based economic programmes that promoted the development of the state's institutional infrastructure (POMED 2012). The alliance's primary parliamentary rival was the JCP (Kirkpatrick 2012' *Libya Herald* 2012; Salem and Kadlec 2012). Both the NFA and the JCP are coalitions that include a multitude of tribes and organizations that are usually bonded together through a range of vested interests, ideological, political, social, and economic. The political divisions that could not be resolved and the power struggle became obvious in the aftermath of failed government negotiations between July and November 2012.[9] During the turbulent political impasse between July 2012 and June 2014, it became clear that the unitary government would collapse. The subsequent political split into two administrative governments supported by rival military networks became apparent in August 2014.

The NFA established the House of Representatives (HoR), initially the only internationally recognized government based in the eastern city of Tubruq. The main opponent to the HoR was formed several months after the split in Tripoli. It consisted of the remaining GNC parliamentarians, the New General National Congress (NGNC) and, under the leadership of the JCP, the largest Islamist party. The result of the political split was a further activation of military networks, which were eventually remodelled into two large alliances. On the one side, the military alliance supporting the HoR had been composed of the Zintan Brigades, based in the western city of Zintan, and the Libyan National Army, including by far its most powerful military ally: 'Operation Dignity', under the leadership of General Khalifa Haftar. Haftar, one of Qaddafi's closest associates during the 1960s, defected to the United States during the 1980s. On the other side, the military alliance supporting the NGNC, the 'Libya Dawn', comprised largely of Islamist militias that had absorbed the most powerful militia group based in the city of Misrata and Amazigh tribal militias in Tripolitania and Fezzan (CFR 2014). This alliance also included the Libya Revolutionaries Operations Room (LROP), originally formed by Abu Sahmain, who belonged to an Amazigh minority and was himself the GNC president between 25 June 2013 and 4 August 2014 – the day of the unitary government's official collapse (Maddy-Weitzman 2015, 2506; see also *France Diplomatie* 2013).

Operation Dignity, under Haftar's leadership, had already begun its military attacks in early May 2014, targeting largely Islamist militias in Benghazi. Two weeks later, they expanded their attacks to Tripoli and other cities in Tripolitania. The clashes between the two sides intensified throughout the summer and fall of

2014, setting in motion a spiralling revenge. The two political adversaries – the HoR in Tubruq and the NGNC in Tripoli, both of which had claimed to be Libya's elected governments – had with their respective military networks become the main parties in the civil war by fall 2014.

It is important to keep in mind that the growing tensions between the Islamists and their nationalist opponents in the original GNC escalated gradually, given the inability to agree on the vital issues concerning wealth and power distribution, but also due to different opinions about the role of the old, Qaddafi-era political elite in the new political system. Another contentious issue has been the political rivals' inability to control their respective military units, with the ensuing increasing insecurity. This situation escalated during the late spring and early summer of 2014, resulting in full-blown battles in the capital (Kirkpatrick 2014). So, Misratan powerful militias, backed by other smaller Islamist militias and frustrated by the stalled political process, claimed that the nationalists (later the HoR) represented the old regime (*adhlaam*) and therefore needed to be excluded from the power-sharing process. The eastern-based nationalist militias – primarily those under the influence of General Haftar and backed by their allies from the western city of Zintan – were in turn concerned with what they saw as the growing influence of Islamist militias.

As a response to the political destabilization and security deterioration, and in order to break the political stalemate, the GNC parliamentarians agreed to hold new elections on 25 June 2014. This time, only independent candidates were allowed to contest the 200 parliamentary seats, and no parties would be allowed to campaign. However, the voter turnout was as low as 18 per cent, resulting in only 30 seats for the Islamist representatives.

Underneath the rhetoric of ideological differences, militias are fighting mainly for the control of the capital and state institutions in order to obtain political power and economic resources (Wehrey 2014). Economic revenues are the key component of a group's ability to wage war. Control of the oil fields, most of which are located in Cyrenaica – as well as the port cities of Ras Lanuf and al-Sidr, with their facilities to load crude oil onto tankers – are of highest strategic value (see Energy Information Administration 2014). These strategic points have in fact been some of the most important battlegrounds between Operation Dignity and the Libya Dawn (Malsin 2014; Wehrey 2015).

A prime example of this ongoing power struggle is General Haftar's armed campaign. With no prior government mandate, he organized Operation Dignity in February 2014 to establish his control over the country's most important cities and regions. By May, his campaign had gained enough momentum for him to demand the suspension of the GNC and of the government (Daragahi 2014). In order to defeat the Islamist militias, he demanded the dissolution of the parliament, where the Islamist party JCP was the second largest party. Considering the JCP as religiously extremist, Prime Minister Zeidan eventually agreed with Haftar and dissolved the government (Gerlach 2014).

Borders became all the more permeable. Due to the worsening security situation in Tripoli, with the Misrata-dominated alliance takeover of the city, the nationalist parliamentarians relocated to Tubruq in early August 2014 (*Economist* 2015). Haftar's May offensive had apparently encouraged coalition building between a number of Islamist militias in Tripoli, all of which became loyal to the JCP. The coalition, composed of various Islamist and Misratan militias under the name of the Libya Dawn, quickly seized many of the vital functions in the capital (Daragahi 2014). The remaining members of the GNC, under the leadership of Abu Sahmain, reconstituted the National Assembly under the name of the New General National Congress. The House of Representatives in Tubruq came to be led by Abdullah al-Thini and received international recognition shortly after its relocation in August 2014. In November, Libya's Supreme Court, most likely under the influence of the NGNC, denied the legality of the HoR (Eljarh 2014).

Sectarian identification in the different tribes was fuelled by the competition for economic resources and political control. Tribal and ethnic identifications are a major source of social and political mobilization (Bruce 2011; Obeidi 2013), including electoral behaviour. Tribes, town-alliances, and regional groups in fact offer a concrete sense of belonging and protection (ICG 2015), orienting towards selective and limited collective goals and commitments. As noted earlier, the Qaddafi regime's purposeful sustainment of tribal divisions for the purpose of maintaining a patrimonial system of governance has had negative consequences in (re-)building the vital state institutions (Bruce 2011; Dehghanpisheh 2011). Inter- and intra-tribal relations produce social ties based on kinship affiliation which, in the case of Libya, jeopardized the development of civic allegiances to and membership in a larger socio-political entity, such as a nation-state. In the wake of the regime's fall and the institutional disintegration, we have witnessed the rapid armament of tribal groups across Libya that have reopened old inter-tribal rivalries and provided opportunities to settle old scores (Markey and El-Yaakoubi 2014; Oborne and Cookson, 2012; Schruf 2014). In fact, a number of armed inter-tribal clashes in the southern regions of Kufra and Sabha (including the whole Fezzan region) confirm both the breakdown of central authority and the revival of a tribal political economy, including disputes about the distribution of revenue coming from the oil and gas exports (Abu Zayd 2012).

Sectarian identification was also fuelled by the ethnic tensions between self-identified Arab and Amazigh (i.e. Berber) tribes (Al Jazeera 2013). In the city of Zuwara, to the east of Tripoli, as well as the Nafusa Mountain on the border with Tunisia, Ibadi Muslim Amazigh tribes have been active in emphasizing their cultural distinctiveness vis-à-vis the Arab-Sunni majority. Their social mobilization has become increasingly political, raising the claim for the establishment of a federalized political system (Maddy-Weitzman 2015; Zurutuza 2013). Even though the Amazigh tribes are not a unified political or military force, they have shared similar negative experiences under Tripoli's political control (Bruce 2011; see Cole and McQuinn 2015). In the far northeast, the armed conflict supported a renewed sense of ethnic pride and the struggle for cultural rights among the Amazigh tribes. Due to the continued political destabilization and the civil war between the Tripoli-based and the Tubruq-based governments, many Tuareg tribes and southern Tobou militias, in addition to transnational jihadi groups, have created security concerns for Libya's neighbours: Chad, Niger, Algeria and, not least, Sudan and Mali. The fluidification of state borders has allowed the movement of people, goods (both legal and illicit), and arms, all of which continues to exacerbate the internal political and ethnic tensions (*Economist* 2015; ICG 2015; Maddy-Weitzman 2015; Malsin 2014; Reeve 2015; Poljarevic 2015).

What is more, ISIS entered the Libyan civil war through its alliance with the local jihadi militias in the eastern city of Derna (Joscelyn 2015). The prolonged nature of the Libyan civil war, and the sense of a rising desire for revenge among a segment of Libyan youth primarily in the cities in the Cyrenaica, have given rise to another militant group, the Islamic State in Syria and Iraq (ISIS) (Dalil 2015; Markey and Elumami 2015). This development has made the already precarious situation even more violent.

The (further) radicalization in the civil war

Within the spiralling dynamic of violence, insecurity, and the reproduction of hostilities discussed above, we also find armed groups mobilized around a militant and narrow interpretation of Islam. These groups are characterized by an uncompromising stance, often embracing indiscriminate war tactics by which to realize their military/political goals (see della Porta and LeFree 2012). In the context of Libyan civil war, Salafi groups primarily targeted what they considered to be signs of heresy in society. Their destruction of Sufi shrines at the al-Shaab Mosque in Tripoli, the tomb of Sidi Abdul-Salam al Asmar al-Fituri in Zliten, and Zubeida in Bani Walid are examples of violence against what they perceived as symbols of blasphemy (UNHR 2012). In the wake of security deterioration, the fluidification of borders, and the failure of institutional transition, this revolutionary form of jihadi militancy became a substantial mobilizing force that spawned several powerful militias, especially in Cyrenaica.

The Ansar al-Shari'ah (AS), headquartered in Benghazi, has probably been the country's most powerful jihadist militia. The initial military success of the core group of members, their puritan religious narrative, and their (initially adamant) moral practices – including an uncompromising stance against old Qaddafi regime operatives – resonated well with a portion of the young urban youth in Benghazi and the surrounding areas (see Dettmer 2013; Maher 2012). The AS's negotiation with the representatives of the HoR from Tubruq were halted before even beginning due to the AS leadership's demand of excluding any known Qaddafi regime supporter from the institution-building process. This insistence put the AS on a collision course with Haftar's Operation Dignity, which is the main backer of the HoR (Mahmoud 2015; MEMO 2014). Throughout the summer of 2014, a series of intense battles in and around Benghazi between the coalition of the AS-affiliated militias and Haftar's nationalist alliance made it clear that there would be no reconciliation between the jihadist militias and the HoR (Ibrahim *et al.* 2014). These battles coincided with the rise of the new transnational jihadi group – ISIS – which has emerged from within the wars in Iraq and Syria.

Initially, battle-hardened militants from the Middle Eastern battlefronts, both Libyan and foreign, flocked to the coastal city of Derna. There, a local jihadist group, the Islamic Youth Shura Council (IYSC) – an offshoot of the larger Islamist Abu Salim Martyrs Brigade (ASMB)[10] – pledged allegiance to the Islamic State in Syria and Iraq in November 2014 (Fowler 2014; Mustafa 2014). The ASMB was one of the first groups, led by the former political inmates of the notorious Abu Salim prison, formed in the uprising against the Qaddafi regime. Since its inception, the group has actively promoted its interpretation of the Islamic moral order within Libya, together with the public provision of social services in Derna. By April 2014, however, a new jihadi group, the IYSC, had emerged, directly challenging the ASMB. The IYSC's demands and ambitions became transnational, indiscriminately violent, and visibly totalitarian, claiming authority over the entire city and beyond. The group soon after pledged its allegiance to ISIS and its caliph, making them the sole representatives of the Caliphate's new province – Tarablous. The ASMB response was to form the Mujahideen Shura Council (MSC), a wider alliance of fighting groups, arguably connected to al-Qaida, in order to counteract the rise of ISIS in Libya.[11] The fighting in and around Derna continued unabated until May 2016, when the city was taken over by the MSC.

ISIS then moved its headquarters to the city of Sirte (Kirkpatrick et al. 2015). The main reason for ISIS' branching out in Libya, besides the ambition to control the whole country, seems to have been the strategic disadvantage in Derna (Cruickshank 2015; Saleh 2015; Torelli and Varvelli 2015). The threat from the MSC was amplified by the aerial bombardment of their positions by the Egyptian and UAE warplanes, approved by the Arab League as a measure by which to support the HoR and Haftar's Operation Dignity (Kirkpatrick 2015). The initial attacks by the Egyptian air force were a response to the ISIS militants' execution of about 20 Egyptian guest workers, who had previously been abducted in Sirte and taken to Derna. ISIS had justified their execution on the grounds of Egypt's covert backing of Haftar's campaign against their positions as early as mid-2014 (Al-Warfalli and Laessing 2014).

Spiralling revenge continued to fuel the continuation of the conflict (*Libyan Gazette* 2016; *Middle East Eye* 2015; Tawil 2015). The prolonged nature of a civil war with little likelihood of peaceful solution gives rise to a generation of battle-hardened militants who are more willing to accept a *radical* form of political order, including an uncompromising stance against the perceived enemies and the use of indiscriminate violence. The conflict between ISIS and al-Qaida affiliated groups can be seen as a process of radicalization directly connected to the protracted civil war (see Bigo et al. 2014; Hellesøy 2013). This does not mean, however, that all Islamists – or for that matter all jihadist groups – are willing to accept ISIS' internationalist or al-Qaida's (inter)nationalist ambitions (Fowler 2014; Wehrey 2015).

A range of heterogeneous and largely uncoordinated militias often view not only Libya Dawn and Operation Dignity as enemies, but also other jihadi groups as rivals. One of the primary obstacles to a large-scale de-radicalization seems to be the effects of the discussed mechanism of (violent conflict) reproduction. The negative effects include the ubiquitous sense of insecurity among the population, spiralling cycles of revenge, and the growth of a war economy that fuel military networks' activities. Such an environment facilitates the growth of uncompromising attitudes and extremist ideologies in the context of which these groups' message has resonance among the most susceptible layers of the population, namely the youth. Evidence of this has been one of the latest efforts to bring the main warring parties to the negotiating table. Despite the UNSMIL-supported talks and the signing of a peace agreement between representatives from the NGNC and the HoR on 17 December 2015, there have been few signs of military de-escalation on the ground (BBC News 2015; *Guardian* 2016; UN News Centre 2015).

Conclusion

This chapter has analysed the context and evolution of the Libyan civil war, including the mechanisms behind the country's failure to make the peaceful transition from totalitarian to democratic rule. The analysis of the causal mechanisms that have contributed to the civil war can be grouped into three main clusters: (1) contextual, path-dependent mechanisms at the onset of the conflict; (2) activating mechanisms that have solidified the war participants' objectives; and (3) mechanisms of reproduction of war efforts.

The chapter demonstrated how the patrimonial networks withered rapidly as a result of the regime's loss of political control. When those interpersonal alliances and the web of economic and political interdependency began to fall apart, the regime's balancing between the important tribes and the defection of key regime figures resulted in the crumbling of the old system. Under the pressure of revolt by populations and foreign intervention, the Qaddafi family could not sustain its power structure.

The transitional period between mid-2012 and mid-2014 revealed the depth of the social fragmentation of Libyan society, including among the political elites. The divided society contained little capacity to produce a citizenship-based political narrative. The rivalry among the political, tribal, ethnic, and economic elites, which either controlled or were allied with an armed group, continued to sustain insecurity and the fluidity of territorial control in the entire country. As a result of the institutional failure, the political destabilization, the security deterioration, and the fluidification of borders ignited the ongoing civil war.

The chapter also discussed the role of military networks in sustaining the political elites' pursuit of tactical goals reproducing the conditions under which the mechanism of radicalization could add a new layer to the war. What is more, the increasing tension between the population's various segments – the Amazigh and

Arab tribes, the urban and rural dwellers, ideological rival groups, but also the older and the younger generations – made extreme ideologies more attractive.

In sum, it has become increasingly clear that all signs of the loosely coordinated social movement mobilization that existed at the outset of the uprising have disappeared. The failure to sufficiently include, coordinate, channel, and institutionalize the multitude of political, economic, and social interests represented by various powerbrokers has ultimately resulted in wide-ranging lawlessness and state collapse (Di John 2008; Fund for Peace 2014).[12] The political elites, despite the repeated and foreign-assisted efforts to build viable state structures, remain deeply divided. Each political faction maintains its own military units and foreign helpers to deter possible political usurpers.

The political elites operate within the zero-sum-game framework. Libya's existing social networks remain based on extended family ties, tribal and sometimes ideological allegiances, and ethnic groups that often serve as interest groups focused on meeting their members' basic needs and their own survival. The endemic socio-political and economic insecurity, spirals of revenge, and activation of military networks have created opportunities for extreme political groups, such as ISIS and the MSC, to permeate important fragments of the disaffected civil society.

Acknowledgements

I wish to thank Donatella della Porta, Teije Hidde Donker, and not least the editors who have contributed with comments and advice on how to improve the text. The work behind this chapter was made possible by PDRA grant #1-0120-14121 from the Qatar National Research Fund (a member of the Qatar Foundation). The findings achieved herein are solely the responsibility of the author.

Notes

1 Noteworthy historical examples are the Pahlavi regime in Iran, the Batista regime in Cuba, the Somoza regime in Nicaragua, and so on.
2 Libya's three administrative regions, *Tripolitania, Fezzan*, and *Cyrenaica* are comprised of some 140 different tribes, 30 of which can be considered as having significant political influence (Bell *et al* 2011, 17): Al-Awager, Warfalla, Tarhona, Wershifana, Al-Fwatir, Awlad Busayf, Al-Zintan, Al-Rijban, Al-Awagir, Al-Abaydat, Drasa, Al-Barasa, Al-Fawakhir, Al-Zuwayya, Al-Majabra, Al-Msmare, Al-Qaddadfa, Al-Magarha, Al-Magharba, Al-Riyyah, Al-Haraba, Al-Zuwaid, Al-Guwaid, Al-Hutman, Al-Hassawna; and also a number of Tuaregh (Amazigh) tribes, Al-Zuwayya; Toubou, and so on.
3 Qaddafi explained his ideas to the nation in his *The Green Book*.
4 See www.ab.ly/ar/.
5 The most noteworthy leader of the LIGF is Abdelhakim Belhadj, who had fought with the *mujahideen* against the Soviet occupation of Afghanistan during the late 1980s. He was later appointed the highest leader of the Libyan Revolutionary Army, and subsequently the leader of the al-Wattan Party; see http://wattan.ly
6 Libya's population in 2007 was about 5.7 million, with a median age of 26, and a youth population that comprised nearly 20 per cent of the general population.
7 Some of these videos can still be accessed at www.livestream.com/libya17feb; see also www.mohamednabbous.com

8 By passing Resolution 2144, the United Nations Security Council created a UN body to facilitate national dialogue among various opposition and social groups in order to promote Libya's transition to a democratic and liberal political order (UNSMIL's mission statement: http://unsmil.unmissions.org/Default.aspx?tabid=3544&language=en-US)

9 One critical event that arguably prompted the solidification of military alliances is the 11 September 2012 attack on the US consulate in Benghazi, most likely by the Ansar al-Shariah militants (see Vandewalle 2012).

10 The group's choice of name is connected to the infamous prison (Abu Salim), where numerous Islamist and other political prisoners were massacred during June 1996. This indicates their vehement opposition to working with any of the overthrown regime's officials (see HRW 2003).

11 The formation of the MSC mirrors a similar change of tactics used by al-Qaida in Iraq during 2007. Most likely, it is a way to demonstrate its rejection of ISIS' legitimacy and claims of political authority (see Felter and Fishman 2011).

12 See Ghani *et al.* (2006) for an overview of the definitional conditions of a failed state. Assertions of (popularly and internationally granted) legitimacy and administrative capacity are two necessary conditions, however insufficient and contingent, for a modern nation-state to function. It is also useful to critically examine the usefulness of the concept 'failed state' more thoroughly. An excellent critique is presented in Call (2010). I am aware of the limitations of such a use of the concept; nevertheless, the term 'failed state' here reflects the Libyan civil society's inability to agree upon a unitary government and even less to sustain a stable institutional framework to represent and serve the country's various groups.

References

Abdel-Baky, Mohamed. 2011. 'Libya protest over housing enters its third day', *Ahraam Online*, 16 January. Available at: http://english.ahram.org.eg/NewsContent/2/8/4032/World/Region/Libyaprotest-over-housing-enters-its-third-day.aspx

Abu Zayd, Sarkis. 2012. 'Has the tribal political life been revived?' (ar.). *Al-Safir*, 12 April. Available at: http://assafir.com/Article/272156

Ahmida, Ali Abdullatif. 1994. *The Making of Modern Libya State Formation, Colonization, and Resistance, 1830–1932*. New York: SUNY University Press.

Ahmida, Ali Abdullatif. 2012. 'Libya: social origins of dictatorship, and the challenge for democracy'. *The Journal of the Middle East and Africa* 3(1): 70–81. doi: 10.1080/21520844.2012.666646.

Al Jazeera. 2011. '"Day of rage" kicks off in Libya'. 17 February. Available at: www.aljazeera.com/news/africa/2011/02/201121755057219793.html

Al Jazeera. 2013. 'Berber protesters enter Libya parliament'. 13 August. Available at: www.aljazeera.com/news/africa/2013/08/201381314533399976.html

Al-Warfalli, Ayman, and Laessing, Ulf. 2014. 'Libyan special forces commander says his forces join renegade general'. Reuters, 19 May. Available at: www.reuters.com/article/2014/05/19/us-libya-violence-idUSBREA4G04A20140519

Amnesty International. 2011a. 'Libyan writer detained following protest call'. Amnesty.org, 8 February. Available at: www.amnesty.org/en/news-and-updates/libyan-writer-detained- following-protest-call-2011–02–08

Amnesty International. 2011b. 'Libya: Writer detained after calling for demonstrations'. Amnesty.org, 5 February. Available at: http://www.amnesty.org/ar/library/asset/MDE19/003/2011/ar/aa60397c-55b4–423e-af3c-6c20e906d1ea/mde190032011en.html

Amnesty International. 2011c. 'Libya must end protest crackdown'. Amnesty.org, 16 February. Available at: www.amnesty.org/en/news-and-updates/libya-urged-end-protest-crackdown-2011–02–16

Amnesty International. 2011d. 'The battle for Libya: killings, disappearances and torture'. Amnesty.org, 13 September. Available at: www.amnesty.org/en/library/info/MDE19/025/2011

Anderson, Lisa. 2011. 'Demystifying the Arab Spring: Parsing the differences between Tunisia, Egypt, and Libya'. *Foreign Affairs*, May/June.

Ashour, Omar. 2011. 'Ex-jihadists in the new Libya'. *Foreign Policy*, 29 August. Available at: www.foreignpolicy.com/2011/08/29/ex-jihadists-in-the-new-libya/

Ashour, Omar. 2012. 'Libyan Islamists unpacked: rise transformation, and future'. Brookings Institute, May. Doha/Washington, DC: Brookings Doha Center.

Bamyeh, Mohammed. 2011. 'Is the 2011 Libyan revolution an exception?' *Jadaliyya*, 25 March. Available at: www.jadaliyya.com/pages/index/1001/is-the-2011-libyan-revolution-an-exception

Barany, Zoltan. 2011. 'Comparing the Arab revolts: the role of the military'. *Journal of Democracy* 22(4): 28–39.

BBC News. 2011. 'Gunfight erupts near Tripoli airport in Libya'. 3 December. Available at: www.bbc.co.uk/news/world-africa-16128837

BBC News. 2015. 'Libya's rival parliament reach tentative agreement'. 6 December. Available at: www.bbc.com/news/world-africa-35020308

Bell, Anthony, Butts, Spencer, and Witter, David. 2011. 'The Libyan Revolution: Part 4 – The tide turns'. Washington, DC: Institute for Study of War.

Bigo, Didier, Ragazzi, Francesco, Guittet, Emmanuel-Pierre, and Bonelli, Laurent. 2014. 'Syria on our minds – fear of youth radicalisation across the European Union'. *Open Democracy*, 4 June. Available at: www.opendemocracy.net/didier-bigo-francesco-ragazzi-emmanuelpierre-guittet-laurent-bonelli/syria-on-our-minds-–-fear-of-youth

Black, Ian. 2011. 'Libyans try to get back property seized by Gaddafi'. *The Guardian*, November 4. Available at: www.guardian.co.uk/world/2011/nov/04/libya-gaddafi-property-restitution-demands

Bruce, Ronald. 2011. 'A guide to protests in Middle East, North Africa'. *National Public Radio*, 13 April. Available at: www.npr.org

Call, C.T. 2010. 'Beyond the "failed state": toward conceptual alternatives'. *European Journal of International Relations*, 17(20).

CFR. 2014. 'Is it too late for Libya?' Council on Foreign Affairs, 3 October. Available at: www.cfr.org/libya/too-late-libya/p33548Cole, Peter, and McQuinn, Brian (eds). 2015. *The Libyan Revolution and its Aftermath*. Oxford: Oxford University Press.

Cruickshank, Paul. 2015. 'United Nations warns of ISIS expansion in Libya', *CNN*, 2 December. Available at: Edition.cnn.com/2015/12/01/politics/isis-united-nations-libya-expansion/

Dalacoura, Katerina. 2012. 'The 2011 uprisings in the Arab Middle East: political change and geopolitical implications'. *International Affairs* 88(1): 63–79.

Dalil, Miriam. 2015. 'Rival Libya factions reject UN deal but promise unity government'. Available at: www.maltatoday.com.mt/news/world/60332/rival_libya_factions_meet_in_malta?#.VnEjQDblw_V

Daragahi, Borzou. 2014. 'Tripoli warns rival militias over airport battle'. *Financial Times*, 17 July. Available at: www.ft.com/cms/s/0/812d4f58–0db1–11e4–815f-00144feabdc0.html#axzz3O3aJLMy0

Dehghanpisheh, Babak. 2011. 'Tribes in Libya are changing the conflict'. *Newsweek*, 13 March. Available at: www.newsweek.com/tribes-libya-are-changing-conflict-66185

della Porta, Donatella, and LaFree, Gary. 2012. 'Processes of radicalization and de-radicalization'. *International Journal of Conflict and Violence* 6(1): 4–10.

Dettmer, Jamie. 2013. 'Jihadists are creeping into Syria's rebel factions'. *The Daily Beast*, 4 January. Available at: www.thedailybeast.com/articles/2013/01/04/jihadists-are-creeping-into-syria-s-rebel-factions.html

Di John, Johnathan. 2008. 'Conceptualising the causes and consequences of failed states: a critical review of the literature'. Working Paper No. 25. London: Crisis States Research Centre.

Dorsey, James M. 2016. *The Turbulent World of Middle East Soccer*. London: C. Hurst & Co.

Economist, The. 2015. 'That it should come to this', 10 January. Available at: www.econo mist.com/news/briefing/21638123-four-year-descent-arab-spring-factional-chaos-it-should-come

Eljarh, Mohamed. 2014. 'The Supreme Court decision that's ripping Libya apart'. *Foreign Policy*, 6 November. Available at: www.foreignpolicy.com/2014/11/06/the-supreme-court-decision-thats-ripping-libya-apart/

Elkin, Mike. 2012. 'Exiles return to Libya contentiously'. *Inter Press News*, 17 February. Available at: www.ipsnews.net/2012/02/exiles-return-to-libya-contentiously/

Energy Information Administration. 2014. 'Independent statistics and analysis, U.S. Energy Information Administration'. Available at: www.eia.gov/countries/cab.cfm?fips=ly

Euronews. 2015. 'Libya's Abdulhakim Belhadj: "We are working to find a solution to end this crisis"'. 3 February. Available at: www.euronews.com/2015/02/03/libya-s-abdulhakim-belhadj-we-are-working-to-find-a-solution-to-end-this-crisis/

Felter, Joseph, and Fishman, Brian. 2011. 'Al-Qa'ida's foreign fighters in Iraq: a first look at the Sinjar records'. West Point: US Military Academy.

Fowler, Evan. 2014. 'From Raqqa to Derna: exceptionalism in expansionism'. *Jadaliyya*, 4 December. Available at: www.profiles.jadaliyya.com/pages/index/20182/from-raqqa-to-derna_exceptionalism-in-expansionism

France Diplomatie. 2013. 'Election of Mr. Nuri Abu Sahmain as President of the General National Congress of Libya'. 26 June. Available at: www.diplomatie.gouv.fr/en/country-files/libya/events-7697/2013/article/libya-election-of-mr-nuri-abu

Freedom House. 2009. 'Freedom in the World Report: Libya'. Available at: www.freedom house.org/report/freedom-world/2009/libya

Fund for Peace, The. 2014. 'Libya in 2014', in *Country Data and Trends*. Washington, DC. Available at: http://ffp.statesindex.org/2014-libya

Gerlach, Daniel. 2014. 'The General National Congress behaves like a dictator!' *Zenith*, 12 June. Available at: www.zenithonline.de/english/home/politics/interview-with-former-libyan-prime-minister-ali-zeidan/

Ghani, Ashraf, Lockhart, Claire, and Carnahan, Michael. 2006. 'An agenda for state-building in the 21st century'. *The Fletcher Forum of World Affairs* 30(1): 101–23.

Goldstone, Jack A. 2002. *Revolutions: Theoretical, Comparative, and Historical Studies*. London: Wadsworth Publishing.

Guardian. 2011a. 'Libyan protesters clash with police in Benghazi'. 16 February. Available at: www.guardian.co.uk/world/2011/feb/16/libyan-protesters-clash-with-police

Guardian. 2011b. 'Libyan protesters prepare for "day of rage"'– 17 February. Available at: www.guardian.co.uk/world/2011/feb/17/libyan-protesters-prepare-for-day-of-rage

Guardian. 2016. 'Libya rivals announce unity government as part of UN-backed plan'. 19 January. Available at: www.theguardian.com/world/2016/jan/19/libya-rivals-announce-unity-government-un-planHellesøy, Kjersti. 2013. 'Civil war and the radi-calization of Islam in Chechnya'. *Journal of Religion and Violence* 1(1): 21–37.

HRW. 2003. 'Libya: June 1996 killings at Abu Salim Prison'. *Human Rights Watch*. Avail-able at: www.hrw.org/sites/default/files/reports/libya2003.pdf

Human Rights Council. 2011. 'Report of the International Commission on the Libyan Arab Jamahiriya'. United Nation Document, 11 June. A/HRC/17/44, para. 36.

Ibrahim, Noora, Adam, Ali, and Ajnadin, Mustafa. 2014. 'Benghazi Revolutionary Council damns revenge killings by armed demonstrators'. *Libya Herald*, 17 October. Available at: www.libyaherald.com/2014/10/17/benghazi-revolutionary-council-damns-revenge-killings-by-armed-demonstrators/#ixzz3Sfs98ZHS

ICG. 2011a. 'Popular protest in North Africa and the Middle East (V): Making sense of Libya'. *International Crisis Group*. Middle East/Africa Report, No.107, 6 June. Available at: www.crisisgroup.org/middle-east-north-africa/north-africa/libya/popular-protest-north-africa-and-middle-east-v-making-sense-libya

ICG. 2011b. 'Holding Libya together: security challenges after Qadhafi.' *International Crisis Group*. Middle East/North Africa Report No.115, 14 December. Available at: www.crisisgroup.org/middle-east-north-africa/north-africa/libya/holding-libya-together-security-challenges-after-qadhafi

ICG. 2015. 'Libya: getting Geneva right'. International Crisis Group. Middle East and North Africa Report No.157, 26 February. Available at: www.crisisgroup.org/~/media/Files/Middle%20East%20North%20Africa/North%20Africa/libya/157-libya-getting-geneva-right.pdf

Jacinto, Leela. 2011. 'Benghazi's Tahrir Square: Times Square style meets revolutionary zeal'. *France24*, 25 April. Available at: www.france24.com/en/20110425-libya-benghazi-tahrir-square-times-reporters-notebook-leela-jacinto

Joscelyn, Thomas. 2015. 'Islamic State "province" in Libya claims capture of town'. *The Long War Journal*, 15 February. Available at: www.longwarjournal.org/archives/2015/02/islamic_state_provin_1.php

Kirkpatrick, Patrik. 2012. 'Election results in Libya break an Islamist wave'. *The New York Times*, 8 July. Available at: www.nytimes.com/2012/07/09/world/africa/libya-election-latest-results.html?pagewanted=all&_r=2&

Kirkpatrick, David. 2014. 'In Libya, parliament convenes amid battles'. *New York Times*, 4 August. Available at: www.nytimes.com/2014/08/05/world/africa/libyas-new-parliament-meets-amid-militia-rivalries.html

Kirkpatrick, David. 2015. 'Egypt launches airstrike in Libya against ISIS branch'. *The New York Times*, 16 February. Available at: www.nytimes.com/2015/02/17/world/middleeast/isis-egypt-libya-airstrikes.html?_r=0

Kirkpatrick, David, Bubbard, Ben, and Schmittnov, Eric. 2015. 'ISIS' grip on Libyan city gives it a fallback'. *New York Times*, 28 November. Available at: www.nytimes.com/2015/11/29/world/middleeast/isis-grip-on-libyan-city-gives-it-a-fallback-option.html?_r=1

Kjaerum, Alexander, Lust, Ellen, Pedersen, Line Fly, and Wichmann, Jakob Mathias. 2013. 'Libyan parliamentary election study'. Working Paper, Copenhagen JMW Consulting.

Lacher, Wolfram. 2011. 'Families, tribes and cities in the Libyan Revolution'. *Middle East Policy* 18(4).

Lacher, Wolfram. 2013. 'Fault lines of the revolution: political actors, camps and conflicts in the New Libya'. SWP Research Paper, Stiftung, Wissenschaft und Politik/German Institute for International and Security Affairs. Available at: www.swp-berlin.org/fileadmin/contents/products/research_papers/2013_RP04_lac.pdf

Libya Herald. 2012. 'Muslim Brotherhood formally launches party'. 3 March. Available at: www.libyaherald.com/2012/03/03/muslim-brotherhood-formally-launches-party/#axzz3PMh5v9uI

Libyan Gazette. 2016. 'Haftar forces suffer major losses in battle with Ansar Al-Sharia and Co'. 29 July. Available at: www.libyangazette.net/2016/07/29/haftar-forces-suffer-major-losses-in-battle-with-ansar-al-sharia-and-co/

Linz, Juan, and Stepan, Alfred. 1996. 'Modern nondemocratic regimes', in *Problems of Democratic Transition and Consolidation*. Baltimore, MD: Johns Hopkins University Press.

Maddy-Weitzman, Bruce. 2015. 'A turning point? The Arab Spring and the Amazigh movement'. *Ethnic and Racial Studies* 38(14): 2499–515.

Maher, Ahmed. 2012. 'Meeting Mohammad Ali al-Zahawi of Libyan Ansar al-Sharia'. BBC News, 18 September. Available at: www.bbc.com/news/world-africa-19638582

Mahmoud, Khalid. 2015. 'Libyan PM will not step down: cabinet source'. *Asharq al-Awsat*, 8 January. Available at: www.aawsat.net/2015/01/article55340228/libyan-pm-will-not-step-down-cabinet-source

Malsin, Jared. 2014. 'Egyptian involvement sparked Libya oil port battle, expert says'. *Times. com*, 19 December. Available at: time.com/3642616/libya-oil-egypt-tobruk-tripoli/

Markey, Patrick, and El-Yaakoubi, Aziz. 2014. 'Libya, security insight'. Reuters, 1 August. Available at: uk.reuters.com/article/2014/08/01/uk-libya-security-insightid UKKBN0G02382014080

Markey, Patrick, and Elumami, Ahmed. 2015. 'Feuds and factions: no easy road to implementing Libya peace deal'. Reuters, 14 December. Available at: af.reuters.com/article/libya News/idAFL8N14328M20151214?feedType=RSS&feedName=libyaNews&utm_ source=feedburner&utm_medium=feed&utm_campaign=Feed%3A+reuters%2FAfrica LibyaNews+%28News+%2F+Africa+%2F+Libya+News%29&rpc=401&sp=true

Mattes, Hanspeter. 2004. 'Challenges to security sector governance in the Middle East: the Libyan case'. Paper presented at Geneva Center for the Democratic Control of Armed Forces (DCAF) as a part of Security Governance in the Mediterranean Project, 13 July.

McGuirk, Russell. 2007. *The Sanusi's Little War: The Amazing Story of a Forgotten Conflict in the Western Desert, 1915–1917*. London: Arabian Publishing.

Media Spy. 2011. 'Online journalist Mohammed Nabbous killed in Libya'. 20 March. Available at: www.mediaspy.org/2011/03/20/online-journalist-mohammed-nabbous-killed-in-libya/

MEMO. 2014. 'Al-Thini's government calls for civil disobedience in Tripoli'. *Middle East Monitor*, 22 October. Available at: www.middleeastmonitor.com/news/africa/14811-al-thinis-government-calls-for-civil-disobedience-in-tripoli

Michael, Maggie. 2011. 'Protesters in Libya demand Gaddafi ouster and reforms'. *The Washington Post*, 17 February. Available at: www.washingtonpost.com/wp-dyn/content/article/2011/02/16/AR2011021607292.html

Middle East Eye. 2015. 'Libya's Haftar confirms military support for Operation Dignity from Egypt and UAE'. 30 January. Available at: www.middleeasteye.net/news/libyas-haftar-confirms-support-operation-dignity-egypt-and-uae-1265705213

Mittelstaedt von, Juliane. 2011. 'Libya's soccer rebellion: a revolution foreshadowed on the pitch of Benghazi'. *Der Spiegel*, 15 July. Available at: www.spiegel.de/international/world/libya-s-soccer-rebellion-a-revolution- foreshadowed-on-the-pitch-of-benghazi-a-774594.html

Mustafa, Ajnadin. 2014. 'Derna's Islamic Youth Council declares allegiance to Daesh: report'. *Libya Herald*, 4 October. Available at: www.libyaherald.com/2014/10/04/dernas-islamic-youth-council-declares-allegiance-to-daesh-report/#ixzz3SlaS7dmU

Obeidi, Amal. 2013. *Political Culture in Libya*. London: Routledge Curzon.

Oborne, Peter, and Cookson, Richard. 2012. 'Libya still ruled by the gun'. *The Telegraph*, 18 May. Available at: www.telegraph.co.uk/news/worldnews/africaandindianocean/libya/9265441/Libya-still-ruled-by-the-gun.html

OECD. 2009. 'Gender equality and social institutions in Libya'. Gender, Institutions and Development Database. Available at: www.oecd.org/dev/genderinstitutionsanddevel opmentdatabase.htm

Pargeter, Alison. 2010. 'Reform in Libya: Chimera or reality?'. *Mediterranean Papers Series*. Available at: www.iai.it/pdf/mediterraneo/GMF-IAI/Mediterranean-paper_08.pdf

Poljarevic, Emin. 2015. '*Les Salafistes* and a French reproduction of certainties in a world of uncertainties'. *American Journal of Islamic Social Sciences* 33(2): 145–55.

POMED. 2012. 'Backgrounder: previewing Libya's elections'. 5 July. Available at: pomed. org/wordpress/wp-content/uploads/2012/07/Previewing-Libyas-Elections.pdfReeve, Richard. 2015. 'Libya's proxy battlefield'. *Oxford Research Group*, 13 January. Available at: www.oxfordresearchgroup.org.uk/publications/briefing_papers_and_reports/briefing_libya_proxy_battlefield

Reporters Without Borders. 2011. 'The birth of "free media" in Eastern Libya'. Paris: International Secretariat – Reporters Without Borders. Available at: http://en.rsf.org/IMG/pdf/libye_2011_gb.pdf

Reuters. 2007. 'Libya says it will lay off 400,000'. *The New York Times*, 22 January. Available at: www.nytimes.com/2007/01/22/world/africa/22libya.html

Reuters. 2011a. 'Militias may drag Libya into civil war: NTC chief'. 4 January. Available at: www.reuters.com/article/2012/01/04/us-libya-idUSTRE80301120120104

Reuters. 2011b. 'Libya sets up $24 bln fund for housing'. 27 January. Available at: www.reuters.com/article/2011/01/27/libya-fund-investment- idUSLDE70Q1ZM20110127

Reuters. 2011c. 'Nervous Libyans ready for first taste of democracy'. 6 July. Available at: www.reuters.com/article/2012/07/06/us-libya-elections- idUSBRE86412N20120706

Reuters. 2015. 'Libya's rival factions agree date to sign U.N. peace deal'. 11 December. Available at: http://reut.rs/1IZWpGt

Saleh, Heba. 2015. 'What is at stake in Libya talks?' *Financial Times*, 11 December. Available at: www.ft.com/intl/cms/s/0/b4fec58a-9f1b-11e5–85ae-8fa46274f224

Salem, Paul, and Kadlec, Amanda. 2012. 'Libya's troubled transition'. Carnegie Paper, June. Available at: http://carnegieendowment.org/2012/06/14/libya-s-troubled-transition/bzw4

Schruf, Naser. 2014. 'Libya: Who's fighting whom?' *Deutsche Welle*, 2 September. Available at: www.dw.de/libya-whos-fighting-whom/a-17894115

Small Arms Survey, (2012. 'Armed groups in Libya: typology and roles'. *Research Notes: Armed Actors*, Number 18, Available at: www.smallarmssurvey.org/fileadmin/docs/H-Research_Notes/SAS-Research-Note-18.pdf

Takeyh, Ray. 2000. 'Qadhafi's Libya and the prospects of Islamic succession'. *Middle East Policy*, 7(2).

Tawil, Camille. 2015. 'Operation Dignity: General Haftar's latest battle may decide Libya's future'. *Terrorism Monitor*, 31 May, 12(11). Available at: www.jamestown. org/programs/tm/single/?tx_ttnews%5Btt_news%5D=42443&cHash=24a38 c40982c66819e7196d24603335b#.VVRtEfntlHw

Torelli Stefano, and Varvelli, Arturo. 2015. 'Competing Jihadist organisations and networks: Islamic State, Al-Qaeda, Al-Qaeda in the Islamic Maghreb and Ansar al-Sharia in Libya'. In Arturo Varvelli (ed.), *Libya's Fight for Survival: Defeating Jihadist Networks*. Brussels: European Foundation for Democracy.

UNDP (2011), 'Human Development Report'. United Nations Development Programme. Available at: http://hdr.undp.org/sites/default/files/reports/271/hdr_2011_en_com plete.pdf

UNHCHR. 1997. 'Country analysis: Libyan Arab Jamahiriya'. Committee on the Rights of the Child, 13–17 October. Available at: www.unhchr.ch/tbs/doc.nsf/(Symbol)/d3d 6f9f2d109255780256559005c5bc7?Opendocument

UNHR. 2012. 'The destruction of cultural and religious sites: a violation of human rights'. UNHR Office of High Commissioner, 24 September. Available at: www.ohchr.org/ EN/NewsEvents/Pages/DestructionShrines.aspx

UN News Centre. 2015. 'UN welcomes "historic" signing of Libyan Political Agreement'. 17 December. Available at: www.un.org/apps/news/story.asp?NewsID=52845#.Vnpu BzblyjQ

UNSC. 2011. 'United Nations Security Council, Resolution 1973'. Security Council 6498th Meeting, 17 March. Available at: www.un.org/press/en/2011/sc10200.doc. html

Vandewalle, Dirk. 2012. 'After Qaddafi: the surprising success of the New Libya'. *Foreign Affairs*, Nov./Dec. Available at: www.foreignaffairs.com/articles/libya/2012–09–16/ after-qaddafi.

Wells, Matt. 2011. 'Mohammed Nabbous, face of citizen journalism in Libya, is killed'. *The Guardian News Blog*, 19 March. Available at: www.guardian.co.uk/world/blog/2011/ mar/ 19/mohammad-nabbous-killed-libya

Wehrey, Frederic. 2014. 'What's behind Libya's spiraling violence?' *Washington Post*, 28 July. Available at: www.washingtonpost.com/blogs/monkey-cage/wp/2014/07/28/ whats-behind-libyas-spiraling-violence/

Wehrey, Frederic. 2015. 'The battle for Libya's oil: on the frontlines of a forgotten war'. *The Atlantic*, February. Available at: www.theatlantic.com/international/archive/2015/02/ the-battle-for-libyas-oil/385285/

Wueger, Diana. 2012. 'Conflict profiles: Libya'. *Women Under Siege*. Available at: www. womenundersiegeproject.org/conflicts/profile/libya

Zurutuza, Karlos. 2013. 'Benghazi "self-rule" resonates with Berbers'. Al Jazeera, 6 November. Available at: www.aljazeera.com/indepth/features/2013/11/benghazi-self-rule-resonates-with-berbers-2013115122219533260.html

5

YEMEN'S FAILED TRANSITION

From peaceful protests to war of 'all against all'

Bogumila Hall

In 2011, tribesmen and fighters left their guns at home to join peaceful protests against the then president, Ali Abdullah Saleh. Today, Yemen's writers, poets and painters are putting down the tools of their creativity and instead picking up steel with which to fight.

(Farea al-Muslimi, 27 May 2016, al-Jazeera)

Introduction

In 2010, Ahmed, then in his early twenties, was learning foreign languages. After quitting university, he tried his chances in the tourism industry. In his makeshift office in Old Sana'a – among the posters of beautiful Yemeni landscapes from Soqotra Island to the Haraz Mountains and the Marib dam – hung a faded poster of then president Ali Abdullah Saleh. Ahmed was not a big fan of Ali Abdullah Saleh, nor was he particularly against him. He was into business, not politics; but as the president enjoyed genuine support in the quarters of the old city and his images were displayed in abundance there, Ahmed, without giving it much thought, had put up the picture too.

About one year later, the doors of his office were shut and the work of the new travel agency suspended. For several months Ahmed was busy on the streets of Sana'a, having joined, after initial doubts, the popular protests against the man whose portrait had decorated his office. In our correspondence, in mixed Arabic and English, Ahmed described the feeling of joining the crowds and chanting slogans as empowering and joyful. He compared the revolution to a holiday (*al-thawra kanat zay al-'aid*). With the statement, 'I was a boy now I am a man', he also described how his continuous presence on the Changes Square led to his gradual politicization.

After 11 months of protests, when the transition agreement was reached and Saleh resigned from power, Ahmed – unlike the majority of more radical members of the youth movement – happily accepted the terms of the deal. He was impatient to return to his business and was hoping the new stability, peace, and capital brought by the transition process would help him in the long term to attract tourists and finally earn some money. Indeed, in early 2013, when the National Dialogue Conference was announced to pave the way for what many called 'the new Yemen' (*al-yemen al-jadida*), small groups of foreign travellers were visiting the country again. Ahmed's hope reflected the attitudes of many ordinary Yemenis: tired after months of protests, deteriorating security, and living conditions, they expected the new government to bring order, justice, and law, but also better employment opportunities, increased salaries, and other tangible improvements. They were yearning for the goals of the revolution to finally materialize. However, as time passed Ahmed grew frustrated with the transition process that left things in Yemen largely the same as before. This looked to him like a mere political game (*la'aba*). Thus, in summer 2014, when the Houthis (Zaydi militants from the northern Saada province) attuned to the anger of people, returned to protests, and soon after seized and took control over Sana'a, Ahmed saw it as a move towards realizing the objectives of the popular uprising. The Houthis, however, did not stop at protests, and moved to expand their territorial control and power, with the country descending into violence and further fragmentation.

'Yemen is in mess', Ahmed told me when his initial enthusiasm cooled down, explaining the bizarre alliances and multiplicity of actors involved in the conflict. There were the Houthis allied with ex-President Saleh, new President Hadi supported by the Islamist party, Islah, but also al-Qaeda, Saudi Arabia, and the United Arab Emirates, according to Ahmed.

After months without communication, by the end of March 2015, Ahmed's messages started to arrive more frequently than ever. This was about the time when Saudi Arabia responded to President Hadi's call for assistance and started an airstrike campaign on Yemen, targeting the Houthis and their allies. Ahmed described the bombardment Yemenis were facing and complained about the international silence, 'bought with the Saudi money', as he put it. With every message, and every death of a family or community member, Ahmed's anger grew. He was also proud of what he called the 'resistance movement' led by the Houthis, sharing photos on Facebook of large-scale demonstrations in Sana'a against the Saudi aggression. The pictures of men marching with Kalashnikovs, little boys and girls dressed in military uniforms, and hardly any women present, stood in striking contrast to the images of peaceful protests in 2011. Eventually, almost every message from Ahmed, known among his friends as the most gentle and peaceful person, expressed his desire to take up arms and join the fight. The last time I heard from Ahmed, he told me his younger brother had already joined, and he was hoping his mother would allow him to do so as well. It was impossible to continue with normal life, the country was in pieces, divided more than ever, and the dignity of Yemenis was at stake, he wrote in his last message in early 2016. I later learnt from his friends that Ahmed had acted on his plans. He first did some military training, and soon afterwards quit and went to fight alongside the Houthi rebels in Jawf province. He phoned his family once to say he was well, but since then his where-abouts have been unknown.

I recall Ahmed's evolution from tourist guide, to peaceful protestor, to finally an armed fighter, not necessarily as an illustration of how peaceful protests turned into bloodshed in Yemen. On the contrary, I acknowledge that his perspective is partial and easily contested by competing narratives of what has happened in Yemen since the 2011 uprising, who is at war, and which actors are to be blamed for what is today the biggest humanitarian crisis in Yemen's history. Nevertheless, the seemingly unique trajectory of Ahmed and his reading of contentious events point to some traits of the process of radicalization into violence in Yemen that we will address in this chapter in detail. First, Ahmed's story reveals that a move from social movement to civil war is not necessarily linear, but maybe – as is the case here – long, contingent on various often unexpected shifts and realignments, and paradoxically preceded by an elite-led transitional process. Among those who fight in Yemen today are rebels, various regime factions, but also international actors, and many individuals like Ahmed who first participated in peaceful protests and later took up arms to defend their dignity or local territory. As this vignette shows, radicalization is related to the particular (domestic and international) context, the interpersonal dynamics, but also, on the individual level, the affective processes whereby a sense of insecurity or desire for revenge justifies recourse to violence. This means that in order to fully understand how peaceful resistance has descended into civil war, the micro, meso, and macro levels of analysis must be taken into account.

Some students of Yemeni politics have argued that the structural features of the weak state, its corrupt elites and divided, heavily armed society made civil war in Yemen inevitable. Indeed, military coups and violent repertoires had been part of Yemen's recent history. Others, however, have praised the popular mobilization as a moment of rupture, which could annul tribal and sectarian identifications and pave the way for a new democratic Yemen. Avoiding the shortcomings of these two perspectives, we adopt here a dynamic and processual approach that, through systematic analysis of the mechanisms at work, aims to showcase how and why the peaceful uprising happened in the first place, how it changed its path, and how it culminated in a war that has resulted in thousands of deaths from violence and fam-ine. In other words, we seek to address the puzzle articulated by Farea al-Muslimi, a Yemeni activist and political analyst, in the opening quote of this chapter: why are those who made the peaceful revolution now 'picking up steel with which to fight'? In order to answer these questions, the chapter traces how the regime's bru-tal response to peaceful resistance made the numbers of protestors grow but also led to the split in the military and defections of the regime's core members, who joined the opposition forces. The activation of military networks changed the course of the protests, marginalizing the youth movement and gradually transforming the popular mobilization into an armed conflict between warring elite factions. This brought an end to the movement's unity, and further led to social fragmentation around sub-national identifications.

While the transition deal brokered at the end of 2011 by the neighbouring Gulf countries briefly averted a further escalation of violence, it did not end it, nor did it solve any of the conflicts haunting Yemen. On the contrary, despite procedural advances, old animosities remained in place, new divisions (mobilized around sectarian language) came into play, and finally a strategic alliance was made between the old enemies – the Houthi rebels and the fallen president Ali Abdullah Saleh – united against the common enemy and for the pursuit of power. As a result of the deal drafted by international actors, the youth who had demanded democratization were further sidelined and the status quo in the country remained largely intact.

Against this backdrop, Yemen-in-transition was torn by political destabilization, economic deterioration, and a security void. All of these triggered multiple 'small' wars fought on the local level, which escalated into a civil war in March 2015 when the Houthis advanced southwards to overthrow President Hadi and his government. The Houthis' expansion was followed by the involvement of the Saudi Arabia-led coalition, turning the Yemeni conflict into a war with domestic and regional dimensions. It has been marked by heavy sectarian undertones and a multiplicity of armed groups, whose fighters joined for a variety of reasons: ideology, self-defence, frustration with the failure of peaceful resistance, and financial rewards. The latter should not come as a surprise in a ruined country, where hunger today is as big a threat to people's lives as are bombs and bullets.

While developments in Yemen may seem particular and rooted in the country's unique features, in fact, the mechanisms that were activated at consequent stages of mobilization and civil war speak forcefully to the theoretical framework elaborated by Donatella della Porta in Chapter 2. To give a comprehensive picture of how Yemen – infamous for tribal, often violent politics – turned towards popular peaceful mobilization to finally end in civil war, the chapter is divided into four main sections that shine light on the relevant causal mechanisms. The first introduces Yemen's structural context and the particular make-up of Ali Abdullah Saleh's regime that set the stage for the 2011 revolution. In particular, it shows how Saleh's rule weakened the state and undermined the country's fragile unity by further dividing society – all of which was later exploited and exacerbated by the entrepreneurs of violence. The second section examines the dynamics of popular mobilization for regime change that began in early 2011. It starts with a description of the peaceful revolution led by the youth, and then traces the transformation of the uprising, in light of the regime's use of violence, splits in the military, and the emergence of new armed actors at the protest sites. It shows how, several months into mobilization, the actors who came to dominate the scene had little to do with the youth, or with ideals of revolution and peaceful tactics. The third section describes what is called here the 'transition to civil war', underlining the formal proceedings of the transitional process and the parallel developments that paved the way to what some observers call the 'war of all against all' in Yemen. This part highlights how the actors, who in 2011, mobilized collectively for regime change fragmented into opposing camps in pursuit of power, sectarian interests, and territorial control, rather than social justice and democracy. The final section scrutinizes the dynamics of the civil war, particularly the emergence of various armed actors and the framing they used to justify their recourse to violence.

Yemen: in the state's void

Divided until fairly recently into North and South Yemen, the history of unified Yemen is quite short. North Yemen was a conservative imamate until 1962; in 1970, after a military coup and a long civil war, the Yemen Arab Republic (YAR) was established. The South was a British protectorate, which became the socialist People's Democratic Republic of Yemen (PDRY) after liberation in 1967. The two states, committed to radically different ideologies and run by different economic systems, merged into one in 1990 under the leadership of Ali Abdullah Saleh, who had previously ruled the YAR since 1978.

Since unification, Yemen has been characterized by relative openness and a vibrant civil society, making its political landscape quite unique in the region. While life in authoritarian security states such as Syria or Libya was marked by fear and public displays of obedience (see, for example, Wedeen 1999), in Yemen, public spaces have often been sites of dissent and debate. Scholars have pointed to the existence of democratic practices in Yemen that could be found anywhere from civil society activism to collective qat chews[1] (Carapico 2007; Wedeen 2003; 2008), thus reaching far beyond formal institutions. In the early years of the unification the levels of repression were low, and a large number of new private media outlets emerged, often overtly critical of the regime's failures and excesses. Ali Abdullah Saleh himself would not escape harsh critique, especially in Englishspeaking magazines such as *Yemen Times*, which accused him, for example, of bribery and buying people's loyalty (Al-Bab 2015).

In April 1993, 'relatively fair, peaceful multi-party elections' (Carapico 1993) were held. Saleh's General People's Congress (GPC) won the majority of the seats in the parliament, followed by al-Islah, a new Islamist party from the North, and the Yemeni Socialist Party (YPS), whose stronghold had been traditionally in the South. Until the 2011 uprising, this constellation of power remained largely intact, with the GPC the governing party, and al-Islah and the YPS acting as the main opposition parties. Importantly, the Islamists had been a crucial ally of the president and its leader, Sheikh Abdullah al-Ahmar, was commonly regarded as 'the second most powerful person in the country' until his death in 2006 (Durac 2013, 179).[2]

The early years of the new republic witnessed a huge increase in the number of civil society organizations operating in the country, many of them funded by foreign money. This financial support reflected the larger efforts of the United States and other Western governments and NGOs to spread democracy in the Middle East (Carapico 2002). The new organizations, working largely in the fields of charity, development, human rights, women's empowerment, and social work (Bonnefoy and Poirier 2009, 11), were designated as agents of social change on the ground, and took up many of the responsibilities of the shrinking state (Carapico 2002). In the 1990s, the United States reportedly spent $6.6 million over a period of eight years to advance their democratization mission in Yemen (Lackner 2016, 151).

However, Yemen does not serve as an example of a successful democracy. The formal liberalization that characterized the early years of the new republic turned out to be a short episode, and repression was soon added to the state's repertoire. The Yemeni state from its birth has been characterized by observers as 'weak', with the central government having little control over the country's remote regions, and definitely lacking the monopoly on violence (Saif 2013). While in other authoritarian countries in the region the state seemed omnipresent, reaching the most private spheres of people's lives (for example, through the infamous intelligence services, *mukhabarat*), in Yemen, it has been more common to hear complaints about the state's absence. '*Ma bish dawla*' ('there is no state') was an oft-repeated complaint of Yemenis lamenting regular power cuts, rubbish lining the streets, or overcrowded schools. People in Sana'a casually complained that there was no law (*qanun*) or system/order (*nithaam*) in Yemen; instead, the country was dragged down by corruption (*fasaad*) and chaos (*fawda*). The parliament was seen as merely a façade and the entire political class was distrusted, perceived by ordinary people as serving only the elites. Most Yemenis regarded them as inefficient, unable to address people's grievances, and hence largely redundant (Durac 2013, 183–4).

At the same time, following the Gulf crisis in the early 1990s and later the economic reforms introduced in 1995 under pressure from the World Bank and the International Monetary Fund, Yemeni society has been undergoing gradual impoverishment. Reforms that were supposed to give more power to the Yemeni private sector have meant in practice an end to subsidies on food and fuel, cuts in public sector employment, and, as a consequence, increased costs of living and higher rates of unemployment (de Regt 2008, 160). The privatization of agriculture and what had previously been public services further contributed to the impoverishment of peasants and limited access to healthcare and education for the poor (Seif 2003, 11).

Add to all this the spread of al-Qaeda in the country since the 2000s, and it comes as little surprise that commentators have repeatedly described Yemen as being in 'chaos' (Blumi 2012), in 'permanent crisis' (Philips 2011), or 'on the brink' of failing (Boucek and Ottaway 2010). In fact, in 2009, al-Qaeda announced that Saleh's regime was so weak that it was not worth targeting as its collapse was imminent (Phillips 2010, 3).

Ali Abdullah Saleh's statecraft: co-opting, dividing, repressing

If the state was as weak as it appeared to most external observers and Yemenis themselves, why then did it take so many years to challenge Saleh's one-man rule? One answer may be that what constituted the 'weakness' of the state was a 'strength' of Ali Abdullah Saleh. Or in other words, Saleh's mode of governance, based on control and co-optation through extended patronage networks, served to secure his personal power and wealth, while at the same time eroded the state's structures. As Khosrokhavar (2012, 135) put it, in Yemen, 'The state is at the service of the ruler, not the opposite.'

When Ali Abdullah Saleh was installed as president of the new republic in 1990, nobody expected he would stay in power so long, especially given Yemen's infamous history of assassinations and the exile of the country's rulers (Lackner 2016). Yet, systematically and skilfully, Saleh from the beginning built a highly personalized system of rule whereby politicians, military men, tribal sheikhs, and religious figures were paid with privileges for their loyalty (Alley 2010; Thiel 2012). The core of the regime was ethnic in nature and built around his family and tribe (Sanhan) members, who occupied the most important military and state security positions. His son Ahmed was the commander of the Republican Guards, his two nephews commanded the Central Security Forces, and his half-brother was a chief in the Air Force (Durac 2013; Phillips 2011; Thiel 2012). Choosing 'co-option, compromise, and divide-and-rule tactics over exclusion and direct confrontation', as Alley observed (2010, 392), Saleh was able to gather around him a vast patronage network of elites who knew very well that their position was predicated on their support for the president. Those who failed to exercise it were punished with violence, or political and economic marginalization. Saleh himself described his ruling technique as 'dancing on the heads of snakes' (Clark 2010), referring to the myriad of alliances he had to make, and forces he had to control, to make his reign possible. In practice, this meant exploiting and deepening tribal and sectarian divisions in the country, fighting for survival, and exploiting (domestic and international) fears of the state's collapse to remain in power (Manea 2015). Besides Saleh's personal skills, the ruling GPC played an important role in Saleh's extensive patronage networks, rewarding the loyal ones and co-opting adversaries (Poirier 2011; Schwedler 2004; Transfeld 2016). The party, which was established in theory as a centre-right organization, lost any ideological coherence and gathered all sorts of personas of different backgrounds, who simply sought privileges, protection, and careers.

Through these techniques as well as personal charisma, Saleh enjoyed a certain popularity.[3] While public displays of popular support such as marches or other public gatherings were largely 'national spectacles' (Wedeen 2003, 692) scripted by the regime, people in private settings often expressed their sympathy for the leader. At least in Sana'a, his pictures decorated people's houses, and a popular story circulated that the president was from a poor family and spent his childhood selling cigarettes – a fact that made him seem closer to ordinary people. One could also hear women praising his manliness (*rujuliyya*) and the urban poor contrasting his alleged honesty with the corruption of the rest of the political class. Many residents of the informal settlements in Sana'a refrained from protesting against him in 2011, arguing that they were for change but not for revolution that betrayed the ruler.[4]

While patronage, bribing, and posing as a friendly figure were part of Saleh's survivalist techniques, repression and control were no less important elements of his statecraft. The despotic elements of Saleh's rule had grown since 1994, when the government defeated the Southern secessionists during the short civil war.[5] Saleh's victory consolidated his rule, which, from that point on, became gradually less democratic. For example, in order to control the South of the country and repress dissent, Saleh made amendments to the Constitution that gave him the power to appoint the vice president, dissolve the parliament, or announce a state of emergency (Phillips 2008). By the mid-1990s, Yemenis' civil liberties had been undermined, freedom of speech was restricted, and human rights activists were regularly intimated, beaten up, threatened, and arrested without charges (Lackner 2016, 150). In addition, Saleh's rule was marked by deaths and disappearances of military and security men who had broken the rules of the patronage game and shown signs of disloyalty (Alley 2010, 403–4).

The growing repression and attacks on personal freedoms were conveniently framed by Saleh in security terms, necessitated by the threat posed to the nation by Islamist terrorism, perpetuated by groups such as al-Qaeda. The Yemeni branch of Al-Qaeda (known since 2009 as al-Qaeda in the Arabian Peninsula or AQAP) has been active since the 1990s but first made global headlines in 2000 with the attack on the *USS Cole* in Aden harbour, and later in 2009 when one of its affiliates tried to blow up a plane on Christmas Day. Saleh, who officially declared his commitment to the US-led 'War on Terror', became an ally of the Bush and Obama administrations, both of which provided the regime with large amounts of money, training, and logistical support (Carapico 2011). In the meantime, it was not a big secret in Yemen that the US money and equipment were deployed to improve the coercive apparatus and fight internal political opposition rather than al-Qaeda. Jokes and anecdotes mocked Saleh's commitments to combat terrorism and indicated that many Yemenis believed that Saleh needed al-Qaeda and terror to maintain power. This is what Sarah Phillips (2010) has referred to as 'the politics of permanent crisis', whereby Saleh's regime actively undermined the security situation in the country in order to receive external financial support. The latter was used to fund his patronage networks, whose functioning further eroded security and the rule of law in Yemen.

Yemen's fragile unity

In Yemen, marked historically by tribal loyalties and other traditional categories of belonging such as sect, region, descent, or occupation, fostering national identity was a challenge for the unified republic. The first attempts to promote national identity in North Yemen began when hierarchical status distinctions were banned after the collapse of the imamate in 1962. The republican leaders, among other actions, abolished slavery and introduced a Constitution that proclaimed the equality of all citizens (Carapico 1996). These efforts to strengthen, or rather project, a sense of national belonging, were taken up by the regime after 1990 in an ambiguous manner. They often took the form of celebrations that accompanied anniversaries of the North-South unification in which, for example, regional dances were blended into one in an attempt to signal the nation's unity (Wedeen 2003). However, the unity represented in these spectacles was far from being achieved. On the contrary, the regime had acted in a manner that fragmented society, through the patronage and divide-and-rule politics described previously. Furthermore, weak state institutions, which seemed detached and ineffective, meant that for many affiliations with a tribe or region were more important than loyalty to the state (Saif 2013, 141).

Regional identifications have been crucial in Yemen, whereby during introductions people are usually asked for their family name, from which the interlocutor can trace a person's tribe and place of origin. Traditionally, much of the collective claims-making in Yemen has been place-based, and those who articulated grievances and staged demands did so as 'Southerners', 'Hadramis', 'tribes of Marib', and so on. Most often, their demands focused on material improvements in their particular localities. While Yemen is also divided into two main religious groups – the Zaydis (an offshoot of Shiite Islam) in the North, and the Sunnis in the South and East – sectarian identifications were of little significance until recently. Even if efforts to exacerbate them were systematically undertaken both by the Saleh's regime and by Saudi Arabia (which spent large sums of money building Salafi mosques and schools in Yemen), until the late 2000s, sectarian language was rarely used in Yemen (al-Muslimi 2015). On the contrary, people frequently dismissed the importance of religious differences, proudly stating that Yemen was not Syria, or that the only difference between the Shias and the Sunnis was a praying technique. Even the distinction between Shia and Sunni mosques came late to Yemen, and was largely influenced by Saudi Arabia.

While ordinary Yemenis cared little if one was a Zaidi or a Sunni, the regional differences – in particular between the North and the South –were very clear and emphasized by people, often in the form of jokes. For example, southerners have traditionally been regarded as more open and better educated than the tribal people (*qabail*) from the North, whose supposed backwardness they casually mocked. 'Dahbashi', a character from a popular TV show, who represented an arrogant fool, became a synonym for a 'northerner' among Yemenis from the South. People from Sana'a, on the other hand, argued jokingly that they were the real Arabs, while people from the South were closer to Indians.

The actual tension between the North and South is, however, not merely about cultural differences, but rather reflects tangible power struggles and southerners' experiences of marginalization. The unification of two previously separate entities that took place in 1990, sold by the Saleh's regime as a success story, for many Southerners became a synonym for the occupation. The concentration of power in the hands of northern elites (with Saleh's control over the presidential council and the Ministry of Finance) meant, in practice, the unequal distribution of wealth and exclusion of southerners from the decision-making processes. Frustrated further by Saleh's corruption, repression, and patronage politics, the southern leaders pushed in 1994 for secession, which led to the outbreak of a civil war. The victory of the northern army, accompanied by tribal militias and jihadi returnees from

Afghanistan, consolidated Saleh's grip over the state and the South's subordination (Carapico 2011; Dahlgren 2010). In the following years, Southerners had to witness economic disenfranchisement and repressive rule but also the imposition of what was regarded as tribal mentality and customs. It is against this backdrop that, in the summer of 2007, the Southern Movement (*al-hirak al-janubi*) emerged, when a group of military officers, who were forced into early retirement after the 1994 civil wars, organized to demand better pensions and job opportunities. When the peaceful sit-ins were crushed by the authorities and people's grievances were left unanswered, the movement grew in numbers and issued more radical demands, calling for secession and independence. Since then, the Southern Movement, although divided over its agenda, has been engaged in anti-Saleh activism, because of which in turn it has been depicted by the regime as a threat to the country's stability and unity, and accused of affiliations with al-Qaeda (Day 2012).

The South-North conflict was not the only one haunting pre-revolutionary Yemen. From 2004, the government was also engaged in six rounds of wars against the Houthis, a revivalist Zaydi movement, which emerged in the northern governorate of Saada in the 1990s. The Houthis, known also as Ansar Allah, organized to protect Zaydi traditions against the growing influence of Salafism and Sunni Islam (spread by Saudi Arabia and the Islah Party respectively), but they soon developed political and military wings and were openly critical of the Yemeni government. Under the leadership of Hussein al-Houthi, the movement attacked the regime's systemic neglect of their region, corruption, and Saleh's plans to transfer the power to his son.[6] In the early 2000s, the Houthis organized a series of demonstrations protesting against Yemen's close alliance with the United States and its active support for the so-called 'War on Terror'. The government responded with repression, and heavy fighting broke out in the Saada province in 2004 when security forces attempted to arrest the group's leader. The armed conflict between the insurgents and the government continued on and off until 2010, leading to deaths, displacement of the population, and severe destruction of the Saada governorate (Durac 2013; Transfeld 2016).

In summary, Yemen on the eve of the 2011 popular mobilization was in chaos – with some even referring to it as a 'failed state'. The Yemeni state was palpably weak due to the rampant corruption of the ruling elites, economic disenfranchisement, the security void, calls for secession in the South, and localized war in the North. However, it was the weakness of the state that enabled Saleh's regime to survive. Saleh's regime relied on the state's coercive apparatus but even more so on patronage networks and personal exchanges of favours. In such a context, alliances within the regime could shift easily, as they were not based on shared principles or ideology but rather on received or expected benefits. Furthermore, the regime's undermining of state institutions and its politics of 'divide and rule' worked against the process of formal 'unification', strengthening instead tribal and regional allegiances. These structural features, as we will see later, all played a role in changing the course of the uprising and of the transitional process. Although society's fragmentation, the 'fluidity of alliances and oppositions' (Khosrokhavar 2012, 136) and sub-national identifications were not the causes of the conflict, they were mobilized in the process of violence radicalization and fuelled the civil war.

The 2011 uprising: from popular mobilization to hijacked revolution

While the South and Saada were major concerns for the regime, being in overt conflict with the central government for many years, grievances and the sense of marginalization articulated by the Houthis and the Hirak movement were not unique. They resonated strongly in all provinces that suffered from underdevelopment, unemployment, and continually rising prices for basic commodities. No matter from which region, the educated youth could not find jobs, the sick could not access healthcare, workers were exploited, farmers lacked water, drivers could not afford fuel, and everyday life was a struggle for the majority of Yemenis, with the exception being the secluded elites.

Protests organized around material grievances and labour rights have recurred in Yemen since the 1990s. In particular, in 1996, 1998, and 2005, Yemenis took to the streets in large numbers to oppose price rises in basic commodities. The protests were labelled by the regime as 'riots' and repressed with armed force (Lackner 2016, 151). For example, in 2005, thousands of angry Yemenis protested in Sana'a against the cuts in fuel subsidies, openly blaming Saleh for the state of affairs. Pictures of the president were burned on the streets, and protestors were heard chanting 'no Sanhan after today', referring to Saleh's tribe (Phillips 2006). The late 2000s also witnessed country-wide mobilization of trade unions demanding labour rights and fair salaries. In 2008, a number of strikes took place, organized, among others, by port workers, teachers, labourers, and professors. Throughout 2009 and 2010, oil workers managed to shut down the oilfields and refineries. Finally, in May 2010, a nationwide general strike was organized by the Yemeni Labour Union, forcing the regime to offer concessions to the workers (Alwazir 2012). When in January 2011, protests were organized to decry the regime's corruption and demand higher salaries and better living conditions, they seemed to constitute just another cycle of contention in Yemen. Yet this time, the dynamics of popular mobilization did not follow the usual path.

The peaceful and popular youth revolution ('Al-Thawra al-shababiyaa al-sha'biyya al-silmiya')

Encouraged by the popular uprisings in Tunisia and Egypt, Yemenis took to the streets in mid-January 2011. In the initial stages, protests were small, their participants not overly enthusiastic, and their claims relatively moderate: they demanded jobs and better living conditions, and they opposed the government's attempts to modify the Constitution in order to prolong Saleh's rule. While some thought the Yemeni protests were slowly moving towards an end, things gained new impetus in February 2011, following the victory of the Egyptian revolution.

On 11 February, when news about Mubarak stepping down and live celebrations from Cairo were broadcast by Al-Jazeera, thousands of Yemenis gathered in the evening in front of the gates of Sana'a University. Inspired and excited by Mubarak's resignation, crowds were heard chanting for the first time well-known slogans from the Egyptian and Tunisian revolutions: 'Down with the regime!' and 'The people want the regime to collapse!' Over the coming days, the demonstrations continued and new slogans were added, expressing the peaceful and popular character of the revolution, calling for Ali Abdullah Saleh to step down, and proclaiming the national character and unity of protestors (with slogans such as 'Revolution oh, Yemen from Sana'a to Aden!', 'Revolution oh, people from north to south!'). While the central Tahrir Square was from early on strategically seized by Saleh and filled with his supporters and thugs, the square near Sana'a University, symbolically renamed by activists as 'Taghyir' (Change), became the main site of protests for the next several months. In addition to the Sana'a protests, demonstrations were held across the country in cities such as Ta'iz, Ibb, Aden, Hodeida, and Mukalla, as well as smaller towns, including Dhamar, Hajja, Lahej, Al Ghaydah, and Mareb (Lackner 2016).

Among those who organized demonstrations and sustained the mobilization, the youth movement (*hirak al-shababi*) played a pivotal role. The 'youth' (*shabab*) did not refer so much to the age of protestors, but rather included all those who shared experiences of frustration, marginalization, and dissatisfaction with the traditional political process in Yemen (Yadav 2015). The latter was well articulated in the revolution's slogan: 'No partisan politics, no political parties, our revolution is a youth revolution' (Alwazir 2016, 171). Although some of the youth had been part of the pre-existing networks of the opposition alliance, the Joint Meeting Parties (JMP), the majority of the '*shabab al-thawra*' had not previously belonged to any political parties or movements, and distanced themselves from established actors related to the old regime. By the end of March 2011, the youth, made up of various independent groups, had formed the Coordination Council for Yemeni Revolutionary Youth (CCYRC). The umbrella organization allowed the *shabab* to unite and articulate a broad but coherent list of demands (Alwazir 2016; Yadav 2011). As soon as the demonstrations erupted in Sana'a and other Yemeni cities, the Houthis announced their support for the revolution and arrived at the Change Square in large numbers. Similarly, the members of the Hirak movement joined in, organizing protests in Aden and other southern cities that called for the regime's fall, rather than southern independence (Durac 2013; Lackner 2016). What emerged thus was a unique 'movement of movements', composed of divergent groups. They came together not through strategic deliberation and organizing, but rather through what Bayat (2005) has called 'imagined solidarity', which allowed heterogeneous actors to envisage their interests and aims as one and the same.

The popular mobilization led by the youth shook the traditional political process in Yemen, which had usually been characterized by tribal negotiations and bargaining with the regime (Yadav 2011, 557). It constituted a rupture with the old modes of doing politics in several ways. First of all, the mobilization was sustained for an extended period of time. Unlike in Egypt or Tunisia, protestors were on the streets for 10 months until Saleh resigned, and then continued with sit-ins, occupations of squares, and demonstrations following Friday prayers until mid-2013.

Second, the revolution gave rise to new political engagements away from usual scripts and repertoires of action. Despite the violent tactics deployed by the regime, the youth were determined to remain peaceful, chanting in the face of security forces and regime thugs, 'Our revolution is peaceful, one hundred per cent peaceful!' (Rosen 2012). The squares around Yemen that became the centre of the revolution were occupied by thousands of participants – camping, singing, reciting poems, dancing, and staging plays (Alwazir 2016; Bonnefoy 2012; Fattah 2011). One interviewed activist recalled how protestors mingled in the squares, sharing smuggled alcohol and stories. Among the revolutionaries, women played an important role. While Tawakol Karman became the face of the protest movement in Yemen, thousands of other women protestors camped for months in 'Change Squares' across the country, contributing to the protest organization and sustainability (Yadav 2011, 558). Unusually for Yemen, tribal men marched unarmed (at least in the early stages of the mobilization), the Houthis protested along with the socialists and some Islah members, and men and women shared tents in the squares – all united in the common goal of toppling the regime.

Through these experiences of being together and sharing the same space, new norms were being coined in a festival-like atmosphere. Many participants whom I interviewed remembered the time of mobilization with nostalgia ('these were the real days', as one activist put it), and described their experiences as transformative: as a lesson in political activism, a moment of breaking the fear and speaking out, and an opportunity to meet new friends and comrades. A young woman quoted in a *New York Times* op-ed (*New York Times* 2011) put it evocatively, 'Before, we were sitting at home like pigeons trapped in a cage. When we arrived at the square, we felt the beauty of freedom. We feel proud now and we want a dignified life.'

All these images speak not only to the new creative ways of collective action in Yemen, but also to new alliances and exceptional unity forged at the sites of demonstrations. The old divisions across ideological, sectarian, regional, gender, or tribal lines were suspended and particular claims seemed to have been forgotten, replaced by new, universally shared objectives of the revolution. Among them were regime change, but also economic reforms, ending corruption and redressing injustice experienced by the southerners and the Houthis, among others (Lackner 2016, 154). The change was felt, as one activist told me, when people in Sana'a chanted 'We are all Taizis' (after the regime's crackdown on protests in Taiz), despite the long history of animosities between the two cities, or when members of conflicted tribes met and reconciled at Change Square. The movement of divergent actors, with otherwise divergent agendas, showed that traditional loyalties and divisions were not eternal or did not determine Yemenis' political behaviour, as had been often portrayed in static representations of Yemeni political culture.

As such, it gave hope to many that a new Yemen was in the making, where patronage networks and regional or tribal affiliations would be slowly dissolved.

Repression, regime defections, and militarization of the uprising

Sheila Carapico, writing in May 2011, observed that '[t]he mass uprising in southern Arabia blends features of the peaceful popular revolutions in Egypt and Tunisia with elements of the state repression in Libya and Syria'. From the very beginning, Saleh adopted a mix of strategies in reaction to the protests, combining violence and repression with what looked like concessions to popular demands. Trying to pacify the demonstrators, as he had done in previous years of public unrest, Saleh announced reforms and promised, among other changes, salary increases, tax cuts, the extension of social welfare, and new subsidies (Durac 2013). At the same time, sites of protests were flooded with armed security forces and paid thugs. In Sana'a, as early as in January, Tawwakul Karman, and a number of other activists were arrested, while others were harassed and beaten. In Taiz, as Human Rights Watch documented, attacks on demonstrations began in February 2011, and by March, 'security forces were firing live ammunition directly at protesters' (HRW 2012).

While the regime's violence seemed to be part of the daily ordeal for the protestors, to which they responded tirelessly with peaceful methods, things started to change in mid-March 2011. On 18 March, snipers opened fire on protestors occupying the Change Square, killing up to 52 people and injuring around 200 (HRW 2013a). The event, dubbed by Yemenis as a 'massacre', turned out to be in many ways a turning point in the Yemeni popular mobilization.

First of all, the indiscriminate brutality of the regime, targeting youth and even children, outraged Yemenis, and convinced many that any negotiations with Saleh were not possible. The next day, Yemenis turned their mourning into rage, organizing a march (Day of Rage) in Sana'a, in which around 150,000 people participated. Over the next days, despite the violence and the announcement of the state of emergency on 23 March, the numbers of protestors and the size of squares started to grow, reaching remote areas of the country (Carapico 2011).

Second, the 18 March Massacre was followed by mass defections of members of the ruling party, civilian officers, and military figures, who joined the opposition. Thus, while the youth sustained their mobilization and commitment to peaceful protest, the character of the uprising changed. Among the crucial figures who abandoned Saleh and offered their support to protestors were General Ali Mohsen Ahmar, the ex-key ally of the president and head of the First Armoured Division (FAD), and sheik Hamid al-Ahmar, one of the leaders of the Hashid tribal confederation, but also a prominent member of the Islamist Islah party and one of the richest businessmen in Yemen. Both families had been part of the inner circle of Saleh's regime for many years (Durac 2013; Fattah 2011; Lackner 2016). Now the two united, and supported by al-Islah turned against the president to compete for power. The elite figures-turned-'dissidents' joined the peaceful movement with the heavily armed units loyal to them – namely, the significant section of the army that followed General Ali Mohsen, and the tribal and Islah militias that backed the al-Ahmar family. The activation of military networks had tremendous conse-quences for the Yemeni uprising. On the one hand, the fact that key allies of the president withdrew their support for him revealed the shaky foundations of Saleh's rule. Their move to stand on the protestors' side gave the youth hope for the regime's imminent collapse, and their tanks and weapons granted protection from the government's violence.

On the other hand, the new actors in the struggle to remove Saleh from power were not necessarily committed to peaceful resistance, and engaged in violent clashes with the government forces. The radical transformation of the protest's character was visible, for example, in May 2011, when heavy fighting escalated between the republican guards loyal to Saleh and the forces of sheikh Sadeq al-Ahmar, head of the Hashid tribal confederation. The clashes in Sana'a's Hasaba district changed the area into a 'military zone' (Fattah 2011, 82) and killed over 100 people. Around the same time in Taiz, after the government's brutal crack-down on Freedom Square that started on 29 May 2011 and killed around 50 people in three days, armed groups made up of tribal forces were formed to pro-tect the sit-ins. Over the course of the next few months, the tribal militias engaged in clashes with government forces, fighting for control of the city. Taiz, once a centre of peaceful and joyful revolution, turned into a site of violence and destruction.

Thus, by early June 2011, sit-ins and protests led by the youth were over-shadowed by clashes between pro- and anti-government tribal forces and military units, and cities had been divided by checkpoints controlled by different factions. For instance, the southern parts of Sana'a were controlled by forces loyal to Saleh, while the neighbourhoods in the north were under the control of the 'defectors' – Ali Mohsen's troops and tribal militias of the al-Ahmar family (Transfeld 2016).

When, in June 2011, the tribal opposition resorted to guerrilla tactics and bombed the presidential palace, seriously injuring Saleh, it became clear that a once peaceful uprising had taken the shape of a war. What we observe thus is the rupture of the seriously weakened regime, the spiralling of violence, and a fragmentation of the protest movement, which lost the unity of its first months. While, in the initial phase of mobilization, divergent actors were committed to the same goal – from the Houthis, southern socialists to tribal men, some al-Islah figures and university students – the regime defectors who joined them had a very different vision of change, and deployed different means to achieve it. The youth movement gained powerful allies on paper, but in reality it lost its independence and its leading role in the uprising (Lackner 2016, 156), which was taken up by the more resourceful actors related to Islah and the First Armed Division. Many youth activists complained that the revolution they had initiated had been hijacked by the regime elites, who were more interested in gaining power than in democratizing Yemen. Similarly, the members of the southern Hirak movement expressed their scepticism towards the revolution led by Saleh's half-brother, General Ali Mohsen al-Ahmar, and forces linked to the Islamist Islah Party. The unsustainability of such an 'alliance' was obvious: those who were now in the revolutionary camp with the youth represented the same repression, corruption, and tribal politics against which young Yemenis had rebelled in the first place. As the 'regime defectors' and Islah militias started to dominate the uprising, many, in particular the Houthis and members of the Southern movement, abandoned the squares (Manea 2015, 169).

Political destabilization and the interference of international actors

At the same time, while the weakened regime directed all its energies into the struggle for survival, the security situation in the whole country started to deteriorate dramatically. In order to protect Saleh, the police and loyal army were concentrated in Sana'a, which led to a security void in the southern and northern provinces. Exploiting the opportunity, various non-state actors took control of towns and villages across the country. Among them were the Houthis, who took control of Saada province in the North, and al-Qaeda, who rapidly expanded in the South. In other words, parallel to the clashes between pro- and anti-government forces, and the peaceful demonstrations still taking place, various groups started to fight their own 'wars' for power and territorial control. Against this backdrop of escalating violence and chaos in the country, at the beginning of June 2011, concerns over an imminent civil war in Yemen were common among the observers.

Among those concerned were the neighbouring countries of the Gulf Cooperation Council (GCC) and other international actors. The rich oil monarchies worried first about the potentially contagious effect of the pro-democracy movement, and the possibility of violence from a Yemeni civil war spilling over the borders. Similarly, the United States had been uncomfortable from the beginning with the Yemeni youth uprising. Despite its declared support for democratization, the Obama administration had a friendly relationship with Saleh, who secured American interests in the Arabian Peninsula and had been a loyal partner in the 'War on Terror'. The United States expressed concern over al-Qaeda's presence and feared its expansion in the event of Saleh stepping down (Kasinof and Sanger 2011). In fact, a similar argument was exploited by Saleh himself in his desperate efforts to hold on to power. Saleh warned against the chaos and sectarian strife that would unfold in his absence, projecting himself as the only one capable of fighting the 'Islamists' and maintaining the unity of the country. In March 2011, he had condemned the protestors for steering the country towards a civil war, warning that the uprising was inescapably leading to inter-tribal fighting and the disintegration of Yemen (CNN 2011). The scenario described by Saleh – 'either me or chaos'[7] as Khosrokhavar (2012) put it – did little to convince Yemenis, many of whom believed that Saleh's actions actually strengthened radical Islamists in the country. For example, when, in mid-2011, al-Qaeda started to take control over cities in southern Yemen, many Yemenis claimed that this was done with the tacit support of Ali Abdullah Saleh, who needed a 'terrorist threat' to claim his own legitimacy.

Nevertheless, Saleh's argument fed into some people's fears, particularly those of the international community. Against the backdrop of escalating violence in

Yemen, the GCC, beginning in April 2011, worked on an agreement between the formal oppositional coalition, JMP, and the president, that would grant Saleh immunity in exchange for a peaceful transfer of power. The deal was initially rejected by Saleh, who instead called for new elections, while his security forces simultaneously continued to fire live ammunition at protestors and fought his new, armed opponents. In June 2011, following the attack on his palace, Saleh left for Saudi Arabia to receive medical treatment, but he did not resign from power, and the violence in the country continued. Eventually, under international pressure from, among others, the UN Security Council, Saleh signed the GCC initiative in Riyadh on 23 November 2011.

Under the terms of the deal, Saleh had to resign, but remained the head of the GPC Party, and he and his family were granted immunity from prosecution. In December 2011, the national unity government was appointed (formed in equal numbers by Saleh's GPC and the opposition JMP), with Muhammad Basindawa from JMP selected as prime minister. In February 2012, Abd Rabbuh Mansour Hadi, the vice president since 1994, was elected president in a single-candidate contest. The deal also provided for an inclusive National Dialogue Conference (NDC) that would draft a new Constitution and lay the groundwork for elections in 2013 (Brehony 2015, 238; Durac 2013; Lackner 2016). With the transition deal reached, external observers and some Yemenis breathed a sigh of relief that the civil war in Yemen appeared to have been averted.

Transition to civil war

Yemen in the context of this book provides an interesting case: the peaceful mobilization did morph into violence, but before descending into full-fledged civil war, the country was momentarily 'pacified' by a deal drafted by diplomats and signed by Yemeni elites. The agreement brokered by the Gulf countries was, not surprisingly, supported by political parties who were promised parliamentary representation, and by the regime defectors who used the opportunity to return to the centre of power. They were the biggest beneficiaries of the transitional process. For example, General Mohsen, who formally lost his position due to the restructuring of the military, maintained his influence in the armed forces and strategic relationship with President Hadi, to the extent that, in 2015, he was appointed Yemen's vice president. Other Islah-related actors were overrepresented in the government and steadily strengthened their position in the country. The military, for its part, was divided into two camps, one that supported the new president and welcomed the transition process, and the other that remained loyal to Ali Abdullah Saleh (Saif 2013, 155).

It seems evident that despite its lofty declarations, the transition deal sponsored by the GCC and supported by western countries and the UN Special Envoy Jamal Benomar cared little about Yemen's democratization, the dismantling of the old regime, or bringing justice to its victims (al-Madhaji 2016). Rather, it was a way to demobilize popular forces and prevent the radical change they demanded, for the simple reason that they threatened the interests and stability of Yemen's neighbours in the Gulf. The counter-revolutionary nature of the deal – which excluded the *shabab* from negotiations and ignored its demands – should not be surprising, considering the long history of the engagement of the United States and the Gulf states in 'retrograde politics' in Yemen, as Carapico (2014) put it. With Yemen shifting from the phase of contentious politics to political transition, the unlikely alliance that came together during the uprising – which included secular groups and Islamists, the Zayidis and the Sunnis, the city men and the tribes, as well as senior military figures – was now dead. Put differently, the unity built around the aforementioned 'imagined solidarities' was dispersed by the old divisions and the fragmentation of actors who returned to their narrow interests and agendas. The national unity government was dominated by Islah and other members of established political parties, with no room for the Houthis, Hirak members, or all those who took to the streets to demand radical change.

As things seemed to be moving towards institutional politics, popular mobilization decreased, but it did not vanish altogether. Unlike established political groups, the vast majority of the youth rejected the transition deal (which they regarded as a betrayal of the revolution's objectives) and continued to demand the prosecution of Ali Abdullah Saleh. While western observers were celebrating the GCC-led initiative, the youth returned to peaceful resistance amidst the growing repression (Alwazir 2016). For instance, to show that the 'revolution continues' until Saleh goes to trial, as one activist put it, the youth movement organized two long distance marches across the country. Drawing on the imagery of Gandhi's famous 'Salt March' in 1930, protestors walked first in December 2011 from Taiz to Sana'a, in what they called the 'Life March', and later in January 2012, from the port city of Hudaydah to Sana'a, in the 'March of Dignity'. Both times, thousands of protestors walked approximately 300 kilometres in the cold for several days to demand justice and the prosecution of the fallen dictator (Yadav 2015). Each time, they were brutally attacked by armed forces still loyal to Saleh, and many were killed. The fact that the spectacular marches attracted very little media coverage in Yemen and outside the country was a sign to the youth that they had been effectively marginalized by the GCC deal and erased from the new power struggles in Yemen.

Similarly, the southern Hirak movement expressed little faith in the transition process. When, in summer 2012, the peaceful sit-ins in Aden were crushed by government forces, the funerals of the dead protestors quickly turned into demonstrations calling for the South's secession. Brutal violence deployed by the new government clearly showcased that the post-revolutionary Yemen differed little from the one ruled by Saleh.

The National Dialogue Conference

Nevertheless, amidst popular objections, the transition was set in motion and its cornerstone, the National Dialogue Conference (NDC), was finally launched in Sana'a on 18 March 2013. The date was symbolic, as it marked the second anniversary of the old regime's massacre of the peaceful protestors. Sana'a was covered with flashy billboards announcing that 'Through Dialogue we build the New Yemen' (Steinbeiser 2015, 7), and Yemenis proudly listened to the international observers and policy-makers, who called on other Arab countries to follow the 'Yemeni model' of transition and political inclusiveness (Yadav 2015, 145). The talks that were aimed at the restructuring of the Yemeni political system and the drafting of a new Constitution lasted 10 months and included representatives from the main political parties, the Houthis, some members of the Southern Movement (although the main figures refused to participate), as well as representatives of civil society, women, and youth.[8] The participants were divided into nine working groups, which addressed the most pressing national issues, including Southern aspirations, the conflict with the Houthis, military reform, and state building.

Despite early optimism and hopes for the 'new Yemen', Yemenis soon became disillusioned with the process. In the end, the NDC came up with some 1,800 recommendations, but consensus around the most contentious issues was not reached (Brehony 2015, 239; Yadav 2015, 161). In addition, new controversies arose when the special committee convened by the president drafted a new map for Yemen, dividing it into six federal regions. The proposed division was widely regarded as unsatisfactory, and confirmed the concerns of many, among them the Houthis and the Hirak movement, that the transition process would not redress past injustices but would rather lead to a further unequal distribution of wealth, resources, and power (Thiel 2015). At the micro level, the transition processes did not bring any improvements in security or living standards for the majority of Yemenis (Salisbury 2016). On the contrary, water supplies were scarce in cities and power cuts were even more frequent than before. While Yemenis have endured poverty for many years and did not expect radical improvements straight away, they had hoped that the new government would at least attempt to root out the corruption and introduce policies centred on a more equal distribution of resources and social justice. None of that was on the horizon, however, and the old habits and ways of doing 'dirty politics' seemed to be back. Furthermore, with a weakened military, divided into two camps, the security situation steadily deteriorated. The fragility was brutally displayed on 21 May 2012, when a suicide bomber killed around 100 soldiers from the Central Security Forces. While al-Qaeda kept on striking, targeting military hospitals, checkpoints but also city centres, US drone strikes, sanctioned by President Hadi in 2012, killed suspected terrorists but more often innocent civilians (HRW 2013b; 2014).

Against this backdrop, the discontent, chaos, and fighting in the country grew. Behind the façade of an inclusive dialogue held in the rooms of the Movenpick Hotel in Sana'a, and away from the flashes of cameras, there was a fragmented nation, haunted by power struggles between competing factions, unresolved conflicts, outbursts of clashes among various groups, and terrorist attacks (Salisbury 2016, 15). While some, like the youth movement, did continue with peaceful tactics and civil initiatives (such as, for example, the Support Yemen media collective), others returned to narrowly defined interests and identifications (around tribes, regions, or sects) and localized, often violent, struggles. In 2013 and 2014, the Houthis engaged in a series of fights in different provinces; tribal groups in Marib attacked gas and oil infrastructure; tribes from Hadramaut clashed with government forces, protesting against the presence of northern military units in the region; and finally, members of the Hirak movement in October 2014 called for the South's independence and expulsion of northerners from their territory (Granzow 2015, 165; Salisbury 2016). The regime defectors were again retaining their grip over power, repressing those whom they had allegedly defended in 2011. It was obvious that despite procedural advances in the period between 2013 and 2014, when Yemen was supposed to transition into a democracy, the country was torn by spiralling violence, divisions, and social fragmentation, with the unity forged during the initial stages of mobilization long disappeared. The various conflicts in Yemen seemed to have intensified rather than diminished.

Rise of the Houthis, return of Ali Abdullah Saleh: the rebels' territorial contests

It was in this context that the Houthi militias, exploiting the security vacuum that had existed since late 2011, started to expand their territorial control beyond their traditional stronghold of Saada. Due to the corruption of the new government, packed with old regime members and unable to provide basic services and stability, the popularity of the Houthis – whose rhetoric focused on social justice – grew and this allowed them to recruit new members (Alwazir 2016). Others, often children, were lured simply by the financial rewards they offered. While in 2013 the Houthis joined the NDC deliberations in Sana'a, and thus the formal political process, outside the capital they resorted to guerrilla tactics. The fighting against government forces allied with the Salafi groups, and tribes loyal to the Ahmar family in particular or Islah in general (Transfeld 2016), accelerated in 2013 and 2014. The clashes culminated in the Houthis' destruction of Dammaj, known as the 'Salafi center of power' (Carvajal 2016a), and later in the rebels' victory over the Hadi and Islah forces. They took control over the city of Amran in July 2014. In August 2014, and on the back of a wave of popular discontent with the rising prices of fuel announced by Hadi, the Houthis entered the capital. The initially peaceful protests developed into violent clashes between the rebels and the Islah-linked militias and the military units. On 18 and 19 September, the Houthi forces attacked the Islah supporters and targeted the military headquarters of General Mohsen. Over 100 people were killed in the fighting in Sana'a. By 21 September, the Houthis had taken over the government headquarters and forced the prime minister to resign, gaining control over Sana'a.

It was soon obvious that the rebels' territorial advances and the quick fall of Sana'a were made possible due to the strategic alliance the Houthis had made with Ali Abdullah Saleh, the ex-president who had preserved his influence in the security and armed forces, but also among tribes in the North. This reshuffling of alliances, which pushed the rebels towards the fallen dictator and against those with whom they had shared protest sites in 2011, is one of the most striking developments that marked Yemen's descent into civil war. The pact may seem paradoxical, considering that the Houthis had been outspoken critics of the president since the 2000s and effectively had engaged in war with his government since 2004. For Yemenis, however, it seemed entirely natural that Ansar Allah and Saleh would unite against a common rival – the allied General Mohsen, the al-Ahmar family, and the Islah Party. All of them had previously been the crucial 'clients' of Saleh and had once constituted the core of the regime until they 'abandoned' the president in March 2011.

For the Houthis, General Mohsen was a personal enemy, as it was his First Armed Division that had fought the insurgents in Saada. Besides the feelings of revenge, the Houthis and Saleh were driven by pragmatic calculations, hoping to undermine the power of al-Islah that was steadily growing in post-revolution Yemen (Transfeld 2016). In other words, the 'rebels' who in 2011 decried the regime's corruption and joined the calls for democratization were now, together with Saleh, targeting al-Islah, motivated not so much by the principles of social justice but rather by their pursuit of power and desire for retaliation. Importantly, the rapprochement between the Houthis – former protestors, and Saleh – former president, annulled the configuration of forces of the popular uprising (opposition versus regime) and put forward new alliances and divisions built around the warring elite factions.

With Sana'a falling into the hands of Ansar Allah and Ali Abdullah Saleh, fears of civil war returned to Yemen. On 21 September 2014, a Peace and National Partnership Agreement was brokered by the UN envoy Jamal Benomar and signed by President Hadi, delegates of the Houthi movement, and leaders of major political parties. The document called for an immediate ceasefire and the formation of a non-partisan 'government of experts', which would include actors marginalized in the transition process, such as the Houthis and the Hirak movement (von Bruck 2014). However, despite the pressure, the Houthis did not withdraw from Sana'a. On the contrary, the rebels cemented their control over the city and started to move beyond the capital. In the first months of 2015, the Houthis, backed by Saleh's forces, managed to gain control over significant parts of the country, justifying their advances as a campaign to bring back security and root out al-Qaeda (Brehony 2015). In some areas the Houthis managed to consolidate their power by providing basic services to local communities and expelling corrupt officials. For example, soon after taking over the city of Sana'a, the Houthis turned the house of their enemy, the exiled General Ali Mohsen al-Ahmar, into a museum that served to expose the lavish lifestyles of the corrupt elites against which they claimed to fight (al-Sakkaf and al-Qalisi 2014). In most cases, however, the expansion of the Houthis and attempts to overthrow the government gave rise to protests. Despite the rebels' rhetoric of social justice and standing up for ordinary people, the Houthis repressed the demonstrations with the same brutality as Saleh used to do (Lackner 2016, 163). The Houthis who had mobilized with the youth against Saleh in

2011 were now allied with the ex-president and shooting at young Yemenis who, unlike them, remained committed to the ideals of peaceful revolution.

Yemen's many wars

The violence in the country escalated further after January 2015, when the Houthis targeted President Hadi and launched a campaign to take control of the entire country. The rebels put Hadi under house arrest and forced him to resign on 22 January 2015, completing the coup d'état in February by dissolving the government and replacing it with the Houthi-led presidential council, known as the 'Supreme Revolutionary Committee' (Salisbury 2016, 24). When Hadi escaped house arrest and fled to Aden, the Houthis followed southwards, fighting tribal militias and peaceful protestors who took to the streets across the country to oppose their territorial advances and takeover of power. President Hadi, in the meantime, retracted his resignation and in February 2011 declared Aden the temporary capital of Yemen and the seat of the legitimate government, calling the Houthis' attempts to govern 'invalid and unconstitutional' (Al-Jazeera 2015). Within a month, however, the Houthis had reached Aden, bombing the presidential palace on 19 March 2015 and taking control of the city a few days later. On 25 March, they took control of Taiz, after the peaceful civil opposition was dispersed by the insurgents with force and the city had to surrender. By that time, Yemen was torn by a fully-fledged civil war, with the Houthis gaining control of numerous towns and cities and attacking those who resisted. As a result of the rebels' takeover, President Hadi fled to Riyadh; upon his request, the Saudi Arabian-led coalition began bombing Yemen on 26 March 2015. Besides airstrikes, 'Operation Decisive Storm', as the campaign was called, included an air and sea blockade of Yemen and the arming of groups opposed to the Houthis, with the aim of reinstating Hadi as president. With the involvement of the Arab coalition, the war was 'internationalized' and several external actors were added to the list of warring parties fighting in Yemen.

Activation of militant networks

While the fighting in Yemen is most often framed as a conflict between two clearly demarcated camps – the Shia rebels allied with Saleh, and the Sunni forces loyal to President Hadi – in reality, as Salisbury (2016, 4) put it, 'Most Yemenis do not support either the president or the northern rebels; rather, they are part of much smaller groups with their own identity, ideology, grievances and political goals. . . .' The new allies Saleh and the Houthis have relied largely on the rebels' militias, and some northern tribal forces, as well as the skills and resources of the army units loyal to the ex-president. The Houthis are also believed to receive support from Iran, although both the rebels and Iran deny the relationship, and Iran's actual role is probably less important than commonly argued.[9]

On the other hand, the loose network of resistance groups that emerged to oppose the Houthi/Saleh advances, when the central government and the state's institutions collapsed, is composed of divergent groups with various ideologies and agendas (Al-Hamdani *et al.* 2015). Among them are Islamists, including the Salafis and members of the Islah Party; members of the Hirak movement; military units loyal to Hadi; tribal forces; and soldiers from the United Arab Emirates. They receive financial and military support from the Arab coalition but otherwise have little in common. While some armed groups pre-existed the conflict, others were born during it. The emergence and rapid spread of armed militias aptly illustrate the mechanism of 'the militarization of networks' that fuels civil wars by turning citizens into soldiers driven by ideological reasons, retribution, or financial rewards. For example, the Hirak movement, which had been known for its rejection of violence and peaceful activism since 2007, took up arms upon the Houthis/ Saleh intrusion into the South in March 2015. Other groups like the Salafis, who had previously been defeated by the Houthis, gained military strength through patronage and financial assistance provided by Saudi Arabia. The trajectory of the Houthis is also interesting: while, in 2011, the Zaydi insurgents left their Kalashnikovs at home and joined protests calling for regime change, when the violence escalated, they returned to their guns and their original chant of 'Death to America! Death to Israel! A curse upon the Jews! Victory for Islam!'

The range of actors on both sides means that today's conflict is made up of many camps and multiple wars. In addition, the engagement of international actors has caused some commentators to draw a distinction between the internal Yemeni conflict, driven largely by the competition for power between the regime factions, and the proxy war between Saudi Arabia and Iran – all of which makes it difficult to distil the ongoing confrontations into a coherent narrative. What for some constitutes a 'civil war' is to others nothing more than Saudi Arabia's aggression that is supported by the international community. For many in Sana'a, the fight is about defending Yemenis' dignity and sovereignty. In Taiz, Yemen's third biggest city and at the time of writing besieged by the Houthis, the narrative and lived experiences of the war differ dramatically. There, the rebels' snipers and landmines constitute the daily terror, against which militants fight, and from which ordinary residents seek to protect themselves. Further south, it is common to hear that the current conflict is a repetition of the 1994 civil war: yet another invasion of the northern forces – in this case, the Houthis and Saleh – aimed at imposing their dominance over the south. In places like Aden, taking up arms has often been about defending local territory and autonomy. While some of the southerners support President Hadi and by extension the Saudi-led airstrikes, others oppose Hadi and Saudi Arabia as much as they do the Houthis. They fight not for Hadi to return, but to re-establish South Yemen as an independent state.

These deep divisions and contested narratives of war came to the fore on the recent Independence Day,[10] which marked the 49th anniversary of South Yemen's independence from the British. Ex-president Saleh used the occasion to deliver a public speech, calling on the Yemeni people to unite and as a Yemeni nation oppose the 'Saudi aggression' and terrorism (Al-Motamarnet 2016). In Aden, however, where celebrations were held, there were no chants of unity; instead, people waved flags of independent South Yemen, and some posters read, 'Thank you, Salman, thank you, Khalifa, thank you, the Arab coalition' (Nasser 2016).[11]

Sectarianism wins

The many perceptions and positions of Yemenis reveal the deep fragmentation of society along regional, tribal, and sectarian lines. If the 2011 uprising was about transgressing divisions and forging new collective identities, the radicalization of political violence brought back old divisions, while new oppositions were formed. Despite the fact that the splits today seem deeply entrenched and perhaps irreversible, it is worth remembering that it was not so long ago that Yemenis managed to put aside their differences and unite for the common goal of regime change. In early 2011, today's enemies – the Houthis, Islah members, and socialists – marched together with young men and women, chanting slogans of popular and peaceful revolution, from 'north to south' (Rosen 2012).

What is most striking is probably not the return to narrow, sub-national identifications, which were common in pre-revolutionary Yemen, but rather the growing use of sectarian language, which was not. Sectarianism, muted during the popular mobilization of 2011, grew with the ongoing conflict, aggravated by all involved sides. For example, in 2013 and 2014, the Houthis started the fight for control over mosques and depicted their opponents as 'Daesh'. Their military advance on Damaj and Amran towns was framed as an attack on hubs of Saudi-sponsored terrorism. Similarly, the rebels' campaign in the South was projected as one targeting al-Qaeda, the Islamic State, and their ally Hadi. The other side of the conflict mirrored the sectarian language, quickly denouncing the Houthis as agents following orders from Iran. For example, the Salafi groups who have become the most crucial allies of the Saudi-led coalition (Carvajal 2016b) referred to themselves as 'lions of the Sunnis' and described the war against the Houthis in terms of 'jihad' (Baron and al-Muslimi 2016). Strikingly, the sectarian language has been used not only by actors driven by clear religious ideologies, but also by the seculars. President Hadi, for example, referred to the Houthis as 'twelver shia' (which is factually wrong), implying their connection to Shiites of Iran, and Yemen's ambassador to the United States stated publicly that the war in Yemen was a struggle between 'the Arabs and the Persians' (al-Muslimi 2015; Baron and al-Muslimi 2016).

Despite this rhetoric, the civil war in Yemen did not start because of the Shia–Sunni conflict, nor should it be read as such. The Zaydi population in the North does not necessarily support the Houthis, and the southerners – especially those affiliated with the socialist party and the Hirak movement – are not known for religious devotion. As we have seen earlier in the chapter, sectarianism in Yemen used to have little currency. Common low-level conflicts between tribes or families have traditionally been about local hatreds, personal animosities, or struggles for resources (and were exploited and fuelled by Saleh, who used the politics of fragmenting society to strengthen his own position). Even the Houthis, who had rebelled against the government since the early 2000s, did so not only in the name of Zaydi traditions, but also out of dissatisfaction with the underdevelopment of their region, the regime's corruption, and its support for the US invasion on Iraq and the 'War on Terror'. While sectarian divisions had pre-existed the conflict, they were of little importance in the early stages of the popular uprising. However, they were mobilized around the power struggles that first crystallized in March 2011 with the splits in the regime, and continued well into the transitional period. Since armed confrontations erupted in March 2015, sectarianism has enabled the war belligerents to recruit fighters, delegitimize enemies, and justify violence. As such, sectarian rhetoric, deployed to spread hatred and draw unpassable boundaries between groups, has fuelled the conflict and, as resentments and divisions have intensified, made escape from the vicious circle of violence difficult to imagine.

Conclusion

The multiplicity of actors involved in Yemen's war(s), and the framing that was used to justify their recourse to violence, aptly reveal the social fragmentation, militarization of networks, and mobilization of sectarianism that were put in motion as what began as civil resistance turned into civil war.

As this chapter has described, the radicalization of political violence in Yemen has been a long, and not necessarily linear, process. It first began in mid-2011 when the popular mobilization was overshadowed by armed clashes between pro- and anti-Saleh armed groups. When, in June 2011, Saleh's rule and life were under threat, the once peaceful uprising was more like a war. The escalating violence was eventually quelled by the power transfer agreement brokered by the GCC countries in November 2011. However, while the deal drafted by international actors subdued the violence, it also subverted the goals of the revolution by privileging established political actors and granting Saleh immunity from prosecution. The NDC proceeded, and enjoyed the praise of international observers, but there was a growing sense among Yemenis that little had changed in the country. Armed confrontations again broke out in Yemen when the Houthis, exploiting a security vacuum, popular discontent over economic deterioration, and splits in the military, moved beyond the northern highlands to seize Sana'a in September 2014. The Houthis characterized the move as a continuation of the popular revolution and an attempt to renegotiate the GGC deal that they said had betrayed Yemenis' popular aspirations. However, when the rebels allied with the ousted president Saleh began to steadily advance outside the capital, brutally suppressing any forms of resistance on the way, the negotiations collapsed and gave way to violence. By mid-March 2015, the country had descended into a civil war that was further exacerbated by the involvement of the Saudi-led coalition. This trajectory reveals that what had started as a democratization movement was gradually hijacked by warring elite factions and their allies, along with self-interested regional powers. The forces that stood up together in 2011 have been scattered, with some, like the Houthis, aligning with the 'old regime' of Saleh, and others with the new regime of Hadi.[12]

In this sense, the alliances and oppositions that emerged around the civil war are radically different from those of the popular uprising.

Importantly, behind the main stage of events between 2011 and 2015, Yemen was punctuated by other, less visible episodes of violence, which took the form of local clashes, terrorist attacks, or drone strikes. This continuous, long-lasting crisis, set within the context of a security void, the collapse of the state's institutions, and economic destitution, was also a factor in fuelling radicalization at the individual level. It pushed many ordinary people to take up arms, out of either frustration with the failed political process, the need to defend one's family, or simply financial despair. As UNICEF's representative in Yemen has estimated, approximately a third of all the combatants in Yemen are children who joined armed groups for the sake of money (Pedrero 2015).

Thus, in analysing the country as a 'battlefield', we should not forget that Yemen today is plagued by a humanitarian crisis as much as by sheer physical violence. At the time of writing, there have been over 11,000 people killed, 3.3 million internally displaced, and 14.1 million – out of a population of 27 million – suffering from food insecurity (Keane 2016).

Although all sides bear responsibility for the violence and its impact, the Saudi-coalition airstrikes and its blockade of Yemen have been the most damaging, turning the country's economy, infrastructure, and heritage sites to ruin. The United States and the United Kingdom have also played a role in inflicting suffering on the Yemeni people by providing arms and intelligence to the Arab coalition. Airstrikes are supposed to target Houthi forces, with the stated aim of bringing peace in the country, but the victims are often civilians killed in their sleep or while out shopping in open-air markets, attending funeral processions or wedding celebrations (OHCHR 2016). Not surprisingly, this fuels, rather than eradicates, radicalization and hatred on the ground. Similar sentiments grow on the other side of the conflict, with those who have borne the brunt of the Houthis' abuses calling for retribution, not reconciliation.

For many in Yemen, hunger is their main fear, rather than war. 'The hunger is harder on us than the bombing', as one Yemeni put it (Abdul-Ahad 2016). This is why Ahmed, described at the opening of the chapter, is considered lucky by his friends: because he went to fight with the Houthis, they speculate, he receives money and does not have to worry about food as they do. Securing food, amidst the scarcity of products and rising prices, is the main preoccupation of many young men who remained in Sana'a with their families. Hussein, Ahmed's good friend, told me, 'All I think about each day is how to provide food for my family and make sure my two kids are not hungry.' And yet, Hussein considers himself relatively 'lucky' too, being based in Sana'a and having friends abroad who can sometimes support him with small amounts of money. 'I don't know how others cope,' he said. The 'others' are Yemenis in towns and cities where the Saudi bombardments have been heavy, or where the Houthis have shelled residential areas, indiscriminately killing their opponents as well as women and children. But the worst off, according to Hussein, are those who live in the countryside, where hospitals are shut down and humanitarian aid cannot reach, due to the Saudi blockade or the Houthis' control. They die of hunger and diseases that could be cured if they had access to basic healthcare.

Yemenis today are torn apart by the war, but they probably agree on one thing: that the world does not seem to care much about their plight. In one of the last messages I received from Ahmed in early 2016, he expressed his frustration with the international community that preaches to Yemenis about peace and democracy, but is silent in face of Yemenis' deaths and suffering. 'We are not humans for them,' he concluded. In one of Ahmed's Facebook posts, he conveyed a similar observation through evocative words:

> I don't believe in UN and human right[s]
> The blind UN, human right[s]
> The deaf UN, human right[s]
> Why there is no eye to see the suffering of Yemeni kids?
> You just see the Saudi money
> And you keep silent and [keep] supporting [the] Saudi[s].

With the world turning a blind eye to the deaths and the humanitarian crisis in Yemen, the concerns of ordinary people, many of whom joined the popular mobilization in 2011, revolve around survival rather than democracy and human rights. Nonetheless, violence has not become the new normal in Yemen, and the youth, in particular, have continued to peacefully oppose both the Houthis' crimes and the airstrikes of the Saudi-led coalition. At the end of March 2015, a social media campaign was launched, using the hashtag 'Kefaya War' [enough war] to shed light on the war crimes committed in Yemen by all sides and to share stories of Yemenis' humanity and resilience.[13] Throughout 2014 and 2015, protests were also organized on the ground, resisting the Houthi militias, calling for the country's unity and the rejection of violence (see, for example, Zunes and Al-Haidary 2015). Today, however, amidst the violence, destitution, and despair, these voices of peaceful resistance have become more and more scattered.

Notes

1 *Qat* leaves are popularly chewed in Yemen for their mildly stimulant effect. *Qat* is chewed in private settings, as well as at weddings, business and political meetings. Lisa Wedeen (2008) has argued that the sites of *q*10 Jan. 1989*at* chews are reminiscent of the Habermasian public sphere, as they provide spaces of dialogue and critical debate.

2 The close relationship between the Islah and the president stood in stark contrast to the position of Islamists in countries such as Tunisia and Egypt, where their political organizations had been banned.

3 Probably less so in the South, traditionally and for good reasons more critical of the president.

4 This argument is in fact very close to the one made by Ali Abdullah Saleh, who called the protests a conspiracy that aimed to destroy the country. See, for example, Carlstrom (2011).

5 The 1994 civil war is briefly discussed in the following section.

6 Amendments to the Constitution that passed in 2001 and extended Saleh's power and term in office made it obvious that the president was slowly preparing the succession of his son Ahmed.

7 Saleh's argument was not unique, but was a common rhetorical device of dictators threatened by the 'Arab Spring' uprisings; very similar statements were given by Qaddafi in Libya or Assad in Syria.

8 Of the 565 seats, only 40 were distributed to representatives of the independent youth (Alwazir 2016, 174–5).

9 According to Saudi Arabia, many Yemenis loyal to President Hadi, and the popular media, the Houthis are supported by Iran, which uses the insurgent group to increase its influence in Yemen and the region. Against these claims, scholars of Yemen point out that Iran's involvement in Yemen before the conflict had been minimal; the Houthis, although likely to receive financial and military assistance from Iran, are driven by their own politics and grievances rather than following external orders. See, for example, Von Bruck (2014) and Carapico and Yadav (2014).

10 Independence Day, celebrated on 30 November, is a national day in Yemen, commemorating South Yemen's independence from the British achieved in 1967.

11 Salman and Khalifa refer to Saudi Arabia's king and the UAE's president, respectively.

12 As mentioned earlier, some groups, like the southern movement, took the anti-Houthi/Saleh position without necessarily granting their support to Hadi and al-Islah.

13 See the Facebook profile: Kefaya War#Our Yemen, available at: www.facebook.com/pg/KefayaWar/about/?ref=page_internal

References

Abdul-Ahad, Ghaith. 2016. '"Everything is over now": the last survivors in Yemen's ground zero'. *The Guardian,* 9 December. Available at: www.theguardian.com/world/2016/dec/09/everything-is-over-now-the-last-survivors-in-yemens-ground-zero

Al-Bab (2015) 'Freedom of the Press in Yemen'. 2015. Al-Bab.com. 6 August. Available at: http://al-bab.com/albab-orig/albab/yemen/media/bwmed.htm

Al-Hamdani, Sama'a, Baron, Adam, and Al-Madhaji, Maged. 2015. 'The role of local actors in Yemen's current war'. 2. Sana'a: Sana'a Center for Strategic Studies. Available at: http://sanaacenter.org/publications/item/18-the-role-of-local-actors-in-yemen's-current-war.html

Al-Jazeera. 2015. 'Yemen's Hadi declares Houthi power grab illegal'. Al-Jazeera, 22 February. Available at: www.aljazeera.com/news/2015/02/yemen-leader-hadi-leaves-sanaa-weeks-house-arrest-150221090018174.html

Alley, April Longley. 2010. 'The rules of the game: unpacking patronage politics in Yemen'. *The Middle East Journal* 64(3): 385–409. doi:10.3751/64.3.13.

al-Madhaji, Maged. 2016. 'How Yemen's post-2011 transitional phase ended in war'. Sana'a: Sana'a Center for Strategic Studies. Available at: http://sanaacenter.org/publications/item/39-how-yemen's-post-2011-transitional-phase-ended-in-war.html

Al-Motamernet. 2016. 'The leader Saleh addresses the Yemeni people on the occasion of the Independence Day (30 November)'. 2016. Almotamernet, 29 November. Available at: www.almotamar.net/news/133686.html

al-Muslimi, Farea. 2015. 'How Sunni-Shia sectarianism is poisoning Yemen'. Carnegie. Middle East Center, 29 December. Available at: http://carnegie-mec.org/diwan/62375

al-Muslimi, Farea. 2016. 'Why I think we failed Yemen'. Al-Jazeera, 27 May. Available at: www.aljazeera.com/news/2016/05/failed-yemen-160511100609704.html

Al-Sakkaf, Nasser, and Al-Qalisi, Mohammed. 2014. 'Ali Mohsen's house: a museum with Houthi tour guides'. *Yemen Times,* 4 November. Available at: www.yementimes.com/en/1830/report/4533/Ali-Mohsen's-house-A-museum-with-Houthi-tour-guides.htm

Alwazir, Atiaf. 2012. 'Garbage collectors and the struggle for workers' rights in Yemen'. *Jadaliyya*, 1 June. Available at: www.jadaliyya.com/pages/index/5788/garbage-collectors-and-the-struggle-for-workers-ri

Alwazir, Atiaf. 2016. 'Yemen's enduring resistance: youth between politics and informal mobilization'. *Mediterranean Politics* 21(1): 170–91. doi:10.1080/13629395.2015.1081446.

Baron, Adam, and al-Muslimi, Farea. 2016. 'The politics driving Yemen's rising sectarianism'. Sana'a: Sana'a Center for Strategic Studies. Available at: http://sanaacenter.org/publications/item/40-the-politics-driving-yemen.html

Bayat, Asef. 2005. 'Islamism and social movement theory'. *Third World Quarterly* 26(6): 891–908. doi:10.1080/01436590500089240.

Blumi, Isa. 2012. *Chaos in Yemen: Societal Collapse and the New Authoritarianism*. London: Routledge.

Bonnefoy, Laurent. 2012. 'The Yemeni revolutionary process: have the "shabab Al-Thawra" lost in the face of institutionalized politics?' In Moulay Hicham Foundation. Available at: http://moulayhichamfoundation.org/sites/default/files/LAURENT%20BONNEFOY_Yemen.pdf

Bonnefoy, Laurent, and Poirier, Marine. 2009. 'Civil society and democratization in Yemen. enhancing the role of intermediate bodies'. Available at: https://halshs.archives-ouvertes.fr/hal-01066200/document

Boucek, Christopher, and Ottaway, Marina (eds). 2010. *Yemen on the Brink*. Washington, DC: Carnegie Endowment for International Peace.

Brehony, Noel. 2015. 'Yemen and the Huthis: genesis of the 2015 crisis'. *Asian Affairs* 46(2): 232–50. doi:10.1080/03068374.2015.1037162.

Carapico, Sheila. 1993. 'Elections and mass politics in Yemen'. *Middle East Research and Information Project*, December. Available at: www.merip.org/mer/mer185/elections-mass-politics-yemen.

Carapico, Sheila. 1996. 'Gender and status inequalities in Yemen: honour, economics, and politics'. In Valentine M. Moghadam (ed.), *Patriarchy and Economic Development: Women's Positions at the End of the Twentieth Century*. Oxford: Clarendon Press, pp. 80–98.

Carapico, Sheila. 2002. 'Foreign aid for promoting democracy in the Arab world'. *Middle East Journal* 56(3): 379–95.

Carapico, Sheila. 2007. *Civil Society in Yemen: The Political Economy of Activism in Modern Arabia*. New York: Cambridge University Press.

Carapico, Sheila. 2011. 'No exit: Yemen's existential crisis'. *Middle East Research and Information Project*, 3 May. Available at: www.merip.org/mero/mero050311–1?ip_login_no_cache=5d2267fcaf95daf21e7829175eadb779

Carapico, Sheila. 2014. 'Of transitology and counter-terror targeting in Yemen'. *Muftah*, 22 April. Available at: http://muftah.org/transitology-counter-terror-targeting-yemen/#.WE0tOWOKNSU

Carapico, Sheila, and Yadav, Stacey Philbrick. 2014. 'The breakdown of the GCC initiative'. *Middle East Report*. Available at: www.merip.org/mer/mer273/breakdown-gcc-initiative

Carlstrom, Gregg. 2011. 'Profile: Ali Abdullah Saleh', Al-Jazeera, November 23. Accessed 19 October 2016. Available at: www.aljazeera.com/indepth/spotlight/yemen/2011/02/201122812118938648.html

Carvajal, Fernando. 2016a. 'Salafis, the vengeful giants (Part I): historical shifts in the balance of power in Central and Southern Yemen'. 14 October. Available at: https://diwansite.wordpress.com/2016/10/14/salafis-the-vengeful-giants-part-i-historical-shifts-in-the-balance-of-power-in-central-and-southern-yemen/

Carvajal, Fernando. 2016b. Salafis, the vengeful giants (Part II). 16 October. Available at: https://diwansite.wordpress.com/2016/10/16/salafis-the-vengeful-giants-part-ii/

Clark, Victoria. 2010. *Yemen: Dancing on the Heads of Snakes*. New Haven, CT: Yale University Press.

CNN. 2011.'Yemen battles al Qaeda as president clings to power'. 27 March. Available at: http://edition.cnn.com/2011/WORLD/meast/03/27/yemen.unrest/

Dahlgren, Susanne. 2010. 'The snake with a thousand heads'. *Middle East Report* 40(256). Available at: www.merip.org/mer/mer256/snake-thousand-heads

Day, Stephen W. 2012. *Regionalism and Rebellion in Yemen: A Troubled National Union*. Cambridge: Cambridge University Press. Available at: http://ebooks.cambridge.org/ref/id/CBO9781139135443

de Regt, Marina. 2008. 'Employing migrant domestic workers in urban Yemen: a new form of social distinction'. *Hawwa* 6(2): 154–75. doi:10.1163/156920808X347241.

Durac, Vincent. 2013. 'Protest movements and political change: an analysis of the "Arab Uprisings" of 2011'. *Journal of Contemporary African Studies* 31(2): 175–93. doi:10.1080/02589001.2013.783754.

Fattah, Khaled. 2011. 'Yemen: A social Intifada in a republic of sheikhs'. *Middle East Policy* 18(3): 79–85. doi:10.1111/j.1475–4967.2011.00499.x.

Granzow, Tanja. 2015. 'Violent vs. non-violent struggle: investigating the impact of frames on movement strategies in Yemen'. *Civil Wars* 17(2): 161–80. doi:10.1080/13698249.2015.1070451.

Human Rights Watch. 2012. '"No safe places". Yemen's crackdown on protests in Taizz. 6 February. New York: Human Rights Watch. Available at: www.hrw.org/report/2012/02/06/no-safe-places/yemens-crackdown-protests-taizz

Human Rights Watch. 2013a. 'Unpunished massacre: Yemen's failed response to the "Friday of Dignity" killings'. New York: Human Rights Watch. Available at: www.hrw.org/report/2013/02/12/unpunished-massacre/yemens-failed-response-friday-dignity-killings

Human Rights Watch. 2013b. '"Between a drone and al-Qaeda": the civilian cost of US targeted killings in Yemen'. 22 October. New York: Human Rights Watch. Available at: www.hrw.org/report/2013/10/22/between-drone-and-al-qaeda/civilian-cost-us-targeted-killings-yemen

Human Rights Watch. 2014. 'A wedding that became a funeral: US drone attack on marriage procession in Yemen'. 19 February. New York: Human Rights Watch. Available at: www.hrw.org/report/2014/02/19/wedding-became-funeral/us-drone-attack-marriage-procession-yemenKasinof, Laura, and Sanger, David E. 2011. 'U.S. shifts to seek removal of Yemen's leader, an ally'. *The New York Times*, 3 April. Available at: www.nytimes.com/2011/04/04/world/middleeast/04yemen.html?pagewanted=all&_r=0

Keane, Fergal. 2016. 'Yemen conflict: UN official accuses world of ignoring crisis'. BBC, 6 December. Available at: www.bbc.com/news/world-middle-east-38220785

Khosrokhavar, Farhad. 2012. *The New Arab Revolutions That Shook the World*. Boulder, CO: Paradigm Publishers.

Lackner, Helen. 2016. 'The change squares of Yemen'. In Adam Roberts, Michael J. Willis, Rory McCarthy, and Timothy Garton Ash (eds), *Civil Resistance in the Arab Spring*. Oxford: Oxford University Press, pp. 141–68.

Manea, Elham. 2015. 'Yemen's Arab Spring: outsmarting the cunning state?' In Larbi Sadiki (ed.), *Routledge Handbook of the Arab Spring: Rethinking Democratization*. London: Routledge, pp. 160–72.

Nasser, Afrah. 2016. 'Fractured unions new and old: South Yemen independence day'. 3 December. Available at: http://afrahnasser.blogspot.it/2016/12/fractured-unions-new-and-old-south.html

New York Times. 2011'Clans and tribes forge new Yemen unity'. 2011. *The New York Times*, 16 June. Available at: www.nytimes.com/2011/06/17/world/middleeast/17yemen.html

Office of the United Nations High Commissioner for Human Rights (OHCHR). 2016. 'Situation of human rights in Yemen'. A/HRC/33/38. Geneva.

Pedrero, Agnes. 2015. 'One third of fighters in Yemen are children, says UNICEF'. *Middle East Eye*, 9 April. Available at: www.middleeasteye.net/news/one-third-fighters-yemen-are-children-says-unicef-734199521

Phillips, Sarah. 2006. 'Foreboding about the future in Yemen'. *Middle East Research and Information Project*, 3 April. Available at: www.merip.org/mero/mero040306

Phillips, Sarah. 2008. *Yemen's Democracy Experiment in Regional Perspective: Patronage and Pluralized Authoritarianism*. New York: Palgrave Macmillan.

Phillips, Sarah. 2010. 'What comes next in Yemen? Al-Qaeda, the tribes, and state-building'. Middle East Program, no. 107. Washington, DC: Carnegie Endowment.

Phillips, Sarah. 2011. *Yemen and the Politics of Permanent Crisis*. Adelphi 420. New York: Routledge for the International Institute for Strategic Studies.

Poirier, Marine. 2011. 'Performing political domination in Yemen: narratives and practices of power in the General People's Congress: performing political domination in Yemen'. *The Muslim World* 101(2): 202–27. doi:10.1111/j.1478–1913.2011.01353.x.

Rosen, Nir. 2012. 'How it started in Yemen: from Tahrir to Taghyir'. In Bassam Haddad, Rosie Bsheer, and Ziad Abu-Rish (eds), *The Dawn of the Arab Uprisings: End of an Old Order?*. New York: Pluto Press, pp. 182–99.

Saif, Ahmed. 2013. 'Void versus presence: the in-between-ness of state and society in Yemen'. In Larbi Sadiki, Heiko Wimmen, and Layla Al-Zubaidi (eds), *Democratic Transition in the Middle East: Unmaking Power*. London: Routledge, pp. 138–58.

Salisbury, Peter. 2016. 'Yemen: stemming the rise of a chaos state'. Middle East and North Africa Programme. Chatham House. Available at: www.chathamhouse.org/publication/yemen-stemming-rise-chaos-state.

Schwedler, Jillian. 2004. 'The Islah Party in Yemen: political opportunities and coalition building in a transitional polity'. In Quintan Wiktorowicz (ed.), *Islamic Activism: A Social Movement Theory Approach*. Bloomington, IN: Indiana University Press, pp. 205–28.

Seif, Huda. 2003. 'Moralities and outcasts: domination and allegories of resentment in Southern Yemen'. PhD dissertation, Columbia University, New York:

Steinbeiser, Stephen. 2015. 'No peace without justice: the Arab Spring, the national dialogue, and Yemen's descent into chaos'. *Arabian Humanities*, no. 4 (January). doi:10.4000/cy.2866.

Thiel, Tobias. 2012. 'After the Arab Spring: power shift in the Middle East? Yemen's Arab Spring: from youth revolution to fragile political transition'. IDEAS reports — special reports. London: London School of Economics and Political Science. Available at: http://eprints.lse.ac.uk/43465/1/After%20the%20Arab%20Spring_Yemen's%20Arab%20Spring(lsero).pdf

Thiel, Tobias. 2015. 'Yemen's imposed federal boundaries'. *Middle East Research and Information Project*, 20 July. Available at: www.merip.org/yemens-imposed-federal-boundaries

Transfeld, Mareike. 2016. 'Political bargaining and violent conflict: shifting elite alliances as the decisive factor in Yemen's transformation'. *Mediterranean Politics* 21(1): 1509. doi: 10.1080/13629395.2015.1081454.

Von Bruck, Gabriele. 2014. 'Revolution Phase II? The Houthi advance on Yemen's capital'. *Le Monde Diplomatique*, 28 October. Available at: http://mondediplo.com/outsidein/the-houthi-advance-on-yemen-s-capital

Wedeen, Lisa. 1999. *Ambiguities of Domination: Politics, Rhetoric, and Symbols in Contemporary Syria*. Chicago: University of Chicago Press.

Wedeen, Lisa. 2003. 'Seeing like a citizen, acting like a state: exemplary events in unified Yemen'. *Comparative Studies in Society and History* 45(4). doi:10.1017/S001041750300032X.

Wedeen, Lisa. 2008. *Peripheral Visions: Publics, Power, and Performance in Yemen*. Chicago: University of Chicago Press.

Yadav, Stacey Philbrick. 2011. 'Antecedents of the revolution: intersectoral networks and post-partisanship in Yemen'. *Studies in Ethnicity and Nationalism* 11(3): 550–63. doi:10.1111/j.1754–9469.2011.01139.x.

Yadav, Stacey Philbrick. 2015. 'The "Yemen Model" as a failure of political imagination'. *International Journal of Middle East Studies* 47(1): 144–7. doi:10.1017/S0020743814001512.

Zunes, Stephen, and Al-Haidary, Noor. 2015. 'Powerful nonviolent resistance to armed conflict in Yemen'. *Open Democracy*, 11 April. Available at: www.opendemocracy.net/ civilresistance/stephen-zunes-noor-alhaidary/powerful-nonviolent-resistance-to-armed-conflict-in-yem

6

YUGOSLAVIA

From social movement to state movement to civil war

Daniel P. Ritter

Introduction

On 25 June 1991, Slovenia declared its independence from Yugoslavia. Although the conflict that immediately followed only lasted ten days, it set the country on the path to a decade of civil strife as it was followed by longer and bloodier conflicts in Croatia, Bosnia-Hercegovina, Kosovo, Serbia, and Macedonia. When the dust had finally settled, an estimated 140,000 people had been killed and four million were displaced (International Center for Transitional Justice 2009). While Yugoslavia's structural conditions arguably made it ripe for, or at least at risk of, civil war, it is nonetheless striking that the country went down the path of ethnic strife at the same time as the rest of Eastern Europe, for the most part, transitioned peacefully to democracy.

What is particularly interesting in the context of this book is the fact that civil society mobilization preceded the civil war in Yugoslavia. As elsewhere in socialist Europe, private citizens mobilized for social change, but in stark contrast to developments in places like Poland, East Germany, and Czechoslovakia, Yugoslavian social movements were unable to steer the nation's development in a peaceful direction. Instead, initiatives for peace, democracy, gay rights, and environmental protection gave way to workers' and nationalist movements that were easily co-opted by shrewd politicians, in particular Slobodan Milošević (Stokes 1993, 235).

In line with the rest of this book, this chapter seeks to understand why social movement mobilization was unable to guide Yugoslavia towards democratization, and instead contributed to the outbreak of civil war. To do so, we identify not only those mechanisms that explain movement weakness, but also those that explain how weak movements become radicalized and – in the course of that process – gateways to civil war. Drawing on the book's general framework, we pinpoint several causal mechanisms of relevance. In the Yugoslavian story, these include the economic deterioration that began as early as the late 1970s and the political destabilization resulting from Josip Broz Tito's death in 1980, the government's eventual activation of military networks in response to the fluidification of borders and the social fragmentation both contributing to and resulting from the country's militarization, as well as sectarian identification and spirals of revenge that emerged as a result of a combination of various structural factors.

The chapter begins with an overview of the historical context and the structural conditions within which nationalism emerged as a source of mass mobilization in the 1980s, including a struggling economy and a political vacuum. Here the emphasis is on what we call 'mechanisms at the onset'. The focus then shifts to the resulting movements. We identify the types of movements that emerged in this period and the social grievances that explain their emergence. Furthermore, we ask why these movements were unable to gather the type of independent momentum that similar movements managed to generate elsewhere in Eastern Europe and instead resulted in social fragmentation. The next section then describes and analyses the process of state-led movement radicalization that eventually helped set Yugoslavia on the path to civil war by challenging national borders and causing the deterioration of citizens' sense of security. Finally, we return to the onset and early stages of the civil war to connect social movements to civil war by briefly considering issues of sectarian identification, the activation of (para-)military networks, and spiralling revenge.

Setting the stage: Yugoslavia, Eastern Europe, and the Cold War

The Yugoslav transition to democracy is arguably the most complex of all Eastern European transitions from state socialism, and without doubt the most violent one. The country's roundabout path towards democratization is puzzling for several reasons. First, on the basis of what we know about democratization processes, it could be argued that Yugoslavia enjoyed the most favourable initial conditions of any country in the region, as the old regime was relatively liberal and was counterbalanced by an indigenous civil society. To make matters more complicated for the socialist government and more favourable for reform-minded activists, an economic crisis in the late 1970s pressured politicians towards reforms while the country's non-aligned status made it less vulnerable to either Western or Eastern influence (Woodward 1995, 1). Had these particular structural conditions been the full story, Yugoslavia might have been able to dissolve without the outbreak of the most violent war Europe has experienced since 1945. However, nationalism would soon make all other factors seem irrelevant.

Indeed, the story of Yugoslavia's bloody transition – or its entire history for that matter – cannot be told without due attention to ethnic and nationalist divisions. After World War II, the country was established – and imposed on the populace – as a federation of six republics and two autonomous provinces by the communists who had recently come to power.[1] Employed as a solution to old ethnic divides (in addition to all its other virtues), communism would eventually prove to be only glue capable of holding the federation together (Stokes 1993, 223). Once that ideological rationale was discredited in the 1980s, Yugoslavia began to collapse.

As has been the case with other new nations elsewhere in the world, one of the most important shortcomings of Yugoslavia's construction was the fact that the geographical borders of its eight member republics did not correspond particularly well with the nationalities of its respective citizens. In time, nationalism would come to trump all other objectives, including the desire for democratization. Valerie Bunce has pointed out that to make matters worse – and unlike the state of affairs in some of the other federal states in Eastern Europe, including Czechoslovakia and the Soviet Union – the federal centre of Yugoslavia was inherently weak, consisting of little more than the Yugoslav National (or People's) Army (JNA). Thus, while it was officially a federation, Bunce goes as far as to call Yugoslavia a 'confederation': unlike the Czechoslovak and Soviet 'actual' federations, which were 'characterized by the existence of shared power based on territorial-administrative divisions', Yugoslavia distinguished itself by 'the domination of the republics over the center' (Bunce 1999, 111). Despite his best efforts, Tito had only managed to bring the six republics together by allowing each of them significant autonomy in a highly decentralized federal structure. For instance, each republic was, following the Soviet Union and the Warsaw Pact's invasion of Czechoslovakia in 1968, allowed its own territorial defence force. Similarly, the Yugoslav market, including its banking system, was segmented along republican lines (ibid., 111). The weakness of Yugoslavia's centre could have been mitigated by Soviet influence, but Tito's break with Stalin in 1948 absolved republican leaders of the overpowering presence of Moscow, causing politicians in the republics to be less intimidated by the federal centre, especially after Tito's death in 1980 (Schaeffer 2000, 49).

In addition to the weaknesses emanating from the structure of the Yugoslavian federation, it is important to note, not least in the context of nationalism and civil wars, that some of the constituent republics were historical enemies. In particular, there was little love lost between the Catholic Croats and the Orthodox Serbs, and during World War II the Ustasha (a Croatian fascist group) fought with the Axis powers against the Serbian Chetniks (Cigar 1993, 299–300). After the war, Tito's solution to the lasting animosities and the horrendous collective memories was to forbid any discussion of what had happened (Pavković 2000, 105–6). While in the short run this allowed Yugoslavia to unite under a common socialist banner, these suppressed memories would re-emerge in the 1980s when socialism had played out its unifying role. At that point there would be few structures in place that could prevent ingrained and repressed nationalist grievances from rising to the surface (Mirkovic 2000). In the explosive context surrounding the end of the Cold War, it is then perhaps little wonder that democratization and other political projects took a back seat to more primordial preoccupations, such as national survival and revenge. In short, Yugoslavia's history had to be resolved before democratization could commence, and the different republics found diverging ways of settling the record.

It is important to note that due to its particular Cold War history, Yugoslavia was a different socialist beast from many of its Eastern European neighbours. In contrast to the Soviet satellite states, Yugoslavia was a relatively liberal country enjoying good relations with the West. By the mid-1980s, the country resembled Hungary in the sense that the political elites in the various republics had begun to lose faith in the communist ideology (Vladisavljević 2008, 47–8). Consequently, its citizens could for the most part travel freely, and opposition groups, particularly in Serbia and Slovenia, enjoyed considerable freedom to voice their opinions, as long as they stayed away from the most sensitive political issues (Stokes 1993, 224–5).

To further emphasize the complex nature of the Yugoslav situation, one scholar points out that on 'the eve of the 1989 revolutions in eastern and central Europe, Yugoslavia was better poised than any other socialist country to make a successful transition to a market economy and the west' (Woodward 1995, 1). Still, Yugoslavia took longer to complete the process and was the only country in the region to go through a civil war. As Stokes (1993, 218) points out,

> Yugoslavia had neither a velvet revolution nor a velvet divorce. Midway through 1991 two of its six constituent republics, Slovenia and Croatia, declared their independence, provoking a vicious civil war that spread in 1992 to Bosnia and Herzegovina. Ethnic emotions run deep throughout Eastern Europe, but nowhere did they reach the level of bestiality as they did in Yugoslavia.

The reason Yugoslavia dissolved by way of civil war, we suggest, is that unlike in other Eastern European countries, nationalism, not democratization, became the most salient political project. This was partly because the lack of democracy was considered less of a problem in Yugoslavia than elsewhere, since political pluralism had already been introduced from above in some of the republics (ibid., 237–8). It is true that nationalism was a factor in some of the other Eastern European transitions as well, including in Czechoslovakia and East Germany, but nowhere else did it have such devastating consequences as it did in Yugoslavia, nor did it derail those countries' democratization efforts. Ironically, then, Yugoslavia's advantageous starting point, seen from a democratization perspective, turned out to be a disadvantage when republican political leaders sought to promote their own political careers by exploiting nationalist concerns and their associated discourses (Pavković 2000, 86).

The historical and structural roots of nationalism: political and economic destabilization

In order to understand the context in which democratizing social movements were replaced by workers' and nationalist movements in the late 1980s and led to severe ethnic conflict, it is necessary to consider Yugoslavia's history. Unlike most Eastern

European countries that cropped up after World War II, the creation of Yugoslavia as a communist state was not the result of Soviet intervention. Rather, socialist Yugoslavia emerged out of the armed struggle waged by the Communist Party of Yugoslavia (CPY) against regional fascist forces that supported the Axis powers during the war. The communists, led by Tito, were able to assert control over what was at the time known as the Kingdom of Yugoslavia, and by 1945 they had succeeded in eliminating the existing multi-party system. In January of 1946, King Peter II was removed from power as the new rulers rewrote the Constitution and changed the country's name to the Socialist Federal Republic of Yugoslavia (SFRY). Composed of six republics (Croatia, Slovenia, Serbia, Bosnia and Herzegovina, Macedonia, and Montenegro) and two autonomous provinces (Vojvodina and Kosovo, both part of Serbia), the new Yugoslavia afforded its member republics significant freedoms and autonomy in a decentralized system that would become even more devolved following the adoption of the Constitution of 1974 (Bunce 1999, 111; Gibianskii 2006, 18).

While initially aligned with Stalin's Soviet Union, the relationship between the two countries collapsed as early as 1948, with Moscow repeatedly accusing Tito of not being staunch enough in his support of the USSR. More specifically, the disagreement centred on Stalin's fear that Tito was trying to establish a Balkan version of the Soviet Union that would constitute a rival communist epicentre in Europe. However, the Kremlin never punished Yugoslavia militarily the way it dealt with East German, Hungarian, and Czechoslovakian dissent. Instead, Yugoslavia was allowed to simply sever relations with the USSR, ties that were later repaired and restored to normality when Yugoslavia joined the group of non-aligned states (Perovic 2007).

Why did Stalin not try to bring the fellow socialist state into the Soviet sphere? Following World War II, at Yalta, Churchill and Stalin had agreed that influence over Yugoslavia should be shared between the East and the West (Licht 2000, 118), and invading obstinate Yugoslavia would therefore come at a much higher price than the invasions carried out in other Eastern European states. Yugoslavia's strained relationship with the Soviet Union did, however, result in Western compensation, as the American and various European governments began to provide Yugoslavia with economic aid in the late 1940s. In the 1950s alone, the United States government provided Yugoslavia with $2.7 billion in non-repayable economic and military aid as part of its policy to assist non-Soviet-aligned dictatorships in Europe. This 'generosity' allowed the Yugoslav economy to grow rapidly, and gave Tito a smoother domestic ride in the early years of his rule (Schaeffer 2000, 49).

Helped by Western economic support, the Yugoslav government sought to develop its own version of a socialist economic system that incorporated some aspects of the capitalist market system. Private businesses were permitted as long as they employed no more than four people, but the state ran all of the major businesses, albeit in a less centralized manner than elsewhere in Eastern Europe. The 'self-management' system meant that workers were in control of their factories and workplaces, and in each factory the workers elected their management through a one-worker-one-vote arrangement. For a while, this system benefited the country greatly, with the economy growing at high rates and with low levels of unemployment (Estrin 1991; Schaeffer 2000, 49; Woodward 1995). However, inefficient use of foreign aid meant that although workers received relatively high salaries in comparison to their Eastern European counterparts, the rate of economic growth slowed down in the 1970s. The subsequent economic downturn was exacerbated by the global economic crisis that occurred around the same time, and when the second oil crisis hit the world in 1979, just a year before Tito's death, 'the Yugoslav miracle' was officially over (Stokes 1993, 229).

The reason the global economic crisis only became problematic for Yugoslavia in the late 1970s was that, like other nations in the region and in Latin America, Yugoslavia had increased its borrowing from the West in order to compensate for lost revenues. As a result, between 1971 and 1975, the country's debt doubled from $2.7 billion to $5.8 billion, reaching a debilitating $20.5 billion in 1981. Lenders now demanded that Yugoslav leaders make tough decisions, including the imposition of structural adjustment policies and various austerity programmes (Schaeffer 2000, 51; Stokes 1993, 229–30). While this eventually helped Yugoslavia stabilize its economy, it came at a terrible political price as workers lost their jobs and consumer prices rose. Before the unpopular economic policies of Ante Marković (Yugoslavia's last prime minister) began to pay off in 1990, the declining economic situation had already led to widespread discontent and worker mobilization in demand of change; mobilization that would eventually stoke the flames of civil war (Stokes 1993, 238–41).

Unfortunately, Yugoslavia's economic problems were not limited to its foreign debt. As a federation, the country consisted of economically diverse republics. The most prosperous ones, Slovenia and Croatia, enjoyed relatively large influxes of foreign capital, due mainly to tourism. While each republic had some autonomy in how it spent the money it generated, much of it was redistributed across the federation. This meant that the richer states contributed disproportionally to the development of the less wealthy parts of Yugoslavia, such as Kosovo and Macedonia. This issue forced the introduction of a new constitution in 1974, and in some way opened the door for the eventual dissolution of the country (Hayden 1992). The new Constitution further decentralized Yugoslavia in a somewhat desperate attempt by the federal elite to keep their political project viable. However, none of the most important republics was happy with the new constitution. Croatia and Slovenia felt that the decentralization efforts did not go far enough, while Serbia, conversely, had hoped to prevent the fragmentation of a federal system in which it was the central power (Stokes 1993, 228).

By the mid-1980s, Yugoslavia's economic system – often referred to as Titoism – was on the verge of collapse, and nationalism was on the rise throughout the federation (Vasilevski 2007, 5). But while all republics suffered economically, the federal composition of the country meant that no republican leader had to assume responsibility for the crisis. This was decidedly different from the rest of Eastern Europe, where the state and the party were indivisible. In the spirit of state socialism elsewhere, Yugoslavia's complex arrangement included a national party, the League of Communists of Yugoslavia (LCY), but also autonomous communist leagues in each of the republics. This had two important consequences. First, the LCY had no meaningful constituency other than its army (JNA). Second, each republic's communist leaders could blame the federal centre for the country's economic problems. Hence, when the economic crisis began to severely affect the country's citizens in the mid-1980s, each republic's party leadership, in an attempt to maintain power and legitimacy, blamed the other republics and the federal centre for the nation's misfortunes (Licht 2000). Not only was this expedient in terms of warding off criticism, but it also resonated well with the burgeoning nationalist movements that were emerging throughout Yugoslavia, especially among Kosovo Serbs and Slovenes.

The economic crisis encouraged communist politicians to refashion themselves as socialist nationalists. Such moves had the potential of saving individual political careers, but they also spelled disaster for the country at large. Evidence of how detrimental this turn of events was for the country is represented by the fact that although Marković's austerity policies largely repaired the Yugoslav economy and managed to persuade foreign investors to return to the country in 1990 and 1991, the republican leaderships by and large refused to execute his economic policies (Glenny 1993, 88). Rather than saving the economy by introducing unpopular reforms, republican leaders jumped on their respective nationalist bandwagons and condemned both the federal leadership and their greedy neighbours (Stokes 1993, 238–41). Virtually overnight, most communist leaders became socialists and distanced themselves from both communist ideology and the single-party system.

While domestic structural factors loom large, the importance of Yugoslavia's international context must also be considered when contemplating the path to civil war. Unlike most Eastern European socialist states, Yugoslavia enjoyed good relations with the West. In addition to resulting in relative economic prosperity, Western relations also seem to have had a liberalizing effect on Yugoslavia as a whole, especially in Slovenia and Serbia. One consequence of Slovenia's proximity to Western Europe was that already in the 1970s Slovenian dissidents enjoyed significant freedoms.

> [W]hen Tito died Slovenia boasted perhaps the most independently minded intelligentsia in Yugoslavia. By the mid-1980s its capital city Ljubljana could boast of an influential student press, a strong group of intellectuals surrounding the avant-garde journal *Nova revija* (New Review), and the first stirrings of alternative movements of feminists, gays, peace activists, and environmentalists.
>
> *(ibid., 236)*

In short, by the end of the 1980s, Yugoslavia harboured two important preconditions for mass mobilization: a faltering economy and a relatively vibrant civil society. While these two preconditions can lead to peaceful protest movements, the added component of nationalism within a contested federal structure meant that civil war rather than democratization from below would eventually become the final outcome (della Porta 2014).

Because of the faltering economy and the fact that a burgeoning civil society already existed in both Slovenia and Serbia in the early 1980s, Yugoslavia was vulnerable to pressures from below. It therefore took relatively little to further destabilize the federal structure of the country, and in 1980 the country experienced an incident that would contribute to the end of the federation within just over a decade. Tito's death on 4 May shocked a country that had grown accustomed to its leader over his 35 years of rule. As the population mourned, Tito's political heirs struggled to keep the deceased strongman's project alive.

However, this was always going to be a difficult task because of the particularities of Yugoslav socialism. Whereas other Eastern European countries had accepted socialism as their sole political ideology, in Yugoslavia that acceptance was coupled with nationalism and the idea of the Yugoslav people. Historically, the different nations that made up the federation had considered themselves distinct from one another, and had often fought wars among themselves. After World War II, Tito managed to put old grudges to rest by authoritatively imposing Yugoslav nationalism upon the country through the proxy of socialism and by forbidding debates over past crimes conducted in the name of nations. This meant that that the two ideologies – nationalism and socialism – were intimately linked and maintained in large part by Tito himself (Banac 2006; Schöpflin 2006; Stokes 1993). As Stokes (1993, 223) explains:

> [T]he linkage of 'Yugoslav' and 'socialist' contained a critical weakness that Tito and his colleagues could never have imagined. As long as the Communist movement remained strong, Yugoslavism was not in danger. If nationalism reared its head the party could and did push it back under the surface. If the League of Communists of Yugoslavia should disintegrate, however, then the Yugoslavism it championed would disintegrate too.

For the federal government, the death of Tito represented the beginning of the disintegration of the LCY, as his passing coincided with the emergence of a new generation of party leaders in the various republics. The generational shift resulted in 'pragmatic relaxation of repressive practices' (Vladisavljević 2008, 47), as younger politicians were much less ready than their predecessors to clamp down on dissidents. Although the entire country experienced an easing of government control, it was particularly salient in Serbia and Slovenia. In these two republics, the new generation of politicians 'tolerated both cultural and political dissent and engaged in informal alliances with protest groups and dissident intellectuals in the second half of the 1980s' (ibid., 48), which naturally emboldened activists and resulted in a reinvigorated civil society.

The main problem now faced by the Yugoslav government was that political power had come to reside in Tito personally. This had long been to the advantage of the Party, but after his death, no politician emerged who could fill his shoes. In office, Tito had been able to manage republican divisions by decentralizing the federation and providing citizens with West-like freedoms, knowing that his personal control over the army and his status as a national hero would prevent republican leaders from opposing the system he had built (ibid., 47–8). However, this 'solution' experienced major systemic problems once Tito was gone. As long as its leader was strong, it mattered relatively little that the state itself was weak. However, without Tito's personal strength, the weakness of the state became evident, and republican politicians were quick to notice.

Tito's death had a tremendous impact on all segments of society, including the federal and republican elites. However, his passing affected these two groups in radically different ways. While federal leaders struggled against pent-up popular frustration over Yugoslavia's economic performance, republican elites enjoyed real independence for the first time in decades. Following Tito's death, the latter sought to exploit the country's federal arrangement and limit the central leadership's power. One way of doing this was through their unprecedented efforts to block economic and political reforms. In December 1987, the Federal Assembly failed, for the first time in the country's history, to pass the budget for the following year. In Tito's lifetime, such heresy would have been inconceivable, but by the mid-1980s the old guard of Tito supporters was rapidly aging and was being replaced by younger career politicians unwedded to the ideological values and the historical legacy of the Party. Not personally linked to Tito, they had no intention of relinquishing power because of economic mistakes committed in the misguided name of socialism (ibid., 126). Thus,

> [B]y 1988 the great majority of Tito's chosen coterie of republics' leaders had been replaced with leaders who had no common loyalties . . . [and] both the Yugoslav federation and the Yugoslav Communist party – the League of Communists – which nominally ruled the country had lost much of their legitimacy.
>
> *(Pavković 2000, 76)*

Unlike their predecessors, the new republican elites now in charge had little incentive to cooperate with one another in a moment of crisis. Consequently, divisions – political, ideological, and generational – grew rapidly (Vladisavljević 2008, 126). By the early 1990s, it had become clear that political elites throughout Yugoslavia had abandoned Tito's socialist approach and had begun to flirt with nationalism as a way of saving their own power (Licht 2000, 113). Simply abandoning the old ideology was not sufficient, as strong currents were brewing throughout the country – the strongest of which was nationalism. Shrewd (or perhaps desperate) politicians capitalized on what they may have perceived as their last chance to cling to power by embracing populist calls and desires in virtually all of the republics. As will become clear in the following sections, nationalist movements had been building at least since 1981, but the Kosovo Serb mobilization in the mid-1980s would play the most important role in Yugoslavia's descent into civil war.

In sum, disparate nationalisms festered in Yugoslavia from the mid-1980s on. While ambitious politicians initially intended for this to be a strategy for achieving increased republican autonomy, the powers set free by these populists could not easily be reined in. A Pandora's box had been opened, and nationalism could not simply be put back inside. One of the many victims of this development was Yugoslavia's civil society, to which we now turn our attention.

Social fragmentation and the failure of civil society

Prior to the late 1980s, Yugoslavia's more participatory political arrangements and its tradition of labour organizing had created a social context in which civic associations were perceived to be less threatening than elsewhere within the socialist sphere (Figa 1997, 168). Nonetheless, human rights and democratization groups would have less of an impact here than, for example, in Czechoslovakia and East Germany, and the same goes for peace and environmental groups. A possible explanation for this might be that simply by virtue of being tolerated, these liberal elements of civil society were less effective. Since freedom of expression was respected to a greater degree than elsewhere in Eastern Europe, calls for democracy and human rights were less salient to the general population, and the associated groups therefore generated less sympathy (Vasilevski 2007, 17). Instead, the groups that were able to mobilize the largest number of protestors were nationalist and workers' groups, and, to a lesser extent, students. As this section demonstrates, the relatively advantageous position of civil society in Yugoslavia failed to generate a pro-democracy challenge to the state, both on the federal and the republican levels, and was quickly marginalized by workers and nationalists, thus contributing to social fragmentation.

This does not mean that civil society groups were unimportant, but their relative weakness contributed to steering Yugoslavia in the direction of ethnic strife and civil war rather than towards democratization. While civil society groups only entered national politics in full force in the 1980s, scholars have dated the beginning of their mobilization to the early 1960s, or at the very latest to 1966–68 when students occupied the University of Belgrade (Licht 2000, 119–20). As in other Eastern European countries, some of the earliest civil society mobilization included calls for democratization and human rights.

The democratization/human rights movement

The early 1970s represented a fairly repressive time in the history of Yugoslavia. When Croatian communists began to speak of secession and were charged by their Serbian counterparts with wanting to destroy the federation, Tito responded with purges. In the aftermath of these destabilizing events, the country witnessed numerous political trials, with many of the defendants receiving prison sentences.

By the mid-1970s, leading dissidents began to ask difficult questions about 'the very nature of the regime' and demanded a change in the direction of 'pluralism and toward a genuine respect for human rights' (Licht 2000, 120). Rather unsurprisingly, these criticisms coincided with the signing of the Helsinki Accords in 1975. In the aftermath of Helsinki, a petition movement emerged in Belgrade in 1976–77 (ibid., 120). The movement was limited, with each petition only attracting between 50 and 300 signatures, but it 'opened up a new stage, which was taken over in debates by the Slovenians on such issues as reproductive rights, gay and lesbian rights, and nuclear energy' (ibid., 120).

The human rights movement then largely disappeared from the Yugoslavian political scene. Whereas activists elsewhere in Eastern Europe clung tightly to the human rights rhetoric as their most potent line of attack on their governments (Ritter 2012a; 2012b), Yugoslav activists appear to have gained little traction from it. There could of course be many reasons for this, but a plausible explanation would suggest that human rights simply was not a salient issue in Yugoslavia. As noted above, the country was the most open socialist state in Europe and enjoyed close ties with the West. As a result, the human rights angle was not successful in terms of generating mass mobilization in Yugoslavia.

It would in fact take another ten years before the democratization/human rights rhetoric re-emerged. Only in 1988, when the rest of Eastern Europe was already on the move, did activist form 'an organization for Yugoslav democratic initiative' with branches throughout the country (Licht 2000, 121). From a theoretical perspective, this is somewhat puzzling: Why did the country that seemed best prepared to take steps toward democratization in the mid-1980s lag behind the more repressive Soviet satellite states? In Poland, Czechoslovakia, and East Germany, activists had been mobilizing continuously since the mid-1970s (Ritter 2012a; 2012b). In addition to the explanation offered above – that Yugoslavia was sufficiently liberal to dissuade a popular uprising in favour of liberal democracy – it seems that the nationalist currents overshadowed demands for democracy and human rights.

There existed, however, one major exception to the general absence of pro-democracy movements in Yugoslavia. In Slovenia, the Committee for the Defense of Human Rights teamed up with the Slovene communists (including its media outlets) and the Catholic Church in 1988 to organize a campaign of protests in defence of the 'Ljubljana Four', a group of journalists who had angered the Yugoslav army by raising questions about its arms sales to Ethiopia. While fought in the name of human rights and judicial fairness in a democratic context, the fact that all Slovenian power holders united behind this campaign betrays its nationalist element. In fact, the movement was a part of a Slovenian strategy for controlling Milošević (Pavković 2000, 109–10).

Unlike much of the rest of Eastern Europe, Yugoslavia's most important pro-democracy movements did not take place until the end of the 1990s and early 2000s. In both Croatia and Serbia, mass mobilization coincided with elections. Supported by Western funders, civil society groups generated massive efforts to get out the vote and to monitor the elections. Whereas in Croatia the democratic opposition was able to rely solely on the elections themselves in order to oust the ruling HDZ, in Serbia mass demonstrations and a general strike were required to end Milošević's rule (Boduszyński 2010; Bunce and Wolchik 2011).

New social movements and student mobilization

What scholars refer to as 'new social movements' (NSMs) flourished in Yugoslavia in the 1980s, particularly in Slovenia and Serbia. The fact that the new ruling elites took a less repressive approach to social control meant that 'non-political' activism was tolerated and at times even supported by official socialist institutions. Civil society mobilization emerged in Slovenia from the culturally driven alternative scene, which in turn grew out of the 1970s punk movement (Figa 1997, 164). As Figa explains,

> [New social movements] addressed issues not faced by the political establishment. They posed a dilemma for the rulers: By permitting NSMs to operate, the party-state allowed them to expand into the space for free expression, thereby giving up control over certain social and political processes, even though the party-state at any time could lay claim to that space if they were prepared to use violence . . . Yugoslavia in general, and Slovenia in particular, were very proud of their progressive and democratic nature vis-à-vis the USSR and its allies. An antidemocratic purge would be embarrassing when Soviet totalitarianism was on the verge of collapse.
>
> *(ibid., 168)*

Slovenian communists knew that the destabilizing potential of NSMs was indeed very real, but by exercising self-restraint and staying away from politically taboo topics Slovenian activists were able to mobilize on a range of issues that were 'rooted in postmodern concerns and included opposition to using violence in any form of human interaction, peace, minority rights, environmental issues, alternative forms of psychotherapy, and gay rights' (ibid., 168–9). It is worth noting that NSM activists not only exercised self-restraint when it came to which issues they addressed, but they also opted for nonviolent methods of struggle (ibid., 169) – tactics radically different from those that would later be used throughout Yugoslavia in the 1990s.

The peace movement was perhaps the most important of Slovenian NSMs. Not because it forced Slovenia to pursue progressive policies – it did not – but because it drove Slovenian leaders onto a collision course with the rest of the federation. The main issue raised by the peace movement organization, which went by the name 'The Working Group for Peace Movements', was that of conscientious objection. Yugoslavia employed broad conscription rules, with the concept of conscientious objection being foreign to the JNA. Under pressure from its own citizens and in the context of Serbian hostility, the Slovenian government agreed to press for changes to the conscription rules on the federal level. As a result, relations between Slovenia, on the one hand, and Serbia and the federal govern-ment, on the other, soured. This development coincided with the 'Ljubljana Four' incident mentioned above, where journalists working for the Slovene publication *Mladina* claimed that the Yugoslav army was illegally selling arms to Ethiopia. In this conflict, the Slovene government, which might already have had its mind set on a divorce from the federation, took the side of the journalists, thus adding fur-ther fuel to the intra-communist conflict (ibid., 170).

Although the Slovenes were the first to organize on peace issues, they were not the only ones. In the mid-1980s, international peace activists helped local organizers in Serbia to form a group dedicated to peace and democracy. The 'Bel-grade Group for Peace and Democracy' was ultimately unable to attract a large membership, as many felt that the word 'democracy' made the group too political. Consequently, the group failed to have an impact comparable to that of its Slove-nian equivalent (Licht 2000, 121). As one Slovenian commentator rather ironically recollects:

> [It is] fascinating how the issues of peace and democracy were not on peo-ple's minds in other parts of the country, including Serbia. They were still impressed by the Yugoslav policy of non-alignment, and believed that the issue of war and peace was simply unimportant for Yugoslavia as a whole.
>
> *(ibid., 121)*

Obviously, war and peace would soon become central concepts in Yugoslavian politics.

Women's movements were perhaps the best organized manifestations of NSMs in Yugoslavia. Unlike most other groups, the women's movement organized itself across and beyond republican borders, and with significant cross-national coopera-tion. The main practical concern of the women's movement was the protection of victims of domestic violence and lobbying on women's reproductive health issues. Lesbian branches of the movement also struggled for equal recognition under the law (Benderly 1997, 186). The destructive developments in the late 1980s and early 1990s reduced the impact of the women's movement and marginalized it as 'more important things' filled the agenda, as women were now expected to be patriotic and have as many children as possible in order to help their respective nations win the war. Some of the structural changes did not help either, as non-communist arrangements following the dissolution of Yugoslavia created high unemployment that hit women particularly hard (ibid., 196–8). Thus, in the years leading up to the civil war, in a context of rising nationalism, 'a rift developed between those feminists who opposed nationalism and those who became more patriotic as they drew parallels between the victimization of women and the victimization of their nation' (ibid., 184).

Yugoslavia also hosted various environmental movements, but these played a limited role on the country's civil society scene. Nonetheless, green groups organized in both Serbia and Slovenia. In Slovenia, the movements' esteem rose in the second half of the 1980s in the wake of global environmental disasters (Figa 1997, 175). In Serbia, a major anti-nuclear energy movement came about in 1986 and 1987. In an impressive effort, the movement gathered hundreds of thousands of signatures, mainly from schools and universities, and actually succeeded in overturning a government decision to build a nuclear power plant (Licht 2000, 120–1).

Although students took some part in the 1980s social movements, they rarely organized independently of other civil society groups. Instead, the impact of student protest was most significant in the beginning of civil society mobilization in the late 1960s and early 1970s, mainly in Croatian protests against Tito and in favour of decentralization (ibid., 120; Rusinow 1977, 296–306). Also, students came to play an important role in the struggle against Milošević after the Dayton Accord had been signed, first in 1996–97, in response to stolen local elections, and then during the Bulldozer Revolution of 2000 when the student-led Otpor emerged as a powerful political player (Marković 2012, 112). While Otpor usually gets most of the credit in analyses of the Serbian case, Bunce and Wolchik (2011, 97) note 'the path-breaking effect' the 80-day student protests in 1996 and 1997 had on the country's political climate. In fact, Otpor grew out of the 1996–97 experience, as many Otpor activists and leaders participated in those earlier student protests (ibid., 100).

As the above makes clear, traditional civil society mobilization failed to have a significant impact on Yugoslavia at the end of the Cold War. However, other forms of mobilization efforts would prove to be more effective. These movements were organized around worker and nationalist demands, often with the two blending into a blue-brown rhetoric of discontent. The next section describes how the void created by the absence of a strong federal state in 1980s Yugoslavia was filled not by liberal civil society groups, but by 'mobilization from above', that is, movements initiated by workers and other social groups that were eventually hijacked by republican politicians, especially Slobodan Milošević. It is at this point that we begin to see the emergence of the type of social fragmentation that we posit figures prominently as an activating mechanism in movement-to-war moments.

Workers' and nationalist movements

Although other social groups also had legitimate grievances to air in the later stages of the Cold War, the Yugoslav workers found themselves in a unique situation. Yugoslavia was per definition a 'workers' state'. This meant that unlike other groups, workers were normally spared criticism from socialist politicians. Until the early 1980s, the working class was largely absent from the political stage, 'despite sharply deteriorating living standards' (Vladisavljević 2008, 111). Strikes and work stoppages did take place, but they did so on what was for the government manageable levels, usually lasting only for a few hours. By 1984, this state of affairs began to change as the number of strikes increased, and by 1987 the situation was spinning out of control. 'In that year', Vladisavljević reports,

There were 1685 registered strikes and roughly 4.3 percent of all employ-ees in the huge state-controlled sector of the economy took part in strikes as opposed to less than 1 percent in previous years. The workers' protests now lasted longer than a day on average and, significantly, the number of strikes in large state enterprises, with more than 500 workers, was sharply on the increase. Roughly half of the strikers came from heavy industries and mining, but strikes in other sectors of the economy, as well as in health services and education, became increasingly frequent. In 1988 the number of strikes and strikers further increased, especially in large enterprises, and strikes became longer on average.

(ibid., 111)

In the early 1980s, when strikes had been fairly limited, worker mobilization had been centred in Slovenia and Croatia, the most developed republics of the fed-eration. But by 1987 these regional differences had nearly completely vanished as workers throughout the country were voicing their discontent with the regime. Protests focused overwhelmingly on economic and workplace-related issues, with political change being a side matter (ibid., 111–12).

While the workers' privileged position within the socialist ideology gave them significant leverage in their protests against the state, it was the emerging national-ist movements that tore Yugoslavia asunder. As noted above, nationalism was not a new phenomenon in Yugoslavia in the 1980s. Although virtually all national groups were mobilized by the end of the decade,

The road to civil war began in March 1981 when Albanian students took their demands for better conditions at the University of Prishtinë to the streets in the time-honored tradition of students everywhere. Their demonstration touched a nerve of Albanian patriotic feeling, and over the next month anti-Serbian demonstrations demanding that Kosovo become a Yugoslav republic became so massive that the federal government sent in troops.

(Stokes 1993, 230)

Serbia, which was in control of the autonomous province of Kosovo, was under-standably not interested in the realization of these demands. Consequently, the movement did not result in much political gain for Kosovo Albanians, but it did contribute to a fragmenting social context in Kosovo. By the mid-1980s, the province's Serbian minority felt sufficiently harassed and discriminated against to demand change. The Kosovo Serb movement began in 1985 with a protest out-side the headquarters of the Kosovo Communist Party. Not receiving the remedy they had demanded, the movement submitted a petition with 2,011 signatures to the presidency of the Serbian Communist Party in early 1986, 'demanding radical measures to stop the continuing harassment of non-Albanians' (Pavković 2000, 83). From this point on, the movement quickly gathered momentum. Pro-test activities similar to the one staged in Belgrade took place in several cities throughout Kosovo and Serbia. Those responsible for organizing these protests came from variety of walks of life, but almost always from non-elite backgrounds, which gave the movement a grassroots feel (ibid., 83).

For politicians, nationalism became the surest path to avoid having to take responsibility for Yugoslavia's economic demise (Licht 2000, 116–17). The politician most talented in this blame game was the Secretary of the League of Communists of Serbia, Slobodan Milošević. Milošević rose to power precisely because of his support for the Serb minority in Kosovo (Popovic 2006, 51). From 1985, Kosovo Serbs had protested against what they perceived to be discrimination at the hands of Kosovo's Albanian majority. Discontented with the Albanian leadership of Serbia's autonomous province, the Kosovo Serbs sought protection from the federal government and from Serbia in particular. In what has been depicted as Milošević's crowning moment, the future dictator addressed a crowd of 15,000 Kosovo Serbs and Montenegrins in the night and early morning of 24 and 25 April 1987. While different accounts of the speech exist, Milošević is supposed to have told the crowd something along the following lines:

> The first thing that I wish to tell you, comrades, is that you must remain here. This is your land, your houses are here, your fields and gardens, your memories . . . It was never characteristic of the spirit of the Serb and Montenegrin people to knuckle under to difficulties, to demobilize itself when it must fight, to become demoralized when the going is tough. You must remain here on account of your ancestors and descendants. Otherwise, we would be shaming the ancestors and disillusioning the descendants.
>
> *(cited in Banac 1992, 176–7)*

In this moment of brilliant opportunism, Milošević turned nationalist complaints *against* Serbia into a political gain. He went from not having done enough to protect Kosovo's Serbian minority to becoming the protector of all Serbs and the most powerful politician in all of Yugoslavia. Once he had consolidated Serbian power, Milošević completed his renunciation of Tito's rule by permitting hitherto forbidden public criticism of the father of the nation. But Milošević did not focus his criticisms of Tito on the old dictator's undemocratic performance. Instead, Tito's most heinous crime was depicted as his preservation of the federalist structure, as well as the fact that he was a Croat. From his position of immense power, Milošević employed the full capacity of Serbia's media, educational, and cultural establishments, as well as its armed forces, 'in the service of Serbian national homogenization and supremacy' (ibid., 178). Put differently, Milošević unleashed and appropriated nationalism. At the same time, other more benign currents within civil society were quickly marginalized to make way for the expedited protection of Serbs throughout Yugoslavia.

Although Milošević was certainly the most radical nationalist leader to emerge in Yugoslavia in the 1980s, he was by no means the only one. In Slovenia, the most liberal republic and the place where civil society had made the biggest inroads, political leaders abandoned socialism in the late 1980s and early 1990s. As their fear of Milošević grew, the Slovenian socialists exploited the situation, hijacked the nationalist agenda of the opposition, and transformed themselves into the Party of Democratic Renewal. The new party tilted towards Europe but made sure to depict itself as 'a national party of all Slovenes' that would not rest until Slovenia had secured its status as a sovereign state within a confederal Yugoslavia. While Slovenian opposition politicians complained that the socialists trespassed on their political ground, this development indicated the manner in which nationalist concerns assumed vastly different shapes in Serbia and Slovenia (Pavković 2000, 110–11).

In Croatia, counter-elites – in particular discredited former Party members – came to dominate the nationalist movement. In Tito's days, the Croatian ex-communists now in charge had belonged to the anti-nationalist wing of the Party and had been put in control of Croatia after Tito purged its nationalist faction in 1971. The memory of this ordeal had turned Croatia into a more repressive place than Serbia and Slovenia as far as dissidents were concerned. The ruling elite tried its best to contain its new nationalists, who were led by a former communist by the name of Franjo Tuđman. However, threatened by Milošević's nationalist rhetoric, the communists-turned-socialists 'found in late 1988 new tolerance for nationalist dissidents' (ibid., 112). By 1989, Tuđman had founded Croatia's first opposition party, the Croatian Democratic Union (HDZ). Once the socialist party had undergone a transformation similar to that of their Slovenian counterparts in the early months of 1990, the HDZ came to power later that year in Croatia's first elections (ibid., 113).

With Slobodan Milošević's rise to power the Serbian nationalist movement gained a powerful supporter. While one should not overlook Milošević's substantial political calculations, there can be little doubt that the Serbian leader felt strongly about the nationalist issue. Like many Serbs, Milošević had no intention of seeing Serbia (or Yugoslavia for that matter) be divided into smaller pieces simply because Kosovo Albanians thought they deserved republican status and sovereignty over a territory in which they were the majority. For Serbs, Kosovo carries strong historical weight since it was there that the Serbs had lost a major battle to the Ottomans in 1389, and Kosovar sovereignty was therefore inconceivable to men like Milošević (Bunce 1999, 116).

Unfortunately, the tensions between Serbs and Albanians quickly reverberated across Yugoslavia as other republican leaders saw Milošević as an advocate of a 'Greater Serbia', a historical concept that had only been repressed by the creation of Yugoslavia (Cigar 1993, 301–2). Consequently, nationalists throughout the federation came to seize on the notion of sovereignty. Pavković explains:

> One of the primary aims of each of the dissident national ideologies was to reaffirm the sovereignty of 'its' nation over the territory that was claimed for it. The Croat and Slovene national ideologues saw the reaffirmation of sovereignty necessitating the creation of national armed forces within a new

Yugoslav confederation or outside Yugoslavia. The reaffirmation of the sovereignty of the Muslims was to be carried out first through the reintroduction of Islamic values in public life and politics and eventually in the creation of an Islamic state. Albanian sovereignty was to be achieved first in a separate Yugoslav republic and then, possibly, in unification with Albania. Serb sovereignty was to be reaffirmed in the unification of all Serbs in a reorganized 'democratic integrative' Yugoslav federation; if this proved to be impossible, in a Serb state without other Yugoslav nations.

(2000, 97)

Needless to say, the simultaneous realization of all of these aspirations was virtually impossible. As a result, society began to fragment, a development that eventually contributed to the causal mechanism we call 'sectarian identification' (see below). At the core of the matter was the issue that some republics wanted more decentralization, or even independence, while Serbia, the heart of Yugoslavia, was not interested in such a development. In a context in which socialism had come into disrepute as an economic and political ideology, few actors had the power, or desire, to stand in the way of the strong nationalist currents that swept the country. As one scholar summarizes the situation, 'nationalism became a dominant political force largely as an unintended outcome of high levels of mobilization and spiralling social, economic and political conflicts in a complex, authoritarian multi-national state which experienced a severe economic crisis' (Vladisavljević 2008, 6). The fact that republican leaders sought to gain personally from the nationalist tendencies within Yugoslavia did little to prevent their repercussions.

Milošević's 'anti-bureaucratic revolution': fluidification of borders and security deterioration

As the preceding sections have demonstrated, civil society groups engaged in limited protest activities throughout Yugoslavia in the 1980s. Prior to that, students had protested in the late 1960s, with mass mobilization taking place in Croatia in 1971–72 after communist leaders there began a campaign to register people (ethnic Croats) in the Party in an attempt to advance nationalist interests. That nationalist movement, which employed strikes and demonstrations, including student strikes, set a troubling precedent for Yugoslavia that would eventually become the norm for mass action in the 1980s: nationalist mobilization (Pavković 2000, 67–9). Similarly, the workers' protests that gathered momentum in 1982 were not part of a democratization movement, but only demanded pay increases and the removal of unpopular managers and directors. In short, what was under attack was not Yugoslavia's political system, but simply its economic shortcomings. By 1987, the strikes had reached enormous proportions, involving 360,000 workers spread out over 1,570 strikes, four times as many participants as in 1985. Consistent with their efforts earlier in the decade, the workers protested against income freezes and the rapidly increasing inflation (ibid., 78).

In the summer of 1988, industrial worker protests reached their crescendo. Vladisavljević (2008, 113–15) lists some of the major protest events, including the following:

- *May 24*: 300 out of 400 miners at the Đurđevik mine in northeast Bosnia marched on Belgrade after a five-day strike failed to have an impact. Having completed the 70-km march, the miners demonstrated in Belgrade until the federal authorities agreed to meet their demands. This particular action was part of a series of miners' protests in response to their deteriorating economic situation.
- *June 17*: 3,000 metalworkers from the Zmaj tractor factory outside Belgrade marched into the capital and demonstrated outside the Federal Assembly building, successfully securing higher wages. Similar protest took place in Maribor, Slovenia, where thousands of TAM (car manufacturer) workers demonstrated for higher wages on that day and the next.
- *July 6*: 5,000 workers from the Croatian Borovo shoe factory near the Serbian border went on strike. When their action failed to have the intended effect, they travelled by bus to Belgrade to express their concerns there. When the Federal Assembly refused to meet with them, the workers forced their way into the parliament building and left only after their demands had been met.
- *July 16*: 1,500 workers from Agrokomerc, a Bosnian agricultural company, staged a protest in Belgrade for higher wages and the resolution of a 1987 scandal involving the company.

Parallel to these developments in the workers' movements, Kosovo Serbs continued to mobilize for their cause by staging large demonstrations in Vojvodina and Montenegro in July and August 1988. It would perhaps have been natural for the Serbian leadership to view these protests as a potential risk and threat to its own position, but rather than perceiving mass mobilization within Serbia (which is where most of the worker and nationalist protests took place) as such, Milošević saw it as an opportunity. He had already achieved the status of a hero with the Kosovo Serbs, and when he skilfully incorporated the workers movement into a common framework – 'the anti-bureaucratic revolution' – Milošević suddenly had a 'powerful tool' at his disposal: mass rallies (Stokes 1993, 235). Similarly to Khomeini's Islamic Revolution in Iran, the genius of the 'anti-bureaucratic revolution' was that it came to mean all things to all people as it placed the blame for Yugoslavia's decline and internal difficulties on faceless bureaucrats. Stokes (ibid., 235) has beautifully captured the irony of this top-down mass movement:

> In the rest of Eastern Europe people power, as it was called after huge popular demonstrations brought Corazon Aquino to power in the Philippines in 1986, was a force for democracy and pluralism. In Serbia, however, Milošević mobilized people power to destroy Yugoslavia and to create the

conditions for civil war. In September and October 1988 thirty thousand, fifty thousand, one hundred thousand, even one million people gathered in Serbian cities to shout their approval of Milošević's effort to subdue Kosovo. When Albanians tried rallies of their own or conducted strikes in the important mining industry, as they did in November 1988, Milošević sent in the riot police and arrested their leaders . . . In the rest of Eastern Europe people power toppled the old Communist regimes in the name of democracy. In Serbia, Milošević manipulated the same force by racist appeals in order to legitimate his transformation of the League of Communists of Serbia into a nationalist party organized on neo-Stalinist principles.

Under the broad 'anti-bureaucratic' umbrella, Milošević mobilized the people of 'Greater Serbia' in an attempt to bring both Vojvodina and Kosovo back under direct Serbian control. The 'anti-bureaucratic revolution' raged between the fall of 1988 and the spring of 1989. Overlapping with this state-organized movement, Kosovo Albanians mobilized for their cause, while others protested against the brewing conflict between Serbia and Slovenia (Vladisavljević 2008, 145). In this contentious context, Milošević had little trouble making his nationalist populism attractive to many Serbs. Uniquely among Eastern European leaders, Milošević relied on what Pavković (2000, 106–7) refers to as a 'rally fever' – known locally as the 'happening of the people' or 'street democracy' – to mobilize the masses. And he did so to great effect. From September 1988 to March 1989, eastern Yugoslavia experienced extraordinary levels of mobilization for an authoritarian country. Protestors employed a wide variety of tactics and strategies, including public meetings, street rallies, strikes, and marches (Vladisavljević 2008, 145).

Thus, at the same time as people throughout the rest of Eastern Europe were mobilizing to abandon state socialism for liberal democracy, Yugoslavia was mobilizing for nationalism. In fact, 'the level of parallel mobilization of ordinary people in Yugoslavia . . . surpassed those in most other East European states, if judged by the numbers of participants, the variety of groups involved and the temporal and geographical extension of mobilization' (ibid., 2). Even when Milošević did not himself attend the protest events, he encouraged them. By September 1988 – again, in a fashion that at the time was almost unique by authoritarian standards – government officials were *de facto* endorsing selected protest groups and their demands, thereby giving the demonstrations an air of legitimacy; they even paid bands of young men to travel around Serbia, Kosovo, and Vojvodina to demonstrate (Glenny 1993, 34). In other words, 'they openly embraced popular participation in politics, albeit on populist terms' (Vladisavljević 2008, 150). Consequently, the national trend of socialist elites unwilling to defend the old Titoist/federal structure of Yugoslavia reached its pinnacle in Serbia. There, the late Tito would not only no longer be defended, he would be thrown to the wolves (Pavković 2000, 105–6).

The anti-bureaucratic revolution went through distinct regional phases. As Table 6.1 indicates, large protests occurred in Vojvodina, Serbia, and Montenegro.

TABLE 6.1 Major 'rallies of support' during the 'anti-bureaucratic revolution'

Location	Date	Number of participants
Smederevo, Vojvodina	3 Sept. 1988	60,000
Kovin, Vojvodina	3 Sept. 1988	10,000
Sombor, Vojvodina	3 Sept. 1988	2,000
Crevanka, Vojvodina	3 Sept. 1988	10,000 (first 'multi-national' rally)
Sremska Mitrovica, Vojvodina	15 Sept. 1988	30,000 (government-organized, including counter-protest)
Nikšić, Montenegro	18 Sept. 1988	50,000 (more radical, 'we want arms)
Cetinje, Montenegro	18 Sept. 1988	30,000 (more radical, 'let's go to Kosovo')
Novi Sad, Vojvodina	25 Sept. 1988	50,000 (demands for the resignation of the Vojvodina leadership)
Andrijevica, Montenegro	25 Sept. 1988	30,000
Bačka Palanka, Novi Sad	5 Oct. 1988	50,000 (demands for the resignation of the Vojvodina leadership) in support of the mayor who made the demand
Rakovica (outside Belgrade)	4 Oct. 1988	5,000 (at the Federal Assembly in Belgrade)Milošević came to speak to demonstrators
Rakovica (outside Belgrade)	5 Oct. 1988	5,000 (inside Federal Assembly in Belgrade)Milošević came to speak to demonstrators
Novi Sad	6 Oct. 1988	100,000 (from all over Vojvodina)
Titograd, Montenegro	7 Oct. 1988	25,000 (economic and education demands)Broken up violently the next day, fizzled out by the 10th
Belgrade	10 Oct. 1988	700,000 (archetypal 'rally of solidarity')
Titograd	10 Jan. 1989	60,000
Titograd	11 Jan. 1989	100,000 (collapse of the Montenegro leadership)

Source: Vladisavljević 2008, 151–66.

What is particularly interesting is that virtually all protests followed the same pattern, namely that of demonstrations, or 'rallies of solidarity' in support of the Kosovo Serbs, thus lending credence to the idea that the 'anti-bureaucratic' was little more than a vague but effective rhetorical device.

Somewhat surprisingly, the most important protests of the anti-bureaucratic revolution did not take place in Serbia. Here, the plight of the Kosovo Serbs needed little agitation to gain the attention of politicians and citizens alike. In Vojvodina and Montenegro, on the other hand, both places where large numbers of Serbs lived, local elites were less enthusiastic about the movement's demands. The protests in Novi Sad (the capital of Vojvodina) in July and August were crucial because they set the pace of the revolution. Not only did this represent a shift in the location of protests from central Serbia to the peripheral areas, but it came to signify a new phase of mobilization. As one scholar explains:

> The protest groups of Kosovo Serbs and their new allies from Vojvodina, Montenegro and central Serbia cast increasingly radical demands and targeted ever more powerful opponents. Unlike their earlier focus on protection for the Serbs by the courts and law enforcement agencies and the politics of inequality in Kosovo, they now principally demanded constitutional change in Serbia and a temporary shutting down of Kosovo's party and state organs. Instead of targeting Kosovo's high officials, they demanded the resignations of high officials of Vojvodina and their other opponents in the party Presidency and the Central Committee of the LCY, and denounced the leadership of Montenegro.
>
> *(Vladisavljević 2008, 139)*

Vojvodina and Montenegro elites feared that the Kosovo Serbs' demands for constitutional changes in Kosovo, which would bring the province back under Serbian control, would spill over and threaten their own autonomy. These fears were indeed well founded. Discontented with their own elites' economic leadership, citizens of Vojvodina joined the Kosovo Serbs' call for the Vojvodina leadership to step down. Initially, the local communists were able to resist the large protests, but their days in power were numbered. Eager to push through constitutional reforms, Milošević and his Serbian colleagues supported the protest movement by helping its leaders gain access to means of transportation and other material resources (ibid., 148).

By early October, the Vojvodina leadership could no longer withstand the popular calls for its resignation. On 6 October 1988, the province's capital, Novi Sad, came to a standstill. Approximately 100,000 people from all over Vojvodina, as well as activists from Serbia and Montenegro, arrived in Novi Sad to participate in what would become known as the 'Yoghurt Revolution'. Faced by demonstrators throwing packs of yoghurt at the Province Committee building, and without federal support, the Vojvodina high officials resigned and were replaced by leaders approved by Milošević and his entourage (ibid., 158).

With Vojvodina now in line with Serbia and Milošević, attention shifted to Montenegro. As in Vojvodina, solidarity rallies for the Kosovo Serbs soon assumed a life of their own, with Montenegrins sensing their opportunity to punish their leaders for the economic crisis. While Montenegro had witnessed ongoing protests since September, possibly with a short break in December, the final push to oust regional leaders began on 10 January. That morning, workers at Montenegro's largest company, Radoje Dakić, marched on the city centre demanding that the republic's leaders resign. They were soon joined in the central square by students and other concerned citizens. Withstanding the cold winter weather, 60,000 people eventually participated in the protest that day. On 11 January, the protests continued as Montenegro came to a halt. In what can only be described as a spontaneous general strike, an estimated 100,000 people took to the streets of Titograd, ultimately convincing Montenegro's high officials to collectively resign (ibid., 164).

As in Vojvodina, the resigning officials' replacements were handpicked by Milošević and his allies. Importantly, and serving as a warning to republican leaders throughout Yugoslavia of the emerging fluidification of borders, this was 'the first instance in post-1945 Yugoslavia that a communist leader from one republic was able to replace the leadership of another republic by his appointees' (Pavković 2000, 106–7). It must be emphasized that events in Serbia, Vojvodina, Montenegro, and Kosovo did not remain regional affairs. Among the remaining republics, only Macedonia's leaders supported the Kosovo Serb movement. In Croatia, Bosnia-Herzegovina, and Slovenia, republican leaders condemned the Kosovo Serb movement and supported the Montenegrin authorities' attempt to quell the protests (Vladisavljević 2008, 180). This of course had little to do with the Kosovo Serb issue per se, and all to do with what was correctly perceived as a Milošević power grab.

In response to what Kosovo Albanians viewed as disastrous developments in Vojvodina and Montenegro, 1,300 Kosovo miners from Stari Trg went on strike several hundred metres below the earth's surface on 20 February 1989. They pledged to come back up only once the new Kosovo leadership, made up of politicians aligned with Milošević, resigned. After a week below ground, it became clear that the miners were serious about their threat, and the politicians they opposed resigned. Triumphantly the miners returned to the surface, only to be arrested for 'counterrevolutionary activities' (Stokes 1993, 235). Furthermore, the three politicians' resignation was simply another Milošević trick, as they were immediately reinstated in their previous positions (Vladisavljević 2008, 184–5). At this stage, only one task remained in order for the anti-bureaucratic revolution to be completed. To that end,

> The Serbian Assembly, along with the assemblies of Kosovo and Vojvodina that Milošević now dominated, approved the new constitutional arrangements, putting the autonomous regions firmly under the control of the Serbian central government in March 1989. Acceptance of the constitutional provisions produced six days of rioting in Kosovo, which Milošević subdued with substantial loss of life (estimates ranged from 20 to 140).
>
> *(Stokes 1993, 235)*

While most Serbs rejoiced in their nation's triumph, Yugoslavs in the other republics did not share in their enthusiasm over Serbia's expansion. Already during the Kosovo Albanian miners' strike, Slovenia's communist leader Milan Kučan stated during a public meeting that the miners 'were defending the very foundation of Yugoslavia' (Pavković 2000, 107) – a less-than-appreciated comment in Serbia, where 'students immediately reacted to Kučan's statement by organizing huge demonstrations at Belgrade University which drew hundreds of thousands of demonstrators' (ibid., 107). Students were not the only ones to react. True to form, Milošević used the Slovenian criticism to rally support around himself, both from the population at large and from the media. Yugoslavia was now on the path to destruction. As Pavković concludes, 'this type of intimidatory and coercive style of politics could neither be contained nor controlled within the framework of the consensus-seeking federal bodies of Yugoslavia' (ibid., 107). Perhaps the most important consequence of Milošević's anti-bureaucratic revolution was that it challenged Yugoslavia's internal borders, which naturally resulted in a significant security deterioration even in those parts of the federation not directly affected by the new political geography. In this highly uncertain context, civil war would soon follow.

From declarations of independence to civil war: sectarian identification, activation of military networks, and spiralling revenge

Milošević's appropriation of Serbian nationalism for his own political purposes caused substantial concern in the other republics. In particular, Slovenian and Croat leaders feared that Milošević's project was one of creating a 'Greater Serbia', which they naturally saw as a threat to their own nationalist aspirations (Cigar 1993, 301–2). As mentioned previously, Croatia and Slovenia were both unhappy with the existing federal arrangements of Yugoslavia, especially with the redistribution of the country's wealth that was highly disadvantageous to them. In the context of socialist Europe's collapse, the combination of structural economic motivations and nationalist tendencies made peaceful secession a clear possibility in the early 1990s.

Slovenian politicians – and Slovenians at large – had long considered independence. A referendum in December 1990 overwhelmingly supported such a move, and the date for the official declaration was set for 26 June 1991. In the days leading up to that date, the federal government proclaimed that the disintegration of Yugoslavia would not be tolerated. Consequently, when the Slovenes made their announcement (eventually on 25 June because of Croatia's actions discussed below), the federal government mobilized the JNA. Military engagement ensued over the next ten days between the federal army and Slovenian territorial defence forces before the Brioni Accord was signed on 7 July with the help of a troika of politicians from the European Community. Seventy-four people died in the course of the 'ten-day war', but these numbers would pale in comparison to the carnage that would soon follow (Glenny 1993, 86–9, 98).

Croatian politicians, especially President Tuđman, had followed Slovenia's path towards independence with great interest. Tuđman had publicly entertained the idea of a revamped federation, but his personal preference was nonetheless for a sovereign Croatia. Once it became clear that Slovenia would indeed go ahead with its declaration of independence, Tuđman reasoned that for tactical reasons Croatia should follow suit, as two secessionists would have better chances of succeeding than one. Much to the dismay of Slovenians, Croatia therefore jumped the line and declared itself independent on 25 June, a day before Slovenia had planned to make its announcement (ibid., 87).

Unlike Slovenia, which was a fairly homogeneous republic, Croatia hosted a 600,000-member strong Serbian minority. When Tuđman's Croatian Democratic Union (HDZ) won the parliamentary elections in April 1990, the country took a turn towards increased nationalism and ethnic strife. Most Croatian Serbs had not voted for Tuđman and his HDZ, and now felt that they were being discriminated against, with many Serbian state officials being replaced by Croats (ibid., 77). In this already deteriorating social context, Croat sectarian symbols, such as the red-and-white-chequered shield displayed on the country's current flag, gained prominence. Such symbols served as a reminder to many Serbs of the Ustasha atrocities committed during World War II and therefore exacerbated ethnic hostilities and the activation of para-military networks. Given these developments, the Croatian declaration of independence was predictably a cause of severe concern for Croatian Serbs, and immediately triggered an escalation of violence between the two groups. The JNA was sent to Croatia to pacify the situation, but since Serbs were over-represented in the Yugoslav army a situation soon emerged in which JNA soldiers fought side by side with Serbian paramilitary groups against 'Croat police and the republic's embryonic army, the National Guard' (ibid., 101).

While armed hostilities had begun as early as March 1991, full-scale war commenced after the Slovenian conflict had ended. The early hostilities had resulted from fear among Serbs living on Croatian territory that the country would secede from Yugoslavia and lead to a deteriorating situation for its minorities (Cigar 1993). Ironically, Croatian moves towards independence therefore seemed to justify the rhetoric Milošević had been employing for the past few years. Indeed, it seemed, Serbian rights and privileges were threatened by its neighbours. The ensuing violence soon became a self-perpetuating and vicious cycle that would prove difficult to break, as killings on one side were avenged against the other. By the time the war came to an end in 1995, an estimated 20,000 people had perished and another 500,000 had been displaced. Of course, war would continue to rage in the Balkans for several more years, with some of the most horrendous crimes yet to be committed: In the subsequent wars in Bosnia and Kosovo, these numbers would be much higher.

Conclusion

This chapter has sought to explain Yugoslavia's march from social movement mobilization to civil war. In addition to being a terrible tragedy, the emergence of civil war in the country also constitutes a formidable social scientific puzzle. At a time when its Eastern European neighbours shook off the shackles of socialism and transitioned to democracy and capitalism, Yugoslavia instead tore itself apart – despite arguably starting off in a more favourable position.

To explain this divergence, we argued that Yugoslavia exhibits many of the same mechanisms highlighted in previous chapters. First, the country entered the 1980s accompanied by political and economic destabilization. The death of Tito removed the charismatic authority that had hitherto provided Yugoslavia with an ideological adhesive. Socialism had, since the establishment of Yugoslavia after World War II, been used to subdue latent, nationalist conflicts between different republics, but with Tito's death the former came into disrepute. This development was further exacerbated by the Soviet Union's decline in the second half of the 1980s, the collapse of the Communist Bloc, and Yugoslavia's economic difficulties. Combined, these political and economic hardships represent the causal mechanisms at the onset of the civil war.

Successful civil society mobilization can provide a strained society with a pathway towards reform and democratization. However, in the case of Yugoslavia, it seems that social movements instead contributed to social fragmentation. It appears that the type of early social movements that elsewhere in Eastern Europe had set the earliest examples for mass mobilization – pro-democracy movements, human rights movements, environmental movements, and other new social movements – were too weak and culturally irrelevant to make a positive contribution. Instead, politicians were able to capitalize on the fact that movements emerging along the lines of workers' rights and national interests came to dominate the civil society scene. Once Milošević had recognized the power potential of nationalist populism, he channelled the energy of the workers and the Kosovo Serbs into a fearsome political force. By challenging and eventually overcoming political opponents in Kosovo, Vojvodina, and Montenegro, he was able to instil enough fear in the remaining republics to perpetuate the social fragmentation that he had originally benefitted from.

With the political borders of Kosovo, Vojvodina, and Montenegro apparently dissolving, the security situation throughout the country deteriorated rapidly. Politicians in other republics such as Slovenia and Croatia capitalized on these developments by advancing their own nationalist discourse, which frightened their Serbian minorities. This was especially the case in the wake of the HDZ's election victory in April 1990, which multiplied the insecurity experienced by Croatian Serbs. At that point, with the metaphorical barrel of gunpowder on the verge of exploding, it did not take all that much for the country to begin to tear itself apart. Slovenia and Croatia declared themselves independent, which caused the still-existent federal government to take action. The resulting violence, especially in Croatia, targeted minorities that in turn mobilized their own para-military networks. As groups clashed along ethnic/sectarian lines, the exacting of revenge soon became a common occurrence. At that point, of course, civil war already seemed inevitable.

Note

1 Yugoslavia as a concept existed before World War II, as a monarchy known as the Kingdom of Yugoslavia (previously the Kingdom of Serbs, Croats, and Slovenes). It was established in 1918, following the fall of the Austro-Hungarian Empire in that moment of intense nationalism.

References

Banac, Ivo. 1992. 'Post-Communism as post-Yugoslavism: the Yugoslav non-revolutions of 1989–1990', in Ivo Banac (ed.), *Eastern Europe in Revolution*. Ithaca, NY: Cornell University Press, pp. 168–87.

Banac, Ivo. 2006. 'The politics of national homogeneity', in B.K. Blitz (ed.), *War and Change in the Balkans: Nationalism, Conflict, and Cooperation*. Cambridge: Cambridge University Press, pp. 30–43.

Benderly, Jill. 1997. 'Feminist movements in Yugoslavia, 1978–1992', in M.K. Bokovoy, J.A. Irvine, and C.S. Lilly (eds), *State-Society Relations in Yugoslavia, 1945–1992*. New York: St. Martin's Press, pp. 183–210.

Boduszyński, Mieczysław P. 2010. *Regime Change in the Yugoslav Successor States: Divergent Paths toward a New Europe*. Baltimore, MD: The Johns Hopkins University Press.

Bunce, Valerie. 1999. *Subversive Institutions: The Design and the Destruction of Socialism and the State*. Cambridge: Cambridge University Press.

Bunce, Valerie J., and Wolchik, Sharon L. 2011. *Defeating Authoritarian Leaders in Postcommunist Countries*. Cambridge: Cambridge University Press.

Cigar, Norman. 1993. 'The Serbo-Croatian War, 1991: political and military dimensions'. *Journal of Strategic Studies* 16(3): 297–338.

della Porta, Donatella. 2014. *Mobilizing for Democracy: Comparing 1989 and 2011*. Oxford: Oxford University Press.

Estrin, Saul. 1991. 'Yugoslavia: the case of self-managing market socialism'. *The Journal of Economic Perspectives* 5(4): 187–94.

Figa, Jozef. 1997. 'Socializing the state: civil society and democratization from below in Slovenia', in M.K. Bokovoy, J.A. Irvine, and C.S. Lilly (eds), *State-Society Relations in Yugoslavia, 1945–1992*. New York: St. Martin's Press, pp. 163–82.

Gibianskii, Leonid. 2006. 'The Soviet-Yugoslav split', in K. McDermott and M. Stibbe (eds), *Revolution and Resistance in Eastern Europe: Challenges to Communist Rule*. Oxford: Berg, pp. 17–36.

Glenny, Misha. 1993. *The Fall of Yugoslavia: The Third Balkan War*. London: Penguin.

Hayden, Robert M. 1992. 'Constitutional nationalism in the formerly Yugoslav Republics'. *Slavic Review* 51(4): 654–73.

International Center for Transitional Justice. 2009. 'Transitional justice in the former Yugoslavia'. Available at: https://ictj.org/sites/default/files/ICTJ-FormerYugoslavia-Justice-Facts-2009-English.pdf

Licht, Sonja. 2000. 'Civil society, democracy, and the Yugoslav wars'. In M. Spencer (ed.), *The Lesson of Yugoslavia*. New York: Elsevier, pp. 111–24.

Marković, Vladimir. 2012. 'A re-examination of the position of the student movement in Serbia'. In R. Hudson and G. Bowman (eds), *After Yugoslavia: Identities and Politics within the Successor States*. Houndmills: Palgrave Macmillan, pp. 105–19.

Mirkovic, Damir. 2000. 'The historical link between the Ustasha genocide and the Croato-Serb civil war: 1991–1995'. *Journal of Genocide Research* 2(3): 363–73.

Pavković, Aleksandar. 2000. *The Fragmentation of Yugoslavia: Nationalism and War in the Balkans* (2nd edn). Houndmills: Macmillan.

Perovic, Jeronim. (2007) 'The Tito–Stalin split: a reassessment in light of new evidence'. *Journal of Cold War Studies* 9(2): 32–63.

Popovic, Srdja. 2006. 'Milošević motiveless malignancy'. In B.K. Blitz (ed.), *War and Change in the Balkans: Nationalism, Conflict, and Cooperation*. Cambridge: Cambridge University Press, pp. 44–56.

Ritter, Daniel P. 2012a. 'Civil society and the paralyzed state: mobilizing for democracy in East Germany'. COSMOS Working Paper 2012/6. Department of Social and Political Science, European University Institute.

Ritter, Daniel P. 2012b. 'Civil society and the Velvet Revolution: mobilizing for democracy in Czechoslovakia'. COSMOS Working Paper 2012/4. Department of Political and Social Sciences, European University Institute.

Rusinow, Dennison. 1977. *The Yugoslav Experiment, 1948–1974*. Berkeley, CA: University of California Press.

Schaeffer, Robert K. 2000. 'Democratization, division and war in Yugoslavia: a comparative perspective', in M. Spencer (ed.), *The Lesson of Yugoslavia*. New York: Elsevier, pp. 47–63.

Schöpflin, George. 2006. 'Yugoslavia: state construction and state failure', in B.K. Blitz (ed.), *War and Change in the Balkans: Nationalism, Conflict, and Cooperation*. Cambridge: Cambridge University Press, pp. 13–19.

Stokes, Gale. 1993. *The Walls Came Tumbling Down: The Collapse of Communism in Eastern Europe*. New York: Oxford University Press.

Vasilevski, Steven. 2007. 'Diverging paths, diverging outcomes: a comparative analysis of post-communist transition in the successor states of Yugoslavia'. *YCISS Post-Communist Studies Programme Research Paper Series*. Toronto: York Centre for International and Security Studies.

Vladisavljević, Nebojša. 2008. *Serbia's Antibureaucratic Revolution: Milošević, the Fall of Communism and Nationalist Mobilization*. Houndmills: Palgrave Macmillan.

Woodward, Susan L. 1995. *Balkan Tragedy: Chaos and Dissolution after the Cold War*. Washington, DC: Brookings Institution.

7

CONCLUSION

Social movements, democratization, and civil wars

Donatella della Porta

Introduction

Episodes of democratization sometimes turn violent. For instance, violence was present in the mobilization for democracy that started in Eastern Europe in 1989 or across the Middle East and North Africa (MENA) region in 2011. On rarer occasions, conflicts have escalated into civil wars. Focusing on a specific path of violent escalation, our research bridges the literatures in the fields of social movement studies, civil wars, nonviolent resistance, and democratization, which have usually proceeded quite apart from each other.

The social science literature on civil wars has singled out various potential causes for their onset, duration, and brutality, mainly drawing on large-N studies. Among these causes are economic modernization, ethnic nationalism, absence of political democracy, rough terrain, cross-border sanctuaries, state weakness (political instability and large country population), distant areas, diasporas or foreign government support, and type of production (high value, low weight). This work has brought about an accumulation of variables defined as root causes for civil wars' onset, intensity, and duration, with some contradictory results. After a focus on grievance theories, addressing human rights deficits and discrimination as well as protracted social conflicts over deprivation, another wave of analysis addressed greed as motivation, highlighting natural resources but also the corruption of governments engaging in rent-seeking and predation or, more generally, neo-patrimonial and personalist regimes (Collier and Hoeffler 2004).

However, large-N studies have often been criticized as inconclusive, as findings are sensitive to coding and measurement procedures of the dependent variable as well as the considerable distance between theoretical constructs and proxies (Kalyvas 2008). On the other hand, detailed case studies have not produced much accumulation of knowledge. We have suggested in this volume that especially social movement studies, but also studies of failed democratization and nonviolent revolutions, could usefully integrate research on civil war through a focus on causal mechanisms. In what follows, we will summarize the results of the empirical chapters.

Political destabilization

In our research, we have focused on democratization episodes that failed, bringing about the onset of civil wars. While democratization is admittedly only one path towards civil war, its analysis allows us to single out some main processes that facilitate conflict escalation at the political level. Social movement studies have pointed to sudden shifts in opportunities, which allow activists to challenge elites. Looking at the exogenous determinants of protest repertoires, social movement scholars have stressed the roles of both stable institutions and contingent developments. Regarding the former, more centralized political power is seen as making political institutions less accessible 'from below' and, thus, fuelling more violent protest (Goodwin 2001). Additionally, conflict escalation has been considered to be more likely when historically rooted ways to deal with opponents orient authorities towards exclusive strategies. Less durable political contingencies, such as the lack of availability and influence of political allies have also been mentioned as closing windows of opportunity for protestors, often producing escalation (see della Porta and Diani 2006, Chapter 8 for a review). Low levels of freedom and democracy have been linked to political violence at the national level, even in Western Europe (Engene 2004), and less proportional electoral systems have been linked to ethnic violence (Crenshaw 2011). The weakness of democracy, civil liberties, human rights, rule of law, and so on are often considered to be root causes for radicalization. While moderation and power-sharing are seen as facilitating peaceful democratization, research on revolutions states that, when normal channels of access to the political system are blocked, violence might be perceived as necessary, as there is 'no other way out' (Goodwin 2001).

Our research confirmed political destabilization as a causal mechanism in episodes of civil war. The perceived appearance of a possibility for regime change is followed by strong reactions from the regime, which, rather than bringing about a defeat of the opposition, lead to its radicalization and to conflict escalation. Actors from below appropriate opportunities to mobilize, but are not strong enough to produce the breakdown of the regime which, in turn, is shattered but not fully defeated. Emerging internal anarchy pushes citizens to take responsibility for their own security (Toft 2003). Our case studies show how opportunities open up during the conflicts through dynamic interactions.

Libya is a case of failed democratization in a weak state, which has been destabilized. In Libya, Colonel Qaddafi, who took power in 1969 through a coup d'état, shifted power to members of relatively disadvantaged (small) Libyan tribes and urban middle-class professionals. Qaddafi's political project then moved towards a totalitarian-style state in which popular rhetoric combined with brutal repression in the control of all elements of civil and political life. State institutions remained underdeveloped, viewed as potential hotspots of opposition, and were left under-developed and disempowered as Qaddafi disbanded the (tribally based) National Congressional Council. The defection by the elites developed quickly, as early as February 2011, with several of the most important government officials resigning from their posts and joining the opposition. During the revolt, representatives of economic interests – such as the Arabian Gulf Oil Company, the second-largest state-owned oil company in Libya – also defected to the rebels, as did Islamic lead-ers and clerics, among them the Network of Free Ulema (the clerics) and some key tribes such as the Warfalla, Tuareg, and Magarha.

The state was stronger in Syria, where 'the dense links between Bashar al-Asad and the regime core prevented elites' abandonment of the president; at the same time, thicker state-society relations in Syria prevented a Libya-style social isolation in the top leadership' (Hinnebusch, Imady, and Zintl 2016, 225). First, the regime enjoyed a nationalist legitimacy, given its stance against Israel; second, neoliberal reforms had enriched the well-connected middle classes in cities like Aleppo and Damascus. Bashar al-Asad followed his father as Syrian president in June 2000, promising political liberalization; however, the president and his close family remained at the core of the regime, occupying leading positions in the army (al-Asad's brother), military intelligence (his brother-in-law and one cousin), and the economy. In general, clan loyalty also played a role, as Alawi elites continued support for the regime, while defectors were Sunnis. However, the wave of pro-tests that spread from Tunisia and Egypt and also to Syria contributed to destabilize the regime by producing cleavages within the elites.

In Yemen as well, the peaceful uprising, inspired by events in Tunisia and Egypt, unsettled the authoritarian power of the country's leader, Ali Abdullah Saleh. Yemen, born out of the unification of North and South Yemen in 1990, was a weak state plagued by poverty, rampant corruption of the ruling elites, and a security void. With the localized wars in the North, calls for secession in the South and presence of al-Qaeda, Yemen's unity was fragile, and national identifications were undermined by regional and tribal affiliations. The regime of Ali Abdullah Saleh relied on repression but also on patronage networks that further fragmented society and weakened the state (Alley 2010). The core of the regime was built around Saleh's family, who occupied the most important military and state secu-rity positions, and other elites allied with the president through personal relation-ships and exchange of favours rather than principles or ideology (Durac 2013; Khosrokhavar 2012). The fluid nature of these alliances was confirmed when, in March 2011, following the massacre of peaceful protestors, core members of the regime defected and joined the opposition. The rupture of the regime led to armed confrontations between Saleh and the defectors, changing the course of the previ-ously peaceful uprising. At the same time, as Saleh and his family directed all their energies into the struggle for survival, the security situation in the whole country started to deteriorate dramatically.

In the 1980s, Yugoslavia was certainly not a weak state and initially seemed to enjoy the best conditions for a peaceful and straightforward democratization process, including a relatively high degree of liberalization, reflected in a comparatively large number of civil society organizations. A looming economic crisis was exacerbated by Tito's death, and the ensuing succession struggle helped usher in a new generation of party leaders in the various republics. The breakdown of Titoism as a political and economic system (Vasilevski 2007, 5) developed with increased internal competition among the republics. By 1988, 'the great majority of Tito's chosen coterie of republics' leaders had been replaced with leaders who had no common loyalties', and 'both the Yugoslav federation and the Yugoslav Communist party – the League of Communists – which nominally ruled the country had lost much of their legitimacy' (Pavković 2000, 76). Socioeconomic and cultural inequalities then fuelled internal conflicts, as political elites at the level of the republics started playing on nationalism as a way of maintaining their own power (Licht 2000, 113). In fact, this happened through the activation of multiple cleavages:

> Old and new divisions in the political class came to the fore, such as between promoters of greater control of Serbia's central government over its autonomous provinces and their foes; between advocates of a stronger federal centre and protectors of the status quo; between proponents of change in the party's Kosovo policy and their opponents; between conservative and liberally minded politicians; between members of various political generations; and between high- and low-ranking officials. Since the divisions often cut across one another and high officials engaged in complex political maneuvering, relations within the political class became rather complicated.
>
> *(Vladisavljević 2008, 126)*

In sum, both weak and less weak states were destabilized through waves of protest for democracy, which challenged regimes that had already shown some signs of stress. We thus observed that in Libya, Syria, Yemen, and Yugoslavia alike, political destabilization was a key mechanism in the overall process of mobilization for democracy radicalizing into civil war. At the same time, our cases show the different roles the mechanism can take in the overall process. In Libya, it intersected with economic conflicts around the oil industry and was exacerbated by social fragmentation around tribes and traditional religious elites. In Syria, social fragmentation instead countered political instability due to the stronger social underpinnings of the regime around President Bashar al-Assad. In Yemen, the destabilization meant the rupture of the regime, accompanied by security deterioration and fragmentation, with new alliances and divisions built around the warring elite factions. In Yugoslavia, finally, political instability also intersected with social fragmentation but within a more nationalist framework and formalized political structure.

Indiscriminate repression

In research on social movements, the policing of protest is considered a central factor in radicalization. Research on the topic has identified a tendency to use harsher styles of protest policing against social and political groups that are perceived as greater threats to political elites, given that they are more ideologically driven or more radical in their aims (see Davenport 2000; della Porta and Fillieule 2004; Earl 2003). Additionally, police repression is more likely to be directed against groups that are poorer in material resources as well as in political connections (della Porta 1998; Earl, Soule, and McCarthy 2003). The form state power takes has a clear impact on the policing of protest. If repression is always much more brutal in authoritarian than in democratic regimes (e.g. Uysal 2005, on Turkey), even authoritarian regimes vary in the amount, forms, and actors of protest they are willing to tolerate, as well as in the forms in which they police the opposition (Boudreau 2004). Violent uprisings seem to develop when very repressive regimes have long thwarted any development of an autonomous associational life – let alone, of social movements (Goodwin 2001). While repression might reduce the individual's availability to participate by increasing the costs of protesting, in some cases a sense of injustice as well as the creation of intense feelings of identification and solidarity can strengthen the motivation to oppose an unjust and brutal regime (Davenport 2005; della Porta and Piazza 2008; Francisco 2005). So, especially when the protest is widespread and well supported, repression can backfire due to outrage about police disrespect for citizens' rights at the national as well as the transnational level (Davenport 2005; Francisco 2005). In general, repression seems able to control low levels of discontent but fuels armed opposition in cases of broader unrest (Regan and Norton 2005).

If repression is a cost, resistance can become a reward in itself. Our research indicated that this tended to happen especially in situations of indiscriminate and inconsistent repression, which left some free space out of the reach of the regime. Past and present brutal repression strongly influenced the activists' choices, reducing faith in a peaceful surrender of incumbents. Similarly, in our cases, memories of regime brutality worked as a constraint to mobilization in some moments, but in others fuelled protest as the only way to express a call for dignity. The costs of compliance with the regime became unbearable. At the same time, brutal repression fuelled counter-violence, with spiralling escalation.

Never a liberalized autocracy, Qaddafi's regime had used extremely high levels of repression of any political dissent (Joffé 2016). At the onset of the conflict, the protest in fact politicized on the issue of repression, with demonstrations organized by the families of prisoners killed in the Abu Salim prison massacre as well as against the growing repression of those very protests, primarily but not only in Benghazi. In February 2011, violence escalated in various parts of the country, as the regime warned citizens that the state security would use force to disperse any collective actions perceived as promoting public sedition (Jacinto 2011). On 27 February, Qaddafi blamed foreign powers for the disorder and called for loyalists to 'cleanse Libya house by house' (Joffé 2016, 132). Indiscriminate police attacks against protestors immediately spiralled into violent confrontations as the regime proved unable to impose order, especially in some regions.

Also in Syria, where repression had thwarted the development of a civil society, the dynamics of the protests dramatically changed during the upheavals when protest was met with brutal repression, but repressed cleavages re-emerged during the uprising. Mobilization started in March 2011 in the southern city of Dara', moving

> From largely peaceful protests (that were immediately repressed using live ammunition by police) to a full out civil war in which an increasing amount of heavily armed and well trained cadre of army defectors, regular Syrian and foreign fighters are staging an armed insurrection against the regime of Bashar al-Asad.
>
> *(Gelvin 2011, 108–9)*

Escalation followed the torture of children, accused of having spray-painted slogans against Assad. Repression then produced further escalation, as 'The regime's forces, lacking training and experience in crowd or riot control, continued to respond with excessive violence, multiplying regime enemies, and making funerals occasions for more confrontations' (Hinnebusch, Imady, and Zintl 2016, 231). Police brutality was in fact taken as proof of the ineffectiveness of the alternative, nonviolent option – especially after the killing of 138 during the first day of Ramadan, and the shelling and takeover of Hama and Deir ez-Zor as well as Idlib and Latakya in August. While the funerals of the victims of regime repression reignited protest, on 19 July 2012 the assassinations of members of the Syrian security elite in Damascus confirmed the vulnerability of the regime to armed attacks.

In Yemen, the rulers of the new republic in the early 1990s had initially allowed for some liberalization, making the country's vibrant civil society and public sphere open to dissent and debate, uniquely in the region (Carapico 2007; Wedeen 2008). The democratic façade started to crumble following the 1994 civil war between the South and the North, with Saleh's rule becoming more overtly authoritarian. Overt political contention was nevertheless widespread in Yemen and protests, organized in particular around social claims, were held regularly throughout the 1990s and the 2000s. They were usually met with a mix of repression and concessions. A similar strategy was adopted by Saleh from January 2011 on, when arrests and harassment of protestors were accompanied by promises of better salaries and other improvements. Gradually, however, more violence was deployed, until on 18 March 2011, snipers fired upon peaceful protestors in Sana'a, killing at least 52 (HRW 2013a; 2013b).

The brutality of the regime outraged Yemenis, leading to the radicalization of people's demands. Over the next days, despite the violence and the announcement of the state of emergency on 23 March 2011, the numbers of protestors grew and demonstrations spread across the country, reaching even the most remote areas (Carapico 2011). While the youth remained committed to peaceful methods, the regime defectors with their army units and tribal militias engaged in armed clashes with forces loyal to Saleh. By mid-June, cities like Sana'a were divided by checkpoints and some neighbourhoods were turned into military zones (Fattah 2011). The escalation of violence was eventually quelled by the transitional deal brokered by the Gulf Cooperation Council in November 2011. The agreement, which forced Saleh to resign but granted him immunity, was rejected by the youth protestors, who saw it as a betrayal of the revolution's objectives. Thus, despite the declaration of the so-called 'transitional period', neither the popular mobilization of the youth nor the brutal repression of resistance ended (Alwazir 2016). At the same time, with the fragmentation of the movement for change, some of its participants, like the Houthis, returned to their narrow interests and more violent repertoires of action.

Repression had at first been weaker in Yugoslavia where, even if purges had occasionally followed calls for reforms, there had been a gradual liberalization. The situation precipitated, however, after the 1990 elections brought Milošević into power as president of Serbia, and the army sided with him in his attempt to conquer part of Croatia and Bosnia. Although no war was declared, a military draft was initiated in May 1991. When violence erupted in the Serbian-inhabited areas of Croatia, the Yugoslav people's army intervened, the Serbian government declared, in order to protect them. This triggered spirals of protest and repression, with the federal army nevertheless unable to impose order in all the republics. The intervention of the army served to quickly radicalize all sides of the conflict, with violence soon spiralling out of control.

Summarizing, while the degree of previous brutality of the regimes we analysed varied, in all cases, initially peaceful protests escalated in response to repression that was considered indiscriminate, but also ineffective in re-establishing order in the national territories.

Social fragmentation

Social movement studies have stressed the importance of coalition building. As in revolutions, the emergence of waves of protest is related to the capacity to activate large networks by bridging already existing connections and creating new ones. As mobilizing networks always involve cooperation but also (potential) competition, mobilization is likely to subside when (especially in declining phases of protest cycles) splits multiply around strategies and ideological divergences (della Porta and Diani 2006). Multi-cleavage environments present even more challenges as they provide increased opportunities for divisions (della Porta 2013). Research on democratization has often suggested that the distribution of power among ethnic groups could jeopardize the search for peaceful solutions. Studies on nonviolent revolutions have considered the unity of the challengers as an important factor to success (Schock 2005). Civil war studies have often mentioned ethnic belonging as a resilient source of conflict, especially when mixed with a perception of discrimination as socioeconomic grievances are triggered by regional political marginalization (Ylönen 2005). Civil wars stem from horizontal inequality and ethno-political discrimination, as 'countries with one or more ethnic group(s) radically poorer than the national average and countries with large groups discriminated from national politics have a significantly higher risk of armed anti-governmental opposition' (Buhaug, Gates and Lujala 2013, 429). In particular, 'large discriminated groups boost the probability of governmental civil wars, in part because of the evident disconnect between demographic power and political privileges' (ibid., 429). Confirming in part these views, one can note that in fact, in our cases as well, the weakness of civil society interacted with (the potential for) ethnic divisions, which in turn fragmented the opposition.

In Libya, in 2011 and 2012, a popular uprising against long-term authoritarianism evolved into a civil war that was ultimately interrupted through the direct military involvement of a coalition of foreign states. The existent tribal divisions and traditional values were utilized by the regime in order to divide and control. Qaddafi, in fact, played the tribes against one another, even while trying to accommodate some of their requests for power resource sharing, privileging some over others. Together with patron-client networks, inter-tribal and inter-ethnic distrust therefore contributed to the dictator's power. A strict form of patrimonialism and clientelism developed, but the country remained politically and administratively fragmented. Latent tribal conflicts had involved Berbers, Warfalla, and Cyrenaica groups in particular, and violent Islamism also played a role. As Anderson (2011: 6) explains:

> Libyan society has been fractured, and every national institution, including the military, is divided by the cleavages of kinship and region. As opposed to Tunisia and Egypt, Libya has no system of political alliances, network of economic associations, or national organizations of any kind. Thus, what seemed to begin as nonviolent protests similar to those staged in Tunisia and Egypt soon became an all-out secession – or multiple separate secessions – from a failed state.

In 2011, protests grew in size and frequency, with one early slogan reading 'Libya free, nation united'. Uprisings started in Eastern Libya, spreading after a few days to Tripoli; Benghazi was the Eastern base of the anti-regime protests, which also grew in the western cities of Zawiya, Misrata, and even in the capital, Tripoli. While the level of violence rose, peaceful unarmed demonstrations also continued: 'as the chaos of war progressed, disrupting communal and distribution services, spontaneous committees began to emerge that took over municipal and communal responsibilities' (Joffé 2016, 132). However, the opposition remained fragmented, with low organizational capacity and a proliferation of heavily armed militias on regional, ethnic, tribal, and religious bases.

The opposition also fragmented in Syria, where the heterogeneity of civil society – with ethnic minorities, including Kurds, Palestinians, and Armenians, as well as religious minorities such as Christians, Druze, Sunnis, Shiites, Alawis, and Ismaelis (as specific Shiite denominations) and small communities of Jews –'had long undermined collective action among the opposition' (Hinnebusch, Imady, and Zintl 2016, 225). As President Hafez al-Asad took power in 1970, he consolidated his control over the armed forces through tribal and family connections, resulting in Alawi domination of sensitive positions in the army (Perthes 1992). Here as well, the regime addressed the various groups through patronage, as 'The army, intelligence services and Ba'ath party organizations became an instrument for institutionalized corruption in which powerful patrons secured support from lower ranking members, via a highly developed clientelist system' (Donker 2012). When the uprising emerged, efforts at mobilizing brought about the creation of an umbrella organization for the local committees – the Local Coordinating Committees of Syria (LCCS) – which especially involved young people without previous experience of political socialization (Hinnebusch 1993). However, the uprising also mobilized long-standing opponents of the regime, including Kurdish parties, the Committees for the Revival of Civil Society (which emerged from the 2001 'Damascus Spring'), as well as elite oppositional leaders who joined the mobilization effort soon after it begun. Even if Kurds, Sunnis, or other minority groups often dominated in terms of numbers, coordination committees aimed at being inclusive. Trans-sectarian appeals were also spread by the movement: 'we Syrians are one people', declared the singer and activist, Fadwa Soliman (Khosrokhavar 2012, 218), and the words of a song read: 'Come on, Bashar, leave . . . You, the US agent! The Syrian people will not accept humiliation any more' (ibid., 241).

But as in Libya, Syrian civil society was weak and its fragmented nature shaped, despite protestors' statements to the contrary, how the uprising developed. As the strong repression of protests had thwarted political organizations, leaving religious, tribal, clan, and family ties as the main bases of identification and networking, protests spread especially in the periphery, based on strong tribal links. Divisions grew in a fragmented Syrian civil society, with a multitude of minorities and experiences of sectarian violence already in the 1980s (with the Muslim Brotherhood's revolt culminating in the massacre of Hama in 1982). As the uprising became more violent, ethnic and sectarian divisions grew ever more polarized – culminating in the eventual emergence of Jihadist movements and the founding of an 'Islamic' State.

In Yemen, the early stages of mobilization brought surprising levels of unity, giving rise to an unlikely alliance among Zaydi rebels, Islamists, socialists, tribal men, and urban youth. The regional and tribal interests seemed to have been suspended and replaced by the shared goal of toppling the regime. Occupied squares across Yemen became 'physical and social spaces where people from all these different groups met and exchanged views, shared living conditions, and generally interacted in a largely unanticipated manner' (Lackner 2016, 164). The unity started to break up, however, when armed factions joined the struggle. Many abandoned the squares, as they felt uncomfortable with the regime defectors becoming the new leaders of the revolution (Manea 2015). The fragmentation further increased with the (internationally reached) power transfer deal. While the youth of the revolution rejected the deal and kept protesting, other actors agreed to it and moved towards institutional politics, or returned to their narrow interests and agendas. During the period of the National Dialogue Conference between 2013 and 2014, despite the talks of unity, the fragmentation in the country deepened, with the Houthis expanding their territorial control, Southerners calling for secession, and tribes engaging in localized struggles for resources or autonomy. Finally, the alignment between the former protestors (the Houthis) and the former president (Saleh) broke up the clearly demarcated camps of the uprising (opposition versus regime), putting forth new alliances and divisions that marked the phase of the civil war.

In Yugoslavia, civil society organizations had developed in various contentious moments. Especially in Slovenia, new social movement claims had spread on issues of reproductive rights, gay and lesbian rights, and nuclear energy (Licht 2000, 120). In the relatively liberal climate of the late 1980s, feminists, environmentalists, and pacifists coordinated their protests (Figa 1997, 169; Benderly 1997, 184), consisting of peaceful, direct actions (Figa 1997, 169). Mainly composed of intellectuals, these groups developed a strong anti-nationalist stance (Bilic 2012, 94). Some characteristics of the Yugoslavian state building, and its position during the Cold War, formed however the preconditions for inter-ethnic conflicts that the federalist asset was not able to address. The weak power of the federation, with the domination of the republics over the centre (Bunce 1999, 111), facilitated fragmentation into multiple states. Additionally, the historical enmities between the Catholic Croats and the Orthodox Serbs – and between the Croatian fascists, the Ustasha, and the Serbian resistance, the Chetniks – were then revived. The effects of economic and cultural inequalities became all the more dramatic, given another characteristic of Tito's Yugoslavia. As he had linked socialism to the nation,

> [This] contained a critical weakness that Tito and his colleagues could never have imagined. As long as the Communist movement remained strong, Yugoslavism was not in danger. If nationalism reared its head the party could and did push it back under the surface. If the League of Communists of Yugoslavia should disintegrate, however, then the Yugoslavism it championed would disintegrate too.
>
> *(Stokes 1993, 223)*

In the years to come, in the face of brutal escalation, Milošević continued to present himself as a reformist communist and a nationalist: he was described, in fact, as

> the proverbial example (though rare in actual fact in the region) of the communist who, recognizing the threats imposed by the dissolution of the communist order, opted nearly overnight (and helped along by audience reactions to a speech given in Kosovo) to redefine himself as a nationalist.
>
> *(ibid., 92)*

As such, social fragmentation can be observed in each of our four cases. But whereas, in Yugoslavia, this fragmentation was linked mostly to nationalism, in Syria, it also translated through sectarian and ethnic differences. In Libya, though also present in the Syrian case, social fragmentation was expressed was specifically through the tribes. In Yemen, the fragmentation was even more multi-layered, with tribal, regional, and sectarian lines of division. This meant that in all cases, social fragmentation intersected with other political and economic mechanisms, but it did so through country-specific institutions.

Fluidification of borders

Political instability sometimes brings about a redefinition of (formal and informal) borders, which can also imply a fluidification of previously existing borders and the setting of new ones. Social movement studies have looked at the creation of free space. In authoritarian regimes, but also in democracies, challengers might constitute spaces in which to prefigure alternative ways of living and social orders. Squatted youth centres or protest camps might be seen as engaged in fluidifying power relations, order, and borders. A fluidification of borders becomes increasingly visible in civil wars as rebels gain control of territories, where an emergent order has to be established. In fact, research on civil wars has focused on territorial contestation, as at their onset there is a fluidification of borders, with some capacity by the rebels to control specific territories. Typically during insurrections, especially in authoritarian regimes, spaces are freed up by the opposition. Our research also pointed to the fluidification of borders as a key mechanism in civil wars dynamics, constituted by the contested reformation of borders and order.

In Libya, the process of fluidification of borders is visible in the focusing of protests in certain geographic areas, given the regime's inability to keep control over parts of its territory. The collapse of the regime was triggered by a loss of support from the key Libyan tribes as well as key individuals within the government and the army, especially those from the eastern region of Cyrenaica (such as the former Minister of Justice and the former Minister of Internal Affairs), while the police and the army withdrew from Benghazi. A quick loss of territorial control by the regime's security forces has been linked to the geographic structure of the country, with the population concentrated in Tripoli and Benghazi and a desert in between. Even after the military conflict ended with the regime's breakdown on 23 October 2011, tensions between tribal elites from east and west (Cyrenaica and Tripolitania), with their respective militia alliances, continued to fuel insecurity under still strained economic conditions.

In Syria, rapid escalation of the uprising was also related to increasing territorial contestation as rebels began to declare cities 'liberated', which the regime would subsequently try (often successfully) to re-occupy. As a reaction, more residents would start to arm themselves and train in order to resist state repression. The most active regions at the time were those around Idlib, Homs, and Hama: a conservative Sunni majority region. Retreating from the latter areas, the regime focused repression on the two main cities of Aleppo and Damascus. In this context, peaceful opposition survived, notwithstanding repression, but increasingly transformed itself into governance-related institutions. Because of

> government services and security break down in many areas, local neighbourhoods organized an alternative local governance set-up, including self-defence groups, an underground clinic systems, schools, media, and transportation services. With the intensification of the armed conflict, local communities became active in human relief.
>
> *(Hinnebusch, Imady, and Zintl 2016, 242)*

This process of redrawing of borders, with some areas freed by the rebels, intensified following the summer of 2012, after the rebel attack on both Damascus and Aleppo.

With the escalation, internationalization also increased. Inside the country, Palestinian refugees had to take positions in the conflict, and Kurds contacted foreign Kurdish parties (mainly the PKK and Iraqi KDP). Some countries provided arms to the regime (Russia and Iran), while others supported rebel factions (from countries such as Saudi Arabia, Qatar, Turkey, and the United States). The growing tensions in the region were reflected in international interventions, with Turkey, Saudi Arabia, and Qatar supporting the opposition, but Iran, Hezbollah, and Iraq supporting the regime. There was, moreover, local control and supply of services by al-Qaeda or the Kurdish Democratic Unionist Party. With this internationalization, rebel groups proved able to control areas south of Damascus, around Hama, and all across the northern parts of the country. As we saw, the enduring loss of regime control over these regions necessitated a further development of governance organizations – a process that turned highly contentious as civil opposition councils, rebel groups, and Islamist movements increasingly struggled among themselves over control and boundaries of the areas they controlled. Added to this situation was an increasing sectarian rhetoric within which IS emerged. Its rise was a response to the militarism of the regime, but also to the vacuum produced by state failure in both Iraq and Syria, with the spreading of sectarian identities, the war economy, and plundering of state resources. Once polarization developed and radical Islamists increased their influence, they were able to bring an Islamic alternative to governance in practice.

In Yemen, where the popular mobilization of 2011 broke from the usual scripts of political engagements in the country, occupied squares, in Sana'a and other cities, gained the status of 'free spaces'. They were not necessarily safe or free of the regime's violence, but nevertheless turned into zones of creativity and encounters among diverse actors, against the rigid social boundaries typical in Yemen (Lackner 2016; Alwazir 2016). Occupation of squares continued well into 2013, to protest – among other things – the outcomes of the transitional agreement that subverted the goals of the popular uprising. For the youth, the interference of international actors clearly revealed that Yemen's future political landscape had to meet the interests of regional powers and not popular aspirations. The decisive role of the neighbouring Gulf monarchies was confirmed when, after the Houthis reached and overran parts of the South in March 2015, the Arab coalition responded with airstrikes and blockades of Yemen (Salisbury 2016). The fluidification of borders took place also at the local level, as during the transitional period, beginning in late 2011, the void in security and state was filled by various groups taking over in particular localities, such as the Houthis in the North, al-Qaeda in some southern cities, and various tribes in areas across the country. In 2013–14, the Houthi rebels managed to move beyond the highlands, contesting new provinces until they reached and seized Sana'a in September 2014. While they initially earned some local support by providing basic services and removing corrupt officials, their expansion southwards gave rise to growing opposition and acts of resistance. With the latter being brutally repressed, the armed confrontations over contested territories followed, resulting in a full-fledged civil war.

In Yugoslavia, as well, borders fluidified quickly. In September 1988, 'high officials of Serbia now effectively certified specific protest groups and their demands and claims as fully legitimate. They openly embraced popular participation in politics, albeit on populist terms' (Vladisavljević 2008, 150). So-called rallies of solidarity in support of the Kosovo Serbs multiplied in Vojvodina, Serbia, and Montenegro, mobilizing tens of thousands – up to 700,000 in Belgrade on 19 October 1988. While the protests were initially mainly nonviolent and moderate in their discourse, they radicalized later on. Initially justifying intervention as the defence of oppressed (Serbian) minorities, during the mobilization, the aims broadened to bringing both Vojvodina and Kosovo under Serbian control. Fearing the increasing power of the Serbian republic, most other federal states declared their independence (Vasilevski 2007). The former communist elites played the most important role in all the new countries, even though, with the exception of Slovenia, democratization was delayed by the internal wars. After 1989 followed the years of dramatic events, such as the wars in Croatia (with about 25,000 people killed) and Bosnia-Herzegovina (with about 200,000 deaths and a million people displaced), plus the 78 days of the NATO bombing campaign, allegedly against violations of human rights in Kosovo, with a rampant economic crisis and mounting corruption.

The fluidification of borders is very pronounced in all our cases. In both Libya and Syria, we see that the loss of regime control over (part of) its territory necessitated the creation of local governance organizations. With their emergence, governance fragments and fluidification set in, as boundaries and authority over territory become contested. But whereas in Libya this mechanism was mostly internal – as no state institutions remained after Gaddafi's removal, tribes and rival governments took over – in Syria and Yemen, it was much more closely linked to sectarian identification and the intervention of foreign actors. Practical governance fell apart along ethnic and sectarian lines, a process that was exacerbated by its resonance among the foreign actors that intervened. In the Yugoslavian case, instead, we observed that the fluidification of borders emerged through questioning the relationship of specific regions to a Serbian nation.

Security deterioration

In both social movement studies and civil war studies, researchers have mainly addressed socioeconomic characteristics as potential sources of grievances. In work on social movements, however, grievances have tended to be dismissed as causal explanations and considered a constant rather than a variable. Moreover, interest in social stratification has been marginal, as social movements have been considered increasingly as post-materialist. Only recently has attention re-emerged for the structural cleavages that might be mobilized during conflicts (della Porta 2013). In research on contentious politics, the type of economic arrangement has been considered relevant in defining specific paths of democratization. In this direction, Elisabeth Wood (2000) pointed to the intertwining of political and economic power in cases of oligarchic regimes in which democratization often involved (at least partially) violent insurgencies. In research on civil wars, grievances related to economic conditions were initially at the centre of attention, especially those operationalized as poverty, inequality, and ethnic discrimination. In fact, social polarization and horizontal social inequality emerged as positively correlated with the onset of the conflict. Economic polarization adds up to ethnic polarization in increasing the risk of violence. We have suggested here, as well, that violence should be considered as affecting economic conditions as much as it is affected by them. Hence, grievances related to inequality can themselves be produced through the act of mobilization, as political destabilization triggers spirals of impoverishment.

In Libya, the economic recession of the mid-1970s, with the related economic liberalization and privatization of state companies, had already affected the state capacity for patronage, increasing the power and revenues of a few protected individuals (Perthes 1992, 124) while social inequalities increased. Since the late 1990s, neoliberal and administrative reforms have unsettled previous social structures. Qaddafi's attempt to normalize relations with the United States and the European Union brought about some, although very limited, liberalization, but also the dismissal of more than a third of those employed in the public administration. In reaction, protesting the delayed completion of housing projects in the coastal regions, people squatted in several hundred uninhabited, half-finished buildings. Local demonstrations also targeted inefficient distribution of government services. Corruption apparently also involved the protection of drug cartels, whose militias were tolerated (Salih 2014). In a country with nearly 70 per cent unemployment among young people, unemployed young men constituted the largest part of the protestors on the streets. In fact, concerns initially addressed material needs. As in Tunisia and Egypt, calls for dignity, freedom, and justice were frequent, sometimes accompanied by claims for more job opportunities, improved economic conditions, and better education (Michael 2011). Civil war clearly contributed to further economic difficulties by increasing social insecurity, with heavy consequences for an already deprived economy.

Similarly, in Syria, neoliberal reforms had brought about a withdrawal from the previous social contract between the regime and the population, with 30 per cent of the population below the poverty line and 11.4 per cent below indigence. Moreover, the neoliberal reforms had weakened the Ba'ath Party's capacity for co-optation, resulting in a small political-economic elite reaping the benefits of economic liberalization, while traditional methods of state-led social support broke down. As the uprising erupted, protestors stigmatized figures like Rami Makhlouf, Assad's cousin and one of the wealthiest people in Syria, for their corrupt business dealings. Even though many of the initial activists were more highly educated Syrians from the middle classes, this spread the image of a disenfranchised mass opposing a regime-linked economic elite.

In Yemen, as well, protests in early January 2011 started as calls for the end of corruption and for better salaries. Concentration of power and money in the hands of the regime's elite seemed all the more outrageous, given the impoverishment of many citizens. Protests about material claims and labour rights had been indeed frequent in the country. When hopes for better living conditions and policies focused on social justice did not materialize during the transitional period, discontent grew. Attuned to the anger of people, in the summer of 2014, the Houthis returned to protests when President Hadi announced cuts in fuel subsidies. Once protests turned into armed clashes and the Houthis took over the capital, the country started its descent into civil war. With the escalation of violence, particularly after Saudi Arabia's involvement, destitution in the poorest Arab country spiralled, fuelling further radicalization but also pushing children and men to join the armed struggle for the pursuit of financial rewards.

In Yugoslavia, the specific version of a socialist economy – with tolerance for small private business and a 'self-management' system that gave workers control of their factories and workplaces by electing their management – initially seemed to benefit the country's development. The situation started to deteriorate, however, in the 1970s, as the oil crisis helped put an abrupt end to the so-called Yugoslav miracle (Stokes 1993, 229), forcing the country to adopt structural adjustment policies within various austerity programmes in order to repay the large accumulated foreign debt (Schaeffer 2000, 51; Stokes 1993, 229–30). Increases in unemployment and prices fuelled discontent among the population (Stokes 1993, 238–41), and workers' strikes multiplied in the 1980s (Vladisavljević 2008, 111). Territorial inequalities also became increasingly dramatic between the relatively rich Slovenia and Croatia, on the one hand, and the much poorer Kosovo and Macedonia, on the other. In this context, the civil war further contributed to impoverishment and inequalities, with a few enriching themselves at the expense of the large majority of the population.

In sum, albeit to different degrees in the different areas, social inequality played a role by spreading grievances that fuelled protest. These critiques involved inequalities among social groups, with the development of kleptocratic regimes, particularly in the Middle East cases, where neoliberal reforms jeopardized previous patronage but also increased the richness of the corrupt few at the expense of the many. In Yugoslavia, while the inequalities were comparatively smaller, socioeconomic differences among the republics fuelled discontent, especially as they interacted with declining socioeconomic standards and increasing political instability. In all cases, the civil war further increased poverty and inequality, with small groups able to enrich themselves in the war economy, often in the informal or even criminal markets.

Activation of military networks

Social movement studies that focused on the dynamics of mobilization have systematically addressed the importance of networks. In fact, the format of these networks but also their content have been studied as generating relevant consequences for social movements. Research on political violence has pointed to the creation of military bodies for self-defence within social movement organizations as a tipping point in the emergence of clandestine political organizations (della Porta 2013). Research on civil wars but also on nonviolence has looked especially at the availability of armaments as triggering conflict militarization. In fact, insurgency has been defined as a specific technology of military conflict, with small and lightly armed bands using guerrilla strategies especially in rural areas (Kalyvas 2008). In particular, research has singled out the role of the military – or, often, multiple military bodies – in terms of strength, cohesion, and loyalty.

In the literature on nonviolent revolutions, Nepstad (2011) noted that while those that win the support of the military tend to succeed, when the military is composed of different ethnic groups, endowed with varying power, it is difficult for the army as a whole to side with the opposition. Rather, there will be defectors, which can cause violent developments. In civil war research, with its emphasis on individual rationalities, scholars have focused on military networks and the reasons to participate in them. In particular, attention has been paid to the agents who do the killing (Mitchell 2004) and to pre-existing networks (Mampilly 2011). The specific dynamics within rebel groups also emerge as crucial in our analysis. As violence generates violence, the armed forces split between those loyal to the regime and those who oppose it. Those who abandon the regime bring with them arms and military skills, which heavily affect the development of the conflicts, although with varying outcomes. As guns become audible, the civil society is silenced. Foreign military intervention challenges the dictators, but also cost many lives among the civil population.

In Libya, the conflict had moved into a pre-civil war phase by March 2011, assisted by an external military intervention. In the distribution of arms and equipment to the army, the dictator had privileged the regions inhabited by loyal tribes and, mistrusting the army, financed his own militia (Khosrokhavar 2012). The regime thus developed an apparently loyal security system: 'The most important characteristic of these security organizations is that they are neither subject to institutional political control nor to control by the public but have been controlled exclusively by the Revolutionary Leadership led by Colonel Qadhafi' (Cerone 2011, 790). By the end of the 1990s, a special elite-military the 'People's Guard', composed of select loyalists, was formed with the task of protecting Qaddafi's family and the regime infrastructure, especially from 'internal enemies' (Mattes 2004). During the protest wave, those who defected from the regime contributed the military leadership of the opposition. The rebels also accumulated arms through raids of local security forces' headquarters. As the brutality of the fighting increased, the UN Security Council approved a resolution imposing a no-fly zone over Libya; soon thereafter, US and French warships in the Mediterranean started bombing Qaddafi's security forces on the outskirts of Benghazi, allowing the rebels to rearm, regroup, and advance towards the west. The opposition then received aid in terms of communications equipment, training, and above all military support from a substantial number of countries and NATO. NATO's aerial forces helped the rebels advance to the east, culminating in the fall of Tripoli on 20 August and the killing of Mu'ammar Qaddafi and one of his sons in Sirte on 20 October.

Similarly in Syria, defecting soldiers, especially among Sunni conscripts, brought armaments to the opposition while hundreds of soldiers were in fact executed for refusing to fire on the population. At the same time, notwithstanding some regime concessions, continued repression inhibited negotiations between the opposition and the regime, and protestors increasingly started to believe that armed protection of nonviolent demonstrations was both justified and necessary in the face of deadly repression. Despite the initial understanding that violence by the protestors was to be avoided as it would fuel violence by the regime, violent defensive reactions to violent regime repression started to spread. On 6 June 2011, at Jisr as-Shourough, one of the first liberations of a town through local residents' ambush of the army and government buildings apparently took place. Notwithstanding heavy army intervention, which allowed the regime to retake control, the example was followed in other cities. The regime, on the other hand, felt justified in using lethal force (including airstrikes and artillery) against what it now, increasingly justifiably, described as an armed insurrection. The violence then became more organized, as Syrian soldiers started to defect. While defecting soldiers never endangered the stability of the Syrian army itself, they did bring military expertise and a belief in the possibility of armed opposition to the uprising.

A turning point in the activation of military networks' spiral of escalation was in fact, on 29 July 2011, the foundation of the Free Syrian Army (FSA), which aimed at promoting desertion from the army and protecting civilians from repression. Though initially intended to become an opposition alternative to the regular Syrian army, it never lived up to its expectations. Initially, militias formed in various parts of the country based on friendships, clan allegiances, and neighbourhood solidarity. As militias became better structured and trained, larger rebel organizations emerged: Liwa al-Tawhid and Nour al-Din al-Zenki are two examples. Jihadists, including Arabs from other countries in the region, also joined militias; al-Qaeda formed their own group, and so the list went on. Many of these groups were largely autonomous, or completely independent, from the FSA. Predatory practices, criminal activities, and warlordism spread, as an activist noted, 'Now everyone in Syria is armed, and weapons bring out the worst in people . . . Weapons and power are addictive' (Hinnebusch, Imady, and Zintl 2016, 243).

In Yemen, as in Syria and Libya, an uprising that was designed as peaceful and popular quickly gained insurgent dimensions. After the March 2011 massacre of over 50 protestors in Sana'a, core members of the regime started to defect, bringing military units, skills, and equipment to the side of the opposition. Their presence, although first welcomed by the protestors, soon changed the course of the revolution, as popular protests were overshadowed by armed confrontations between Saleh and regime defectors. Four years later, when the transitional period reached a dead end, the contest between the Houthis and President Hadi was accompanied by the emergence of militarized groups on both sides. The Houthis, now allied with Saleh, relied on army units and tribes loyal to the former president, while the groups of the anti-Houthi camp received military assistance from Saudi Arabia. With the escalating violence and abundance of weapons, many previously peaceful protestors, like members of the southern Hirak movement, were transformed into soldiers in the course of the war.

In Yugoslavia, military networks were eventually activated as a result of rising uncertainty. As nationalist Croatian politicians began to discriminate against ethnic Serbs living within the borders of that country in the early 1990s, the minority Serbs perceived themselves under siege. When the spectre of Croatian independence became a reality in June 1991, the worst fears of the Serbian minority seemed to have been realized. Unable to rely on 'their' government for protection against regional militias, the Serbs armed themselves and soon received the backing of the Yugoslav army – by now controlled by politicians, mainly Serbian by nationality, defiant about the prospect of the country's break-up. However, faced with the disintegration of the Yugoslav army, the civil war was fought mainly by militias. In Croatia and Bosnia,

> [conflicts] were spawned not so much by the convulsive surging of ancient hatreds or by frenzies whipped up by demagogic politicians and the media as by the administrations of small – sometimes very small – bands of opportunistic marauders recruited by political leaders and operating under their general guidance. Many of these participants were drawn from street gangs or from bands of soccer hooligans. Others were criminals specifically released from prison for the purpose. Their participation was required because the Yugoslav army, despite years of supposedly influential nationalist propaganda and centuries of supposedly pent-up ethnic hatreds, substantially disintegrated early in the war and refused to fight.
>
> *(Mueller 2000, 42)*

While agreement on separatism remained weak in the population, support was manipulated through selective incentives (including food and liquor) as high rates of desertion from the armed forces served to arm the locals, who formed para-military units. Paramilitary gangs and foreign mercenaries, among them convicted criminals, were responsible for some of the most violent episodes during the Yugoslav wars.

Thus, we can conclude from the case studies that the activation of military networks is an indispensable part of the transition to civil war. At the same time, we were able to observe that in each case this mechanism intersected differently with other mechanisms constituting the overall process towards civil war. In Libya, the initial militias were tribally based and quickly turned to offensive as an international coalition provided support. In Syria, militias emerged around much smaller units but eventually institutionalized along ethnic and sectarian boundaries, weakening the overall military capabilities of the opposition. In Yemen, with the splits in the military and the sponsorship of Saudi Arabia, armed militias emerged on both sides of the conflict. Ironically, the rebels relied on the army men of Saleh, while the anti-Houthi camp was composed of various groups armed by Saudi Arabia. Yugoslav militias were often just as fragmented as in Libya and Syria, but would align along nationalist defined identities.

Spiralling revenge

Social movement studies have sometimes pointed at the vicious circles that emerge during protest cycles, bringing about ideological and strategic transformation in social movement repertoires through the activation of some specific emotional tensions. In particular, motives and feelings change in action, during interactions with allies and opponents. Escalation might happen in spirals of reciprocal revenge, which bring about an intensification of emotions (della Porta 2013). Approaches to civil war also stressed these dynamics, pointing in particular to the combination of various types of emotions in intense time as enhancing the propensity to violence. Once again, while focusing especially on the onset of civil wars, our case studies pointed at its persistence through aroused emotions, with spirals of reciprocal revenge.

In Libya, about 300–400 people were killed in the first half of February (Schemm 2011), while violent clashes spread quickly. The killing of protestors fuelled a narrative of revenge. At the same time, however, there was also a quick development of NGOs to support and protect the communities. In March, a Coalition of Libyan NGOs was created, grouping 240 NGOs (Quesnay 2013, 124). With the spread of the armed conflicts, brutality increased on the side of the regimes, but also in the emerging militias. Even after the end of the regime, violence remained high, as episodes of brutality among different groups of the population spiralled into reciprocal revenge.

In Syria, too, the regime continued to use live ammunition, although it was still unable to suppress the opposition. The situation thus escalated, notwithstanding LCCS calls for peaceful protest. At the start of Ramadan of 2011, after about five months of mobilization, 2,000 had been killed, with another thousand slain by the end of the month. Violence then increased on the part of the protestors as well, initially mainly in little-organized attacks against regime officials, security services, army personnel, and the Ba'ath Party buildings. In fact, the situation became increasingly difficult to address, given the spiral of reciprocal brutalization, as:

> Red lines around the use of particular weapons systems were overstepped one by one: a spiral of violence leading from bullets to bombs and from snipers to sarin was set in motion. As civilians on both sides were targeted, the security dilemma gave the conflict an additional dimension: each side, to feel secure, created armed groups that made all less secure. Proponents of non-violent struggle were not only marginalized but also, like vast parts of the initially uninvolved civilian population, driven out of their homes, injured or killed, with many going into exile to escape the violence, leaving the field to the armed factions.
>
> *(Hinnebusch, Imady, and Zintl 2016, 235–6)*

On 18 July 2012, the FSA and the Jihadi group Liwa al-Islam (Brigade of Islam) claimed responsibility for the killing of Asef Shawkat (the Minister of Defence) and three other elite security leaders. This would prove to be the signal the opposition needed to start an armed assault on Damascus and Aleppo that proved to be the turning point in the transformation of a peaceful Syrian uprising to a civil war. In mid-June 2012, more than 8,000 people had already died; by 18 July the civil war had claimed 20,000 victims and twice as many in November of the same year. As the opposition became increasingly fragmented, brutality (and ensuing fears as well as revenge) also spiralled among its ranks.

In Yemen, the feelings of retribution have been a particularly important force in strengthening divisions and leading to the realignments that changed the course of the popular mobilization. During the transitional period, which was meant to lead to Yemen's democratization, the Houthis and the ousted President Saleh united against the common political enemy – Hadi and al-Islah – in what many Yemenis saw as an 'alliance of revenge'. Their rapprochement annulled the clearly demarcated camps that characterized the popular uprising (opposition versus the regime) and put forward new divisions and coalitions built around the warring elite factions. Later, once the violence radicalized and spread – particularly after the Arab coalition airstrikes – sentiments of retaliation intensified, with the Houthi and anti-Houthi camps accusing each other of war crimes.

In collapsing Yugoslavia, insecurity was fuelled by historically grounded expectations about bad intentions. Croats and Serbs escalated demands on one another, as Croats denied Serbs equal status and Serbians reacted belligerently. Similarly, Kosovo Albanians reacted to Serbian provocations. So, as in these examples, groups negotiate less and less, reaching fewer and fewer agreements and instead escalating their demands. In this process, groups might become more secretive about their military plans in emerging anarchy, which can also cause them to underestimate the adversary's strength (Rose 2000). As Kaldor (2006) noted, in Bosnia-Herzegovina, the most ethnically mixed state, ethnic cleansing was performed by militias armed from outside by Milošević and Tuđman. The area was characterized by both tolerance and fear, in a most militarized country with paramilitary, foreign mercenaries, and local police. With the formal economic collapse, the siege of Bosnian cities followed a typical path:

> First, the regular forces would shell the area and issue frightening propaganda so as to instill a mood of panic. Then the paramilitary forces would close in and terrorize the non-Serb residents with random killing, rape and looting. Control over local administration would then be established. In the more extreme cases, non-Serb men were separated from the women and killed or taken to detention centres. Women were robbed and/or raped and allowed to go or taken to rape detention centres. Houses and cultural buildings such as mosques were looted, burned or blown up. The paramilitary groups also seemed to have lists of prominent people – community leaders, intellectuals, SDA members, wealthy people – who were separated from the rest and executed.
>
> *(ibid., 54)*

Similar patterns developed in areas controlled by the Croatians. Paramilitaries with economic motivations were hired to do the dirty jobs, and ethnic cleansing followed the logic of guerrillas, who rely on support by the population.

In sum, civil wars develop upon emotional mechanisms that are linked, in particular, to spirals of revenge. As fear spread in all our cases, based on feelings of increasing insecurity, people within the different groups became outraged by the deeds and narratives of extreme brutality against fellow group members. Spirals of reciprocal revenge caused that brutality to escalate.

Sectarian identification

Social movement studies and civil war studies have long shared a focus on (often distant) causes. More recently, in both areas, researchers have noted that motivations as well as conditions emerge in action – they are that is, at least to a certain extent, endogenous and processual. Social movement studies have pointed to identification processes as a relevant activity of social movement organizations. Promoting collective action implies first of all a process of identification with the others. That is, individual identities need to be transformed into collective identities and then politicized. Also in studies on civil wars, a constructivist approach contrasted primordialist visions of ethnicity. In fact, the very concept of ethnic conflict has been criticized as addressing phenomena that are too heterogeneous (Gilley 2004). In our cases, religious and ethnic narratives of enmities were, in fact, mobilized, fuelling the continuation of civil wars.

In Libya, we find a different type of religiously fuelled tension from the other cases, as the population is overwhelmingly Sunni. The rising popularity and public expressions of Salafism, a strict and often militant form of Sunni Islam, had caused tensions between Salafis and Sufis. In the immediate aftermath of the regime collapse there have been numerous instances of the destruction of Sufi shrines, all of which indicate a rise in sectarian violence (UNHR 2012). It can also be argued that with the emergence of ISIS in 2014, intra-Sunni sectarian tensions have intensified.

In Syria, even though Friday prayers were the occasion for people to gather, the claims were initially overwhelmingly non-religious, targeting the (power of) the security services and corruption, and calling for political liberalization. Later, sectarian rhetoric increased as the conflict radicalized. With the passing of time, 'The uprising has taken an increasingly sectarian tone, pitting the Sunni majority against the Alawi minority, and has shown the lengths to which the regime and its supporters will go to defend their own survival' (Donker 2012). Sectarian-based attacks became more frequent among opposition and regime-linked militias alike. In combination with the vacuum produced by state failure in both Iraq and Syria, with the spreading of a war economy and plundering of state resources, this provided the context in which IS could emerge. By mid-2015, 4 million out of 21 million inhabitants had left the country. So, 'the processes that led to and fostered sectarian strife fed into an apparent drive for establishment of "sectarian-cleansed" regions secure from the threat of the "other," raising the possibility of post-war fragmentation of Syrian territory along confessional lines' (Hinnebusch, Imady, and Zintl 2016, 239). This was all the more the case as Sunni Islamists consolidated control of the borders with Sunni-dominated Iraq, Jordan, and Turkey, thus 'raising the specter of state boundaries being redrawn along sectarian and/or ethnic lines. Thus, militarization and sectarianization proved to be mutually reinforcing' (ibid., 239). Similarly, narratives of oppression and resistance later supported the institution of a Kurdish state at the northern border.

In Yemen, where national loyalties had traditionally been weaker than tribal or regional allegiances, the early stages of popular mobilization brought surprising levels of unity, with divergent actors emphasizing the pan-Yemeni character of the uprising (Lackner 2016; Yadav 2015). Gradually, however, old divisions came back into play, with many groups – such as the Houthis, tribes, or southern secessionists – turning to their narrow identifications and localized interests. Once the competition between the Houthis/Saleh and Hadi/Islah took the shape of a war, both sides resorted to a sectarian rhetoric, which was previously unusual in Yemeni politics. Sectarianism has enabled all parts of the conflict to recruit fighters, delegitimize enemies, and justify violence. With the divisions exacerbated by sectarian hatred, the calls for revenge spiralled even further.

In Yugoslavia, historical conflicts between Serbs and Croats – as well as (in part overlapping) – between Catholic, Protestant, and Muslim groups – represented historical memories, sleeping but still there to be revived. During the conflict, exclusive nationalist narratives were mobilized. Serbs were praised as the brave soldiers who had protected Austria from the Turks. Even the Chetniks, who had collaborated with the Nazis, were seen in a positive light, as freedom lovers. In contrast, the Croats were the murderers, traitors, and Serb-haters, as were (even if less central) the Turks and the Austro-Hungarians (Malešević 2002). The mentioned variety of autonomous civil society organizations notwithstanding, nationalist groups sponsored from above came to dominate the public sphere by the end of the 1980s. This was the case especially in Serbia, where an aggressive framing about 'great Serbia' developed, activating past memories. Similarly, in Croatia, former party members came to lead the nationalist movement. Feeling threatened by Milošević's nationalist rhetoric, they tried to increase popular support by linking up with nationalist dissidents (Pavković 2000, 112).

Using nationalist propaganda that stressed the past and present victimization of the Serbs, Milošević was able to exploit the support for the Serb minority in Kosovo, which had been protesting since 1985 against the perceived discrimination by Kosovo's Albanian majority. Initially, Serbian nationalism pushed for defensive frames. The relations between Kosovo Albanians and Kosovo Serbs then degenerated, as the Serbs staged rallies in Belgrade: 'The organisers of these protests were Serb and Montenegrin farmers, skilled workers, teachers and low-ranking communist officials. This gave the movement the look of an anti-elite, grassroots movement of harassed Serb and Montenegrin minorities in Kosovo' (ibid., 83). As a turning point, on the night and early morning of 24 and 25 April 1987, Milošević addressed a gathering of 15,000 Kosovo Serbs and Montenegrins with inflammatory words. As other republican leaders started to fear Milošević as a proponent of a Greater Serbia, they reacted by mobilizing for their own sovereignty. In this way, 'nationalism became a dominant political force largely as an unintended outcome of high levels of mobilization and spiralling social, economic and political conflicts in a complex, authoritarian multi-national state which experienced a severe economic crisis' (Vladisavljević 2008, 6).

In sum, in our four cases, emotional and cognitive mechanisms interacted in sustaining civil wars. Exclusive forms of group identification developed during intense interactions that contributed to reactivate and fuel narratives of historical animosity. A Manichean rhetoric was used by leaders to strengthen symbolic incentives towards mobilization against the (ethnic, religious, national) other. Identities emerged as based on ethnicity or religion in all four cases, with tribal identification politicized in the Middle Eastern examples.

Conclusion

The aim of this volume has been to develop some theoretically driven analysis of cases of escalation from peaceful social movements for democracy into civil wars. To this end, building upon studies of other forms of political violence, we have identified some mechanisms that we singled out in part deductively – bridging the analysis of civil wars with social science literature on social movements, nonviolent revolutions, and democratization – but also in part inductively, from some studies on critical cases, looking at the presence and different combinations of these mechanisms at the onset of civil wars and in their development. Our main message is that, beyond root causes, understanding when and how civil wars emerge requires an analysis of the emergent characteristics of violence, as it triggers specific dynamics and constellations of mechanisms that produce and reproduce the conditions for its own survival.

Admittedly, our aim is to contribute to theory building, rather than to test existing theories. Indeed, we have identified the way in which a set of mechanisms emerge and relate, rather than considering them as either necessary or sufficient causes. Additionally, we used some process-tracing analysis of what we considered as relevant cases. This approach resulted in mapping the ways in which a variety of mechanisms can interrelate in constituting a transformative process of mobilization for democracy into civil war.

While focusing on some recent moments of failed attempts at democratization during the Arab Spring, we added an historical case in another area in order to reflect on the robustness of our mechanisms. But our sample was far from representative: much more systematic analysis is necessary to investigate the capacity of the selected mechanisms to travel in space and in time. Finally, while we have elsewhere analysed the involvement of civil society in more successful democratization processes (della Porta 2014; 2016), a systematic comparison of positive and negative cases remains to be undertaken.

References

Alley, April Longley. 2010. 'The rules of the game: unpacking patronage politics in Yemen'. *The Middle East Journal* 64(3): 385–409. doi:10.3751/64.3.13.

Alwazir, Atiaf. 2016. 'Yemen's enduring resistance: youth between politics and informal mobilization'. *Mediterranean Politics* 21(1): 170–91. doi:10.1080/13629395.2015.1081446.

Anderson, Lisa. 2011. 'Demystifying the Arab Spring: parsing the differences between Tunisia, Egypt, and Libya'. *Foreign Affairs* (May/June).

Benderly, Jill. 1997. 'Feminist movements in Yugoslavia, 1978–1992'. In M.K. Bokovoy, J.A. Irvine, and C.S. Lilly (eds), *State-Society Relations in Yugoslavia, 1945–1992*. New York: St. Martin's Press, pp. 183–210.

Bilic, Bojan. 2012. *We Were Gasping for Air*. Baden-Baden: Nomos.

Boudreau, Vincent. 2004. *Resisting Dictatorship: Repression and Protest in Southeast Asia*. Cambridge: Cambridge University Press.

Buhaug, Halvard, Gates, Scott, and Lujala, Päivi. 2013. 'Geography, rebel capability, and the duration of civil conflict'. *Journal of Conflict Resolution* 53(4): 544–69. doi:10.1177/0022002709336457.

Bunce, Valerie. 1999. *Subversive Institutions: The Design and the Destruction of Socialism and the State*. Cambridge: Cambridge University Press.

Carapico, Sheila. 2007. *Civil Society in Yemen: The Political Economy of Activism in Modern Arabia*. Cambridge: Cambridge University Press.

Carapico, Sheila. 2011. 'No exit: Yemen's existential crisis'. Middle East Research and Information Project, May 3. Available at: www.merip.org/mero/mero050311–1?ip_login_no_cache=5d2267fcaf95daf21e7829175eadb779

Cerone, John. 2011. 'Documents on Libya, introductory note'. *International Legal Materials* 505.

Collier, Paul, and Hoeffler, Anke. 2004. 'Greed and Grievance in Civil War'. *Oxford Economic Papers* 56(4): 563–95. doi:10.1093/oep/gpf064.

Crenshaw, Martha. 2011. *Explaining Terrorism: Causes, Processes and Consequences*. London: Routledge.

Davenport, Christian (ed.). 2000. *Paths to State Repression: Human Rights Violations and Contentious Politics*. Boulder, CO: Rowman & Littlefield.

Davenport, Christian. 2005. 'Repression and mobilization: Insights from political science and sociology'. In Christian Davenport, Hank Johnston, and Carol Mueller (eds), *Repression and Mobilization: Social Movements, Protest, and Contention*. Minneapolis, MN: The University of Minnesota Press.

della Porta, Donatella. 1998. 'The political discourse on protest policing'. In Mario Giugni, Doug McAdam, and Charles Tilly (eds), *How Movements Matter*. Minneapolis, MN: The University of Minnesota Press.

della Porta, Donatella. 2013. *Clandestine Political Violence*. Cambridge: Cambridge University Press. http://dx.doi.org/10.1017/CBO9781139043144.

della Porta, Donatella. 2014. *Mobilizing for Democracy: Comparing 1989 and 2011*. Oxford: Oxford University Press.

della Porta, Donatella. 2016. *Where Did the Revolution Go?*, Cambridge: Cambridge University Press.

della Porta, Donatella, and Diani, Mario (2006) *Social Movements: An Introduction*. Oxford: Blackwell.

della Porta, Donatella, and Fillieule, Olivier. 2004. 'Policing social movements'. In David A. Snow, Sarah A. Soule, and Hanspeter Kriesi (eds), *The Blackwell Companion to Social Movements*. Oxford: Blackwell, pp. 217–41.

della Porta, Donatella, and Gbikpi, Bernard. 2012. 'The riots: A dynamic view'. In Seraphim Seferiades and Hank Johnston (eds), *Violent Protest, Contentious Politics and the Neoliberal State*. Farnham: Ashgate, pp. 87–102.

della Porta, Donatella, and Piazza, Gianni. 2008. *Voices of the Valley. Voices of the Straits: How Protest Creates Community*. New York: Berghahn.

Donker, Teije H. 2012. *Mobilizing for Democracy in Syria*. Available at: http://cosmos.sns.it.

Durac, Vincent. 2013. 'Protest movements and political change: an analysis of the "Arab Uprisings" of 2011'. *Journal of Contemporary African Studies* 31(2): 175–93. doi:10.1080/02589001.2013.783754.

Earl, Jennifer. 2003. 'Tanks, tear gas and taxes'. *Sociological Theory* 21: 44–68.

Earl, Jennifer, Soule, Sarah A., and McCarthy, John. 2003. 'Protest under fire? Explaining protest policing'. *American Sociological Review* 69: 581–606.

Engene, Jan Oscar. 2004. *Terrorism in Western Europe*. Cheltenham: Edward Elgar.

Fattah, Khaled. 2011. 'Yemen: A social Intifada in a republic of sheikhs'. *Middle East Policy* 18 (3): 79–85. doi:10.1111/j.1475–4967.2011.00499.x.

Figa, Jozef. 1997. 'Socializing the state: civil society and democratization from below in Slovenia'. In M.K. Bokovoy, J.A. Irvine, and C.S. Lilly (eds), *State-Society Relations in Yugoslavia, 1945–1992*. New York: St. Martin's Press, pp. 163–82.

Francisco, Ronald A. 2005. 'The dictator's dilemma'. In Christian Davenport, Hank Johnston, and Carol Mueller (eds), *Repression and Mobilization*. Minneapolis, MN: The University of Minnesota Press.

Gelvin, James L. 2011. *Divided Loyalties: Nationalism and Mass Politics in Syria at the Close of Empire*. 3rd edn. Berkeley, CA: University of California Press.

Gilley, Bruce. 2004. 'Against the concept of ethnic conflict'. *Third World Quarterly* 25(6): 1155–66. doi:10.1080/0143659042000256959.

Goodwin, Jeff. 2001. *No Other Way Out: States and Revolutionary Movements, 1945–1991.* Cambridge: Cambridge University Press.

Hinnebusch, Raymond A. 1993. 'State and civil society in Syria'. *The Middle East Journal* 47 (2): 243–57.

Hinnebusch, Raymond, Imady, Omar, and Zintl, Tina. 2016. 'Civil resistance in the Syrian uprising: from peaceful protest to sectarian civil war'. In Adam Roberts, Michael Willis, and Timothy Garton Ash (eds), *Civil Resistance in the Arab Spring: Triumphs and Disasters.* Oxford: Oxford University Press, pp. 223–47.

HRW. 2013a. 'Unpunished massacre: Yemen's failed response to the "Friday of Dignity" killings'. Available at: www.hrw.org/report/2013/02/12/unpunished-massacre/yemens-failed-response-friday-dignity-killings

HRW. 2013b. 'Between a drone and Al-Qaeda. The civilian cost of US targeted killings in Yemen'. 22 October. New York: Human Rights Watch. Available at: www.hrw.org/report/2013/10/22/between-drone-and-al-qaeda/civilian-cost-us-targeted-killings-yemen

Jacinto, Leela. 2011. 'Benghazi's Tahrir Square: Times Square style meets revolutionary zeal'. *France24,* 25 April. Available at: www.france24.com/en/20110425-libya-benghazi-tahrir-square-times-reporters-notebook-leela-jacinto

Joffé, George. 2016. 'Civil resistance in Libya during the Arab Spring'. In Adam Roberts, Michael Willis, and Timothy Garton Ash (eds), *Civil Resistance in the Arab Spring: Triumphs and Disasters.* Oxford: Oxford University Press, pp. 116–40.

Kaldor, Mary. 2006. *New and Old Wars.* Cambridge: Polity.

Kalyvas, S.N. 2008. 'Promises and pitfalls of an emerging research program: the microdynamics of civil war'. In Stathis N. Kalyvas, Ian Shapiro, and Tarek Masoud (eds), *Order, Conflict, and Violence.* Cambridge: Cambridge University Press, pp. 397–421. Available at: http://ebooks.cambridge.org/ref/id/CBO9780511755903A028

Khosrokhavar, Farhad. 2012. *The New Arab Revolutions That Shook the World.* Boulder, CO: Paradigm Publishers.

Lackner, Helen. 2016. 'The change squares of Yemen'. In Adam Roberts, Michael J. Willis, Rory McCarthy, and Timothy Garton Ash (eds), *Civil Resistance in the Arab Spring,* pp. 141–68. Oxford: Oxford University Press. Available at: www.oxfordscholarship.com/view/10.1093/acprof:oso/9780198749028.001.0001/acprof-9780198749028-chapter-6

Licht, Sonja. 2000. 'Civil society, democracy, and the Yugoslav wars', in M. Spencer (ed.), *The Lesson of Yugoslavia.* New York: Elsevier, pp. 111–24.

Malešević, Siniša. 2002. *Ideology, Legitimacy and the New State: Yugoslavia, Serbia and Croatia.* London: Frank Cass.

Mampilly, Zachariah Cherian. 2011. *Rebel Rulers: Insurgent Governance and Civilian Life during War.* Ithaca, NY: Cornell University Press.

Manea, Elham. 2015. 'Yemen's Arab Spring: outsmarting the cunning state?' In Larbi Sadiki (ed), *Routledge Handbook of the Arab Spring: Rethinking Democratization.* New York: Routledge, pp. 160–72.

Mattes, Hanspeter. 2004. 'Challenges to security sector governance in the Middle East: the Libyan case'. Paper presented at Geneva Centre for the Democratic Control of Armed Forces (DCAF) as a part of Security Governance in the Mediterranean Project, 13 July.

Michael, Maggie. 2011. 'Protesters in Libya demand Gaddafi ouster and reforms'. *The Washington Post*, 17 February. Available at: www.washingtonpost.com/wp-dyn/content/article/2011/02/16/AR2011021607292.html

Mitchell, Neil J. 2004. *Agents of Atrocity: Leaders, Followers, and the Violation of Human Rights in Civil War*. New York: Palgrave Macmillan.

Mueller, John. 2000. 'The banality of "ethnic war"'. *International Security*, 25(1): 42–70.

Nepstad, Sharon Erickson. 2011. *Nonviolent Revolutions: Civil Resistance in the Late 20th Century*. Oxford: Oxford University Press.

Pavković, Aleksandar. 2000. *The Fragmentation of Yugoslavia: Nationalism and War in the Balkans*. 2nd edn. Houndmills: Macmillan.

Perthes, Volker. 1992. 'The Syrian private industrial and commercial sectors and the state'. *International Journal of Middle East Studies* 24(2): 207–30.

Quesnay, Arthur 2013. 'L'insurrection libyenne, un movement révolutionnaire decentralize', in Amin Allal and Thomas Pierret (eds), *Au cœur des révolte arabes. Devenir revolutionaries*. Paris: Armand Colin, pp. 113–32.

Regan, Patrick, and Norton, Daniel. 2005. 'Greed, grievance, and mobilization in civil war'. *Journal of Conflict Resolution* 49(3): 319–36.

Rose, William. 2000. 'The security dilemma and ethnic conflict: some new hypotheses'. *Security Studies* 9(4): 1–51. doi:10.1080/09636410008429412.

Salih, Yassin Al-Haj. 2014. 'The Syrian Shabiha and their state – statehood & participation'. Heinrich Böll Stiftung. Available at: https://lb.boell.org/en/2014/03/03/syrian-shabiha-and-their-state-statehood-participation

Salisbury, Peter. 2016. 'Yemen: stemming the rise of a chaos state'. Middle East and North Africa Programme. Chatham House. Available at: www.chathamhouse.org/publication/yemen-stemming-rise-chaos-state

Schaeffer, Robert K. 2000. 'Democratization, division and war in Yugoslavia: a comparative perspective'. In M. Spencer (ed.), *The Lesson of Yugoslavia*. New York: Elsevier, pp. 47–63.

Schemm, Paul. 2011. 'Battle at army base broke Gadhafi hold in Benghazi'. *The Washington Post*, 25 February. Available at: www.washingtonpost.com/wp-dyn/content/article/2011/02/25/AR2011022505021.html

Schock, Kurt. 2005. 'Unarmed insurrections: people power movements in nondemocracies', in *Social Movements, Protest, and Contention*, vol. 22. Minneapolis, MN: University of Minnesota Press.

Stokes, Gale. 1993. *The Walls Came Tumbling Down: The Collapse of Communism in Eastern Europe*. New York: Oxford University Press.

Toft, Monica. 2003. *The Geography of Ethnic Violence: Identity, Interests, and the Indivisibility of Territory*. Princeton, NJ: Princeton University Press.

UNHR. 2012. 'The destruction of cultural and religious sites: a violation of human rights'. UNHR Office of High Commissioner, 24 September. Available at: www.ohchr.org/EN/NewsEvents/Pages/DestructionShrines.aspx

Uysal, Ayshen. 2005. 'Organisation du maintien de l'ordre et répression policière en Turquie', in Donatella della Porta and Olivier Fillieule (eds), *Maintien de l'ordre et police des foules*. Paris: Presses de Science Po.

Vasilevski, Steven. 2007. 'Diverging paths, diverging outcomes: a comparative analysis of post-communist transition in the successor states of Yugoslavia'. YCISS Post-Communist Studies Programme Research Paper Series. Toronto: York Centre for International and Security Studies.

Vladisavljević, Nebojša. 2008. *Serbia's Antibureaucratic Revolution: Milošević, the Fall of Communism and Nationalist Mobilization*. Houndmills: Palgrave Macmillan.

Wedeen, Lisa. 2008. *Peripheral Visions: Publics, Power, and Performance in Yemen*. Chicago: University of Chicago Press.

Wood, Elisabeth Jean. 2000. *Forging Democracy from below: Insurgent Transitions in South Africa and El Salvador*. Cambridge: Cambridge University Press.

Yadav, Stacey Philbrick. 2015. 'The "Yemen Model" as a failure of political imagination'. *International Journal of Middle East Studies* 47(1): 144–7. doi:10.1017/S0020743814001512.

Ylönen, Aleksi. 2005. 'Grievances and the roots of insurgencies: Southern Sudan and Darfur'. *Peace, Conflict and Development: An Interdisciplinary Journal* 7: 99–134.

INDEX